The Newest

Air Fry

Cookbook

2024

1800 *Days Effortless and Delicious Air Fryer Recipes That Anyone Can Easily Learn | Fry, Bake, Grill & Roast Most Wanted Family on a Budget*

Catharine O. Rolfson

Table of Contents

INTRODUCTION

Do you crave the crispy, mouthwatering goodness of fried food, but feel guilty about indulging in it? Fear not, my fellow foodies! The air fryer is here to save the day (and your waistline). As a nutritionist and an air fryer enthusiast, I've seen firsthand the amazing things this kitchen appliance can do. The air fryer is like a magic wand that can transform any food into a crispy and healthy delight. It's like having your own personal sous chef that can whip up delicious, healthy meals in a flash.

As a nutritionist, I'm always looking for ways to make healthy eating more enjoyable and sustainable. And the air fryer does just that. With its hot air circulation technology, the air fryer allows you to indulge in your favorite fried foods without the added fat and calories. It's like a superhero that swoops in to save the day when you're craving something indulgent but don't want to compromise your health.

So, my fellow foodies, whether you're a health-conscious cook or just looking for a new and exciting way to prepare your meals, the air fryer is the way to go. Trust me, once you try it, you'll wonder how you ever lived without it.

An Appliance Full of Magic and Power

Think of the air fryer as a magical genie that grants your food wishes without all the greasy consequences. You no longer have to choose between enjoying the crispy, delicious taste of fried food and maintaining a healthy lifestyle. The air fryer uses hot air to circulate your food, creating that crispy crunch we all crave, without the need for excessive oil. It's like a fairy godmother that transforms your favorite foods into guilt-free delights. With the air fryer, you can indulge in your favorite foods without worrying about the harmful effects of excess oil or unwanted calories.

Not only is the air fryer a healthier option for cooking your favorite fried foods, but it's also incredibly convenient. No more waiting for the oil to heat up or dealing with messy cleanups. With the air fryer, you can have dinner on the table in no time. It's like having a personal assistant in the kitchen, taking care of all the hard work so you can focus on enjoying your meal. With the air fryer, you can say goodbye to the hassle of deep frying and hello to hassle-free cooking.

And the best part? The air fryer is incredibly versatile. From crispy chicken wings to savory veggies to sweet treats, this kitchen gadget can do it all. Whether you're cooking up a quick weeknight dinner or preparing for a big party, the air fryer has got your back. It's like a jack-of-all-trades that can handle anything you throw at it. And the best part is, it does it all without sacrificing taste or quality. So, get ready to revolutionize the way you cook and eat with the help of the amazing air fryer.

Your Magic Journey Begins

In the pages that follow, you'll find a variety of delicious, healthy, and easy-to-make recipes that are specifically designed for the air fryer. No more slaving away in the kitchen for hours on end. With the air fryer, you can whip up a feast fit for a king (or queen) in no time at all. And the best part? You won't have to sacrifice taste for health, because the air fryer works its magic to make your food crispy on the outside and juicy on the inside.

So, let's get cooking and let the air fryer do its thang. Who knows, you may just become the air fryer master chef you never knew you were meant to be.

Chapter 1   Breakfasts

Whole Wheat Banana-Walnut Bread

Prep time: 10 minutes | Cook time: 23 minutes | Serves 6

Olive oil cooking spray	2 tablespoons raw honey
2 ripe medium bananas	1 cup whole wheat flour
1 large egg	¼ teaspoon salt
¼ cup nonfat plain Greek yogurt	¼ teaspoon baking soda
¼ cup olive oil	½ teaspoon ground cinnamon
½ teaspoon vanilla extract	¼ cup chopped walnuts

1. Preheat the air fryer to 360°F(182°C). Lightly coat the inside of a 8-by-4-inch loaf pan with olive oil cooking spray. (Or use two 5 ½-by-3-inch loaf pans.) 2. In a large bowl, mash the bananas with a fork. Add the egg, yogurt, olive oil, vanilla, and honey. Mix until well combined and mostly smooth. 3. Sift the whole wheat flour, salt, baking soda, and cinnamon into the wet mixture, then stir until just combined. Do not overmix. 4. Gently fold in the walnuts. 5. Pour into the prepared loaf pan and spread to distribute evenly. 6. Place the loaf pan in the air fryer basket and bake for 20 to 23 minutes, or until golden brown on top and a toothpick inserted into the center comes out clean. 7. Allow to cool for 5 minutes before serving.

Coconut Brown Rice Porridge with Dates

Prep time: 10 minutes | Cook time: 23 minutes | Serves 1 to 2

1 cup canned coconut milk	¼ teaspoon ground cardamom
½ cup cooked brown rice	4 large Medjool dates, pitted
¼ cup unsweetened shredded coconut	and roughly chopped
¼ cup packed dark brown sugar	Heavy cream, for serving (optional)
½ teaspoon kosher salt	

1. In a cake pan, stir together the coconut milk, rice, shredded coconut, brown sugar, salt, cardamom, and dates and place in the air fryer. Bake at 375°F (191°C) until reduced and thickened and browned on top, about 23 minutes, stirring halfway through. 2. Remove the pan from the air fryer and divide the porridge among bowls. Drizzle the porridge with cream, if you like, and serve hot.

White Bean–Oat Waffles

Prep time: 10 minutes | Cook time: 20 minutes | Serves 2

1 large egg white	and rinsed
2 tablespoons finely ground flaxseed	1 teaspoon coconut oil
½ cup water	1 teaspoon liquid stevia
¼ teaspoon salt	½ cup old-fashioned rolled oats
1 teaspoon vanilla extract	Extra-virgin olive oil cooking spray
½ cup cannellini beans, drained	

1. In a blender, combine the egg white, flaxseed, water, salt, vanilla, cannellini beans, coconut oil, and stevia. Blend on high for 90 seconds. 2. Add the oats. Blend for 1 minute more. 3. Preheat the waffle iron. The batter will thicken to the correct consistency while the waffle iron preheats. 4. Spray the heated waffle iron with cooking spray. 5. Add ¾ cup of batter. Close the waffle iron. Cook for 6 to 8 minutes, or until done. Repeated with the remaining batter. 6. Serve hot, with your favorite sugar-free topping.

Two-Cheese Grits

Prep time: 10 minutes | Cook time: 10 to 12 minutes | Serves 4

⅔ cup instant grits	3 ounces (85 g) cream cheese, at room temperature
1 teaspoon salt	
1 teaspoon freshly ground black pepper	1 tablespoon butter, melted
¾ cup milk, whole or 2%	1 cup shredded mild Cheddar cheese
1 large egg, beaten	1 to 2 tablespoons oil

1. In a large bowl, combine the grits, salt, and pepper. Stir in the milk, egg, cream cheese, and butter until blended. Stir in the Cheddar cheese. 2. Preheat the air fryer to 400°F (204°C). Spritz a baking pan with oil. 3. Pour the grits mixture into the prepared pan and place it in the air fryer basket. 4. Cook for 5 minutes. Stir the mixture and cook for 5 minutes more for soupy grits or 7 minutes more for firmer grits.

Cheesy Bell Pepper Eggs

Prep time: 10 minutes | Cook time: 15 minutes | Serves 4

4 medium green bell peppers	chopped
3 ounces (85 g) cooked ham, chopped	8 large eggs
¼ medium onion, peeled and	1 cup mild Cheddar cheese

1. Cut the tops off each bell pepper. Remove the seeds and the white membranes with a small knife. Place ham and onion into each pepper. 2. Crack 2 eggs into each pepper. Top with ¼ cup cheese per pepper. Place into the air fryer basket. 3. Adjust the temperature to 390°F (199°C) and air fry for 15 minutes. 4. When fully cooked, peppers will be tender and eggs will be firm. Serve immediately.

French Toast Sticks

Prep time: 10 minutes | Cook time: 9 minutes | Serves 4

Oil, for spraying	1 teaspoon ground cinnamon
6 large eggs	8 slices bread, cut into thirds
1⅓ cups milk	Syrup of choice, for serving
2 teaspoons vanilla extract	

1. Preheat the air fryer to 370°F (188°C). Line the air fryer basket with parchment and spray lightly with oil. 2. In a shallow bowl, whisk the eggs, milk, vanilla, and cinnamon. 3. Dunk one piece of bread in the egg mixture, making sure to coat both sides. Work quickly so the bread doesn't get soggy. Immediately transfer the bread to the prepared basket. 4. Repeat with the remaining bread, making sure the pieces don't touch each other. You may need to work in batches, depending on the size of your air fryer. 5. Air fry for 5 minutes, flip, and cook for another 3 to 4 minutes, until browned and crispy. 6. Serve immediately with your favorite syrup.

Everything Bagels

Prep time: 15 minutes | Cook time: 14 minutes | Makes 6 bagels

1¾ cups shredded Mozzarella cheese or goat cheese Mozzarella	vinegar
2 tablespoons unsalted butter or coconut oil	1 cup blanched almond flour
1 large egg, beaten	1 tablespoon baking powder
1 tablespoon apple cider	⅛ teaspoon fine sea salt
	1½ teaspoons everything bagel seasoning

1. Make the dough: Put the Mozzarella and butter in a large microwave-safe bowl and microwave for 1 to 2 minutes, until the cheese is entirely melted. Stir well. Add the egg and vinegar. Using a hand mixer on medium, combine well. Add the almond flour, baking powder, and salt and, using the mixer, combine well. 2. Lay a piece of parchment paper on the countertop and place the dough on it. Knead it for about 3 minutes. The dough should be a little sticky but pliable. (If the dough is too sticky, chill it in the refrigerator for an hour or overnight.) 3. Preheat the air fryer to 350°F (177°C). Spray a baking sheet or pie pan that will fit into your air fryer with avocado oil. 4. Divide the dough into 6 equal portions. Roll 1 portion into a log that is 6 inches long and about ½ inch thick. Form the log into a circle and seal the edges together, making a bagel shape. Repeat with the remaining portions of dough, making 6 bagels. 5. Place the bagels on the greased baking sheet. Spray the bagels with avocado oil and top with everything bagel seasoning, pressing the seasoning into the dough with your hands. 6. Place the bagels in the air fryer and bake for 14 minutes, or until cooked through and golden brown, flipping after 6 minutes. 7. Remove the bagels from the air fryer and allow them to cool slightly before slicing them in half and serving. Store leftovers in an airtight container in the fridge for up to 4 days or in the freezer for up to a month.

Homemade Cherry Breakfast Tarts

Prep time: 15 minutes | Cook time: 20 minutes | Serves 6

Tarts:	Frosting:
2 refrigerated piecrusts	½ cup vanilla yogurt
⅓ cup cherry preserves	1 ounce (28 g) cream cheese
1 teaspoon cornstarch	1 teaspoon stevia
Cooking oil	Rainbow sprinkles

Make the Tarts 1. Place the piecrusts on a flat surface. Using a knife or pizza cutter, cut each piecrust into 3 rectangles, for 6 total. (I discard the unused dough left from slicing the edges.) 2. In a small bowl, combine the preserves and cornstarch. Mix well. 3. Scoop 1 tablespoon of the preserves mixture onto the top half of each piece of piecrust. 4. Fold the bottom of each piece up to close the tart. Using the back of a fork, press along the edges of each tart to seal. 5. Spray the breakfast tarts with cooking oil and place them in the air fryer. I do not recommend stacking the breakfast tarts. They will stick together if stacked. You may need to prepare them in two batches. Bake at 375°F for 10 minutes. 6. Allow the breakfast tarts to cool fully before removing from the air fryer. 7. If necessary, repeat steps 5 and 6 for the remaining breakfast tarts. Make the Frosting 8. In a small bowl, combine the yogurt, cream cheese, and stevia. Mix well. 9. Spread the breakfast tarts with frosting and top with sprinkles, and serve.

Spinach and Bacon Roll-ups

Prep time: 5 minutes | Cook time: 8 to 9 minutes | Serves 4

4 flour tortillas (6- or 7-inch size)	4 slices turkey bacon
4 slices Swiss cheese	Special Equipment:
1 cup baby spinach leaves	4 toothpicks, soak in water for at least 30 minutes

1. Preheat the air fryer to 390°F (199°C). 2. On a clean work surface, top each tortilla with one slice of cheese and ¼ cup of spinach, then tightly roll them up. 3. Wrap each tortilla with a strip of turkey bacon and secure with a toothpick. 4. Arrange the roll-ups in the air fryer basket, leaving space between each roll-up. 5. Air fry for 4 minutes. Flip the roll-ups with tongs and rearrange them for more even cooking. Air fry for another 4 to 5 minutes until the bacon is crisp. 6. Rest for 5 minutes and remove the toothpicks before serving.

Whole Wheat Blueberry Muffins

Prep time: 10 minutes | Cook time: 15 minutes | Serves 6

Olive oil cooking spray	1½ cups plus 1 tablespoon whole wheat flour, divided
½ cup unsweetened applesauce	½ teaspoon baking soda
¼ cup raw honey	½ teaspoon baking powder
½ cup nonfat plain Greek yogurt	½ teaspoon salt
1 teaspoon vanilla extract	½ cup blueberries, fresh or frozen
1 large egg	

1. Preheat the air fryer to 360°F(182°C). Lightly coat the inside of six silicone muffin cups or a six-cup muffin tin with olive oil cooking spray. 2. In a large bowl, combine the applesauce, honey, yogurt, vanilla, and egg and mix until smooth. 3. Sift in 1½ cups of the flour, the baking soda, baking powder, and salt into the wet mixture, then stir until just combined. 4. In a small bowl, toss the blueberries with the remaining 1 tablespoon flour, then fold the mixture into the muffin batter. 5. Divide the mixture evenly among the prepared muffin cups and place into the basket of the air fryer. Bake for 12 to 15 minutes, or until golden brown on top and a toothpick inserted into the middle of one of the muffins comes out clean. 6. Allow to cool for 5 minutes before serving.

Buffalo Egg Cups

Prep time: 10 minutes | Cook time: 15 minutes | Serves 2

4 large eggs	2 tablespoons buffalo sauce
2 ounces (57 g) full-fat cream cheese	½ cup shredded sharp Cheddar cheese

1. Crack eggs into two ramekins. 2. In a small microwave-safe bowl, mix cream cheese, buffalo sauce, and Cheddar. Microwave for 20 seconds and then stir. Place a spoonful into each ramekin on top of the eggs. 3. Place ramekins into the air fryer basket. 4. Adjust the temperature to 320°F (160°C) and bake for 15 minutes. 5. Serve warm.

Pumpkin Donut Holes

Prep time: 15 minutes | Cook time: 14 minutes | Makes 12 donut holes

1 cup whole-wheat pastry flour, plus more as needed	pumpkin purée (not pumpkin pie filling)
3 tablespoons packed brown sugar	3 tablespoons 2% milk, plus more as needed
½ teaspoon ground cinnamon	2 tablespoons unsalted butter, melted
1 teaspoon low-sodium baking powder	1 egg white
⅓ cup canned no-salt-added	Powdered sugar (optional)

1. In a medium bowl, mix the pastry flour, brown sugar, cinnamon, and baking powder. 2. In a small bowl, beat the pumpkin, milk, butter, and egg white until combined. Add the pumpkin mixture to the dry ingredients and mix until combined. You may need to add more flour or milk to form a soft dough. 3. Divide the dough into 12 pieces. With floured hands, form each piece into a ball. 4. Cut a piece of parchment paper or aluminum foil to fit inside the air fryer basket but about 1 inch smaller in diameter. Poke holes in the paper or foil and place it in the basket. 5. Put 6 donut holes into the basket, leaving some space around each. Air fry at 360°F (182°C) for 5 to 7 minutes, or until the donut holes reach an internal temperature of 200°F (93°C) and are firm and light golden brown. 6. Let cool for 5 minutes. Remove from the basket and roll in powdered sugar, if desired. Repeat with the remaining donut holes and serve.

Veggie Frittata

Prep time: 7 minutes | Cook time: 21 to 23 minutes | Serves 2

Avocado oil spray	3 ounces (85 g) shredded sharp Cheddar cheese, divided
¼ cup diced red onion	
¼ cup diced red bell pepper	½ teaspoon dried thyme
¼ cup finely chopped broccoli	Sea salt and freshly ground black pepper, to taste
4 large eggs	

1. Spray a pan well with oil. Put the onion, pepper, and broccoli in the pan, place the pan in the air fryer, and set to 350°F (177°C). Bake for 5 minutes. 2. While the vegetables cook, beat the eggs in a medium bowl. Stir in half of the cheese, and season with the thyme, salt, and pepper. 3. Add the eggs to the pan and top with the remaining cheese. Set the air fryer to 350°F (177°C). Bake for 16 to 18 minutes, until cooked through.

Savory Sweet Potato Hash

Prep time: 15 minutes | Cook time: 18 minutes | Serves 6

2 medium sweet potatoes, peeled and cut into 1-inch cubes	2 tablespoons olive oil
	1 garlic clove, minced
½ green bell pepper, diced	½ teaspoon salt
½ red onion, diced	½ teaspoon black pepper
4 ounces (113 g) baby bella mushrooms, diced	½ tablespoon chopped fresh rosemary

1. Preheat the air fryer to 380°F(193°C). 2. In a large bowl, toss all ingredients together until the vegetables are well coated and seasonings distributed. 3. Pour the vegetables into the air fryer basket, making sure they are in a single even layer. (If using a smaller air fryer, you may need to do this in two batches.) 4. Roast for 9 minutes, then toss or flip the vegetables. Roast for 9 minutes more. 5. Transfer to a serving bowl or individual plates and enjoy.

Simple Scotch Eggs

Prep time: 5 minutes | Cook time: 25 minutes | Serves 4

4 large hard boiled eggs	8 slices thick-cut bacon
1 (12-ounce / 340-g) package pork sausage	4 wooden toothpicks, soaked in water for at least 30 minutes

1. Slice the sausage into four parts and place each part into a large circle. 2. Put an egg into each circle and wrap it in the sausage. Put in the refrigerator for 1 hour. 3. Preheat the air fryer to 450°F (235°C). 4. Make a cross with two pieces of thick-cut bacon. Put a wrapped egg in the center, fold the bacon over top of the egg, and secure with a toothpick. 5. Air fry in the preheated air fryer for 25 minutes. 6. Serve immediately.

Onion Omelet

Prep time: 10 minutes | Cook time: 12 minutes | Serves 2

3 eggs	1 large onion, chopped
Salt and ground black pepper, to taste	2 tablespoons grated Cheddar cheese
½ teaspoons soy sauce	Cooking spray

1. Preheat the air fryer to 355°F (179°C). 2. In a bowl, whisk together the eggs, salt, pepper, and soy sauce. 3. Spritz a small pan with cooking spray. Spread the chopped onion across the bottom of the pan, then transfer the pan to the air fryer. 4. Bake in the preheated air fryer for 6 minutes or until the onion is translucent. 5. Add the egg mixture on top of the onions to coat well. Add the cheese on top, then continue baking for another 6 minutes. 6. Allow to cool before serving.

Scotch Eggs

Prep time: 10 minutes | Cook time: 20 to 25 minutes | Serves 4

2 tablespoons flour, plus extra for coating	1 tablespoon water
	Oil for misting or cooking spray
1 pound (454 g) ground breakfast sausage	Crumb Coating:
4 hard-boiled eggs, peeled	¾ cup panko bread crumbs
1 raw egg	¾ cup flour

1. Combine flour with ground sausage and mix thoroughly. 2. Divide into 4 equal portions and mold each around a hard-boiled egg so the sausage completely covers the egg. 3. In a small bowl, beat together the raw egg and water. 4. Dip sausage-covered eggs in the remaining flour, then the egg mixture, then roll in the crumb coating. 5. Air fry at 360°F (182°C) for 10 minutes. Spray eggs, turn, and spray other side. 6. Continue cooking for another 10 to 15 minutes or until sausage is well done.

Broccoli-Mushroom Frittata

Prep time: 10 minutes | Cook time: 20 minutes | Serves 2

1 tablespoon olive oil	½ teaspoon salt
1½ cups broccoli florets, finely chopped	¼ teaspoon freshly ground black pepper
½ cup sliced brown mushrooms	6 eggs
¼ cup finely chopped onion	¼ cup Parmesan cheese

1. In a nonstick cake pan, combine the olive oil, broccoli, mushrooms, onion, salt, and pepper. Stir until the vegetables are thoroughly coated with oil. Place the cake pan in the air fryer basket and set the air fryer to 400°F (204°C). Air fry for 5 minutes until the vegetables soften. 2. Meanwhile, in a medium bowl, whisk the eggs and Parmesan until thoroughly combined. Pour the egg mixture into the pan and shake gently to distribute the vegetables. Air fry for another 15 minutes until the eggs are set. 3. Remove from the air fryer and let sit for 5 minutes to cool slightly. Use a silicone spatula to gently lift the frittata onto a plate before serving.

Vanilla Granola

Prep time: 5 minutes | Cook time: 40 minutes | Serves 4

1 cup rolled oats	¼ teaspoon vanilla
3 tablespoons maple syrup	¼ teaspoon cinnamon
1 tablespoon sunflower oil	¼ teaspoon sea salt
1 tablespoon coconut sugar	

1. Preheat the air fryer to 248°F (120°C). 2. Mix together the oats, maple syrup, sunflower oil, coconut sugar, vanilla, cinnamon, and sea salt in a medium bowl and stir to combine. Transfer the mixture to a baking pan. 3. Place the pan in the air fryer basket and bake for 40 minutes, or until the granola is mostly dry and lightly browned. Stir the granola four times during cooking. 4. Let the granola stand for 5 to 10 minutes before serving.

Denver Omelet

Prep time: 5 minutes | Cook time: 8 minutes | Serves 1

2 large eggs	peppers
¼ cup unsweetened, unflavored almond milk	2 tablespoons diced green onions, plus more for garnish
¼ teaspoon fine sea salt	¼ cup shredded Cheddar cheese (about 1 ounce / 28 g) (omit for dairy-free)
⅛ teaspoon ground black pepper	
¼ cup diced ham (omit for vegetarian)	Quartered cherry tomatoes, for serving (optional)
¼ cup diced green and red bell	

1. Preheat the air fryer to 350°F (177°C). Grease a cake pan and set aside. 2. In a small bowl, use a fork to whisk together the eggs, almond milk, salt, and pepper. Add the ham, bell peppers, and green onions. Pour the mixture into the greased pan. Add the cheese on top (if using). 3. Place the pan in the basket of the air fryer. Bake for 8 minutes, or until the eggs are cooked to your liking. 4. Loosen the omelet from the sides of the pan with a spatula and place it on a serving plate. Garnish with green onions and serve with cherry tomatoes, if desired. Best served fresh.

Classic British Breakfast

Prep time: 5 minutes | Cook time: 25 minutes | Serves 2

1 cup potatoes, sliced and diced	1 tablespoon olive oil
2 cups beans in tomato sauce	1 sausage
2 eggs	Salt, to taste

1. Preheat the air fryer to 390°F (199°C) and allow to warm. 2. Break the eggs onto a baking dish and sprinkle with salt. 3. Lay the beans on the dish, next to the eggs. 4. In a bowl, coat the potatoes with the olive oil. Sprinkle with salt. 5. Transfer the bowl of potato slices to the air fryer and bake for 10 minutes. 6. Swap out the bowl of potatoes for the dish containing the eggs and beans. Bake for another 10 minutes. Cover the potatoes with parchment paper. 7. Slice up the sausage and throw the slices on top of the beans and eggs. Bake for another 5 minutes. 8. Serve with the potatoes.

Hole in One

Prep time: 5 minutes | Cook time: 6 to 7 minutes | Serves 1

1 slice bread	1 tablespoon shredded Cheddar cheese
1 teaspoon soft butter	
1 egg	2 teaspoons diced ham
Salt and pepper, to taste	

1. Place a baking dish inside air fryer basket and preheat the air fryer to 330°F (166°C). 2. Using a 2½-inch-diameter biscuit cutter, cut a hole in center of bread slice. 3. Spread softened butter on both sides of bread. 4. Lay bread slice in baking dish and crack egg into the hole. Sprinkle egg with salt and pepper to taste. 5. Cook for 5 minutes. 6. Turn toast over and top it with shredded cheese and diced ham. 7. Cook for 1 to 2 more minutes or until yolk is done to your liking.

Homemade Toaster Pastries

Prep time: 10 minutes | Cook time: 11 minutes | Makes 6 pastries

Oil, for spraying	2 cups confectioners' sugar
1 (15-ounce / 425-g) package refrigerated piecrust	3 tablespoons milk
6 tablespoons jam or preserves of choice	1 to 2 tablespoons sprinkles of choice

1. Preheat the air fryer to 350°F (177°C). Line the air fryer basket with parchment and spray lightly with oil. 2. Cut the piecrust into 12 rectangles, about 3 by 4 inches each. You will need to reroll the dough scraps to get 12 rectangles. 3. Spread 1 tablespoon of jam in the center of 6 rectangles, leaving ¼ inch around the edges. 4. Pour some water into a small bowl. Use your finger to moisten the edge of each rectangle. 5. Top each rectangle with another and use your fingers to press around the edges. Using the tines of a fork, seal the edges of the dough and poke a few holes in the top of each one. Place the pastries in the prepared basket. 6. Air fry for 11 minutes. Let cool completely. 7. In a medium bowl, whisk together the confectioners' sugar and milk. Spread the icing over the tops of the pastries and add sprinkles. Serve immediately

Italian Egg Cups

Prep time: 5 minutes | Cook time: 10 minutes | Serves 4

Olive oil	cheese
1 cup marinara sauce	Salt and freshly ground black
4 eggs	pepper, to taste
4 tablespoons shredded	Chopped fresh basil, for
Mozzarella cheese	garnish
4 teaspoons grated Parmesan	

1. Lightly spray 4 individual ramekins with olive oil. 2. Pour ¼ cup of marinara sauce into each ramekin. 3. Crack one egg into each ramekin on top of the marinara sauce. 4. Sprinkle 1 tablespoon of Mozzarella and 1 tablespoon of Parmesan on top of each egg. Season with salt and pepper. 5. Cover each ramekin with aluminum foil. Place two of the ramekins in the air fryer basket. 6. Air fry at 350°F (177°C) for 5 minutes and remove the aluminum foil. Air fry until the top is lightly browned and the egg white is cooked, another 2 to 4 minutes. If you prefer the yolk to be firmer, cook for 3 to 5 more minutes. 7. Repeat with the remaining two ramekins. Garnish with basil and serve.

Spinach and Mushroom Mini Quiche

Prep time: 10 minutes | Cook time: 15 minutes | Serves 4

1 teaspoon olive oil, plus more for spraying	½ cup shredded Cheddar cheese
1 cup coarsely chopped mushrooms	½ cup shredded Mozzarella cheese
1 cup fresh baby spinach, shredded	¼ teaspoon salt
4 eggs, beaten	¼ teaspoon black pepper

1. Spray 4 silicone baking cups with olive oil and set aside. 2. In a medium sauté pan over medium heat, warm 1 teaspoon of olive oil. Add the mushrooms and sauté until soft, 3 to 4 minutes. 3. Add the spinach and cook until wilted, 1 to 2 minutes. Set aside. 4. In a medium bowl, whisk together the eggs, Cheddar cheese, Mozzarella cheese, salt, and pepper. 5. Gently fold the mushrooms and spinach into the egg mixture. 6. Pour ¼ of the mixture into each silicone baking cup. 7. Place the baking cups into the air fryer basket and air fry at 350°F (177°C) for 5 minutes. Stir the mixture in each ramekin slightly and air fry until the egg has set, an additional 3 to 5 minutes.

Buffalo Chicken Breakfast Muffins

Prep time: 7 minutes | Cook time: 13 to 16 minutes | Serves 10

6 ounces (170 g) shredded cooked chicken	as Frank's RedHot
3 ounces (85 g) blue cheese, crumbled	1 teaspoon minced garlic
2 tablespoons unsalted butter, melted	6 large eggs
	Sea salt and freshly ground black pepper, to taste
⅓ cup Buffalo hot sauce, such	Avocado oil spray

1. In a large bowl, stir together the chicken, blue cheese, melted butter, hot sauce, and garlic. 2. In a medium bowl or large liquid measuring cup, beat the eggs. Season with salt and pepper. 3. Spray 10 silicone muffin cups with oil. Divide the chicken mixture among the cups, and pour the egg mixture over top. 4. Place the cups in the air fryer and set to 300°F (149°C). Bake for 13 to 16 minutes, until the muffins are set and cooked through. (Depending on the size of your air fryer, you may need to cook the muffins in batches.)

Western Frittata

Prep time: 10 minutes | Cook time: 19 minutes | Serves 1 to 2

½ red or green bell pepper, cut into ½-inch chunks	Salt and freshly ground black pepper, to taste
1 teaspoon olive oil	1 teaspoon butter
3 eggs, beaten	1 teaspoon chopped fresh parsley
¼ cup grated Cheddar cheese	
¼ cup diced cooked ham	

1. Preheat the air fryer to 400°F (204°C). 2. Toss the peppers with the olive oil and air fry for 6 minutes, shaking the basket once or twice during the cooking process to redistribute the ingredients. 3. While the vegetables are cooking, beat the eggs well in a bowl, stir in the Cheddar cheese and ham, and season with salt and freshly ground black pepper. Add the air-fried peppers to this bowl when they have finished cooking. 4. Place a cake pan into the air fryer basket with the butter using an aluminum sling to lower the pan into the basket. Air fry for 1 minute at 380°F (193°C) to melt the butter. Remove the cake pan and rotate the pan to distribute the butter and grease the pan. Pour the egg mixture into the cake pan and return the pan to the air fryer, using the aluminum sling. 5. Air fry at 380°F (193°C) for 12 minutes, or until the frittata has puffed up and is lightly browned. Let the frittata sit in the air fryer for 5 minutes to cool to an edible temperature and set up. Remove the cake pan from the air fryer, sprinkle with parsley and serve immediately.

Hearty Blueberry Oatmeal

Prep time: 10 minutes | Cook time: 25 minutes | Serves 6

1½ cups quick oats	1 teaspoon vanilla extract
1¼ teaspoons ground cinnamon, divided	1 egg, beaten
½ teaspoon baking powder	2 cups blueberries
Pinch salt	Olive oil
1 cup unsweetened vanilla almond milk	1½ teaspoons sugar, divided
¼ cup honey	6 tablespoons low-fat whipped topping (optional)

1. In a large bowl, mix together the oats, 1 teaspoon of cinnamon, baking powder, and salt. 2. In a medium bowl, whisk together the almond milk, honey, vanilla and egg. 3. Pour the liquid ingredients into the oats mixture and stir to combine. Fold in the blueberries. 4. Lightly spray a baking pan with oil. 5. Add half the blueberry mixture to the pan. 6. Sprinkle ⅛ teaspoon of cinnamon and ½ teaspoon sugar over the top. 7. Cover the pan with aluminum foil and place gently in the air fryer basket. 8. Air fry at 360°F (182°C) for 20 minutes. Remove the foil and air fry for an additional 5 minutes. Transfer the mixture to a shallow bowl. 9. Repeat with the remaining blueberry mixture, ½ teaspoon of sugar, and ⅛ teaspoon of cinnamon. 10. To serve, spoon into bowls and top with whipped topping.

Sausage Stuffed Poblanos

Prep time: 15 minutes | Cook time: 15 minutes | Serves 4

½ pound (227 g) spicy ground pork breakfast sausage	and green chiles, drained
4 large eggs	4 large poblano peppers
4 ounces (113 g) full-fat cream cheese, softened	8 tablespoons shredded Pepper Jack cheese
¼ cup canned diced tomatoes	½ cup full-fat sour cream

1. In a medium skillet over medium heat, crumble and brown the ground sausage until no pink remains. Remove sausage and drain the fat from the pan. Crack eggs into the pan, scramble, and cook until no longer runny. 2. Place cooked sausage in a large bowl and fold in cream cheese. Mix in diced tomatoes and chiles. Gently fold in eggs. 3. Cut a 4-inch to 5-inch slit in the top of each poblano, removing the seeds and white membrane with a small knife. Separate the filling into four servings and spoon carefully into each pepper. Top each with 2 tablespoons pepper jack cheese. 4. Place each pepper into the air fryer basket. 5. Adjust the temperature to 350°F (177°C) and set the timer for 15 minutes. 6. Peppers will be soft and cheese will be browned when ready. Serve immediately with sour cream on top.

Breakfast Cobbler

Prep time: 20 minutes | Cook time: 30 minutes | Serves 4

Filling:	spread for dairy-free), softened
10 ounces (283 g) bulk pork sausage, crumbled	¾ cup beef or chicken broth
¼ cup minced onions	Biscuits:
2 cloves garlic, minced	3 large egg whites
½ teaspoon fine sea salt	¾ cup blanched almond flour
½ teaspoon ground black pepper	1 teaspoon baking powder
	¼ teaspoon fine sea salt
1 (8-ounce / 227-g) package cream cheese (or Kite Hill brand cream cheese style	2½ tablespoons very cold unsalted butter, cut into ¼-inch pieces
	Fresh thyme leaves, for garnish

1. Preheat the air fryer to 400°F (204°C). 2. Place the sausage, onions, and garlic in a pie pan. Using your hands, break up the sausage into small pieces and spread it evenly throughout the pie pan. Season with the salt and pepper. Place the pan in the air fryer and bake for 5 minutes. 3. While the sausage cooks, place the cream cheese and broth in a food processor or blender and purée until smooth. 4. Remove the pork from the air fryer and use a fork or metal spatula to crumble it more. Pour the cream cheese mixture into the sausage and stir to combine. Set aside. 5. Make the biscuits: Place the egg whites in a medium-sized mixing bowl or the bowl of a stand mixer and whip with a hand mixer or stand mixer until stiff peaks form. 6. In a separate medium-sized bowl, whisk together the almond flour, baking powder, and salt, then cut in the butter. When you are done, the mixture should still have chunks of butter. Gently fold the flour mixture into the egg whites with a rubber spatula. 7. Use a large spoon or ice cream scoop to scoop the dough into 4 equal-sized biscuits, making sure the butter is evenly distributed. Place the biscuits on top of the sausage and cook in the air fryer for 5 minutes, then turn the heat down to 325°F (163°C) and bake for another 17 to 20 minutes, until the biscuits are golden brown. Serve garnished

with fresh thyme leaves. 8. Store leftovers in an airtight container in the refrigerator for up to 3 days. Reheat in a preheated 350°F (177°C) air fryer for 5 minutes, or until warmed through.

Chocolate Doughnut Holes

Prep time: 10 minutes | Cook time: 8 to 12 minutes per batch | Makes 24 doughnut holes

1 (8-count) can refrigerated biscuits	3 tablespoons melted unsalted butter
Cooking oil spray	¼ cup confectioners' sugar
48 semisweet chocolate chips	

1. Separate the biscuits and cut each biscuit into thirds, for 24 pieces. 2. Flatten each biscuit piece slightly and put 2 chocolate chips in the center. Wrap the dough around the chocolate and seal the edges well. 3. Insert the crisper plate into the basket and the basket into the unit. Preheat the unit by selecting AIR FRY, setting the temperature to 330°F (166°C), and setting the time to 3 minutes. Select START/STOP to begin. 4. Once the unit is preheated, spray the crisper plate with cooking oil. Brush each doughnut hole with a bit of the butter and place it into the basket. Select AIR FRY, set the temperature to 330°F (166°C), and set the time between 8 and 12 minutes. Select START/STOP to begin. 5. The doughnuts are done when they are golden brown. When the cooking is complete, place the doughnut holes on a plate and dust with the confectioners' sugar. Serve warm.

Peppered Maple Bacon Knots

Prep time: 5 minutes | Cook time: 7 to 8 minutes | Serves 6

1 pound (454 g) maple smoked center-cut bacon	¼ cup brown sugar
¼ cup maple syrup	Coarsely cracked black peppercorns, to taste

1. Preheat the air fryer to 390°F (199°C). 2. On a clean work surface, tie each bacon strip in a loose knot. 3. Stir together the maple syrup and brown sugar in a bowl. Generously brush this mixture over the bacon knots. 4. Working in batches, arrange the bacon knots in the air fryer basket. Sprinkle with the coarsely cracked black peppercorns. 5. Air fry for 5 minutes. Flip the bacon knots and continue cooking for 2 to 3 minutes more, or until the bacon is crisp. 6. Remove from the basket to a paper towel-lined plate. Repeat with the remaining bacon knots. 7. Let the bacon knots cool for a few minutes and serve warm.

Golden Avocado Tempura

Prep time: 5 minutes | Cook time: 10 minutes | Serves 4

½ cup bread crumbs	and sliced
½ teaspoons salt	Liquid from 1 can white beans
1 Haas avocado, pitted, peeled	

1. Preheat the air fryer to 350°F (177°C). 2. Mix the bread crumbs and salt in a shallow bowl until well-incorporated. 3. Dip the avocado slices in the bean liquid, then into the bread crumbs. 4. Put the avocados in the air fryer, taking care not to overlap any slices, and air fry for 10 minutes, giving the basket a good shake at the halfway point. 5. Serve immediately.

Berry Muffins

Prep time: 15 minutes | Cook time: 12 to 17 minutes | Makes 8 muffins

1⅓ cups plus 1 tablespoon all-purpose flour, divided	2 eggs
¼ cup granulated sugar	⅔ cup whole milk
2 tablespoons light brown sugar	⅓ cup safflower oil
2 teaspoons baking powder	1 cup mixed fresh berries

1. In a medium bowl, stir together 1⅓ cups of flour, the granulated sugar, brown sugar, and baking powder until mixed well. 2. In a small bowl, whisk the eggs, milk, and oil until combined. Stir the egg mixture into the dry ingredients just until combined. 3. In another small bowl, toss the mixed berries with the remaining 1 tablespoon of flour until coated. Gently stir the berries into the batter. 4. Double up 16 foil muffin cups to make 8 cups. 5. Insert the crisper plate into the basket and the basket into the unit. Preheat the unit by selecting BAKE, setting the temperature to 315°F (157°C), and setting the time to 3 minutes. Select START/STOP to begin. 6. Once the unit is preheated, place 4 cups into the basket and fill each three-quarters full with the batter. 7. Select BAKE, set the temperature to 315°F (157°C), and set the time for 17 minutes. Select START/STOP to begin. 8. After about 12 minutes, check the muffins. If they spring back when lightly touched with your finger, they are done. If not, resume cooking. 9. When the cooking is done, transfer the muffins to a wire rack to cool. 10. Repeat steps 6, 7, and 8 with the remaining muffin cups and batter. 11. Let the muffins cool for 10 minutes before serving.

Sausage and Egg Breakfast Burrito

Prep time: 5 minutes | Cook time: 30 minutes | Serves 6

6 eggs	chicken sausage
Salt and pepper, to taste	½ cup salsa
Cooking oil	6 medium (8-inch) flour
½ cup chopped red bell pepper	tortillas
½ cup chopped green bell pepper	½ cup shredded Cheddar cheese
8 ounces (227 g) ground	

1. In a medium bowl, whisk the eggs. Add salt and pepper to taste. 2. Place a skillet on medium-high heat. Spray with cooking oil. Add the eggs. Scramble for 2 to 3 minutes, until the eggs are fluffy. Remove the eggs from the skillet and set aside. 3. If needed, spray the skillet with more oil. Add the chopped red and green bell peppers. Cook for 2 to 3 minutes, until the peppers are soft. 4. Add the ground sausage to the skillet. Break the sausage into smaller pieces using a spatula or spoon. Cook for 3 to 4 minutes, until the sausage is brown. 5. Add the salsa and scrambled eggs. Stir to combine. Remove the skillet from heat. 6. Spoon the mixture evenly onto the tortillas. 7. To form the burritos, fold the sides of each tortilla in toward the middle and then roll up from the bottom. You can secure each burrito with a toothpick. Or you can moisten the outside edge of the tortilla with a small amount of water. I prefer to use a cooking brush, but you can also dab with your fingers. 8. Spray the burritos with cooking oil and place them in the air fryer. Do not stack. Cook the burritos in batches if they do not all fit in the basket. Air fry at 400°F (204°C) for 8 minutes. 9. Open the air fryer and flip the burritos. Cook for an additional 2 minutes or until crisp. 10. If necessary, repeat steps 8 and 9 for the remaining burritos. 11. Sprinkle the Cheddar cheese over the burritos. Cool before serving.

Not-So-English Muffins

Prep time: 5 minutes | Cook time: 10 minutes | Serves 4

2 strips turkey bacon, cut in half crosswise	stems removed
2 whole-grain English muffins, split	¼ ripe pear, peeled and thinly sliced
1 cup fresh baby spinach, long	4 slices Provolone cheese

1. Place bacon strips in air fryer basket and air fry at 390°F (199°C) for 2 minutes. Check and separate strips if necessary so they cook evenly. Cook for 3 to 4 more minutes, until crispy. Remove and drain on paper towels. 2. Place split muffin halves in air fryer basket and cook for 2 minutes, just until lightly browned. 3. Open air fryer and top each muffin with a quarter of the baby spinach, several pear slices, a strip of bacon, and a slice of cheese. 4. Air fry at 360°F (182°C) for 1 to 2 minutes, until cheese completely melts.

Breakfast Pita

Prep time: 5 minutes | Cook time: 6 minutes | Serves 2

1 whole wheat pita	¼ teaspoon dried oregano
2 teaspoons olive oil	¼ teaspoon dried thyme
½ shallot, diced	⅛ teaspoon salt
¼ teaspoon garlic, minced	2 tablespoons shredded
1 large egg	Parmesan cheese

1. Preheat the air fryer to 380°F (193°C). 2. Brush the top of the pita with olive oil, then spread the diced shallot and minced garlic over the pita. 3. Crack the egg into a small bowl or ramekin, and season it with oregano, thyme, and salt. 4. Place the pita into the air fryer basket, and gently pour the egg onto the top of the pita. Sprinkle with cheese over the top. 5. Bake for 6 minutes. 6. Allow to cool for 5 minutes before cutting into pieces for serving.

Lemon-Blueberry Muffins

Prep time: 5 minutes | Cook time: 20 to 25 minutes | Makes 6 muffins

1¼ cups almond flour	3 tablespoons melted butter
3 tablespoons Swerve	1 tablespoon almond milk
1 teaspoon baking powder	1 tablespoon fresh lemon juice
2 large eggs	½ cup fresh blueberries

1. Preheat the air fryer to 350°F (177°C). Lightly coat 6 silicone muffin cups with vegetable oil. Set aside. 2. In a large mixing bowl, combine the almond flour, Swerve, and baking soda. Set aside. 3. In a separate small bowl, whisk together the eggs, butter, milk, and lemon juice. Add the egg mixture to the flour mixture and stir until just combined. Fold in the blueberries and let the batter sit for 5 minutes. 4. Spoon the muffin batter into the muffin cups, about two-thirds full. Air fry for 20 to 25 minutes, or until a toothpick inserted into the center of a muffin comes out clean. 5. Remove the basket from the air fryer and let the muffins cool for about 5 minutes before transferring them to a wire rack to cool completely.

Maple Doughnuts

Prep time: 10 minutes | Cook time: 14 minutes | Makes 8 doughnuts

1 (8-count) can jumbo flaky refrigerator biscuits	3 tablespoons milk
Cooking oil spray	2 cups confectioners' sugar, plus more for dusting (optional)
½ cup light brown sugar	
¼ cup butter	2 teaspoons pure maple syrup

1. Insert the crisper plate into the basket and the basket into the unit. Preheat the unit by selecting AIR FRY, setting the temperature to 350°F (177°C), and setting the time to 3 minutes. Select START/STOP to begin. 2. Remove the biscuits from the tube and cut out the center of each biscuit with a small, round cookie cutter. 3. Once the unit is preheated, spray the crisper plate with cooking oil. Working in batches, place 4 doughnuts into the basket. 4. Select AIR FRY, set the temperature to 350°F (177°C), and set the time to 5 minutes. Select START/STOP to begin. 5. When the cooking is complete, place the doughnuts on a plate. Repeat steps 3 and 4 with the remaining doughnuts. 6. In a small saucepan over medium heat, combine the brown sugar, butter, and milk. Heat until the butter is melted and the sugar is dissolved, about 4 minutes. 7. Remove the pan from the heat and whisk in the confectioners' sugar and maple syrup until smooth. 8. Dip the slightly cooled doughnuts into the maple glaze. Place them on a wire rack and dust with confectioners' sugar (if using). Let rest just until the glaze sets. Enjoy the doughnuts warm.

Parmesan Sausage Egg Muffins

Prep time: 5 minutes | Cook time: 20 minutes | Serves 4

6 ounces (170 g) Italian sausage, sliced	Salt and ground black pepper, to taste
6 eggs	3 ounces (85 g) Parmesan cheese, grated
⅛ cup heavy cream	

1. Preheat the air fryer to 350°F (177°C). Grease a muffin pan. 2. Put the sliced sausage in the muffin pan. 3. Beat the eggs with the cream in a bowl and season with salt and pepper. 4. Pour half of the mixture over the sausages in the pan. 5. Sprinkle with cheese and the remaining egg mixture. 6. Bake in the preheated air fryer for 20 minutes or until set. 7. Serve immediately.

Greek Bagels

Prep time: 10 minutes | Cook time: 10 minutes | Makes 2 bagels

½ cup self-rising flour, plus more for dusting	4 teaspoons everything bagel spice mix
½ cup plain Greek yogurt	Cooking oil spray
1 egg	1 tablespoon butter, melted
1 tablespoon water	

1. In a large bowl, using a wooden spoon, stir together the flour and yogurt until a tacky dough forms. Transfer the dough to a lightly floured work surface and roll the dough into a ball. 2. Cut the dough into 2 pieces and roll each piece into a log. Form each log into a bagel shape, pinching the ends together. 3. In a small bowl, whisk the egg and water. Brush the egg wash on the bagels. 4. Sprinkle 2 teaspoons of the spice mix on each bagel and gently press it into the dough. 5. Insert the crisper plate into the basket and the basket into the unit. Preheat the unit by selecting BAKE, setting the temperature to 330°F (166°C), and setting the time to 3 minutes. Select START/STOP to begin. 6. Once the unit is preheated, spray the crisper plate with cooking spray. Drizzle the bagels with the butter and place them into the basket. 7. Select BAKE, set the temperature to 330°F (166°C), and set the time to 10 minutes. Select START/STOP to begin. 8. When the cooking is complete, the bagels should be lightly golden on the outside. Serve warm.

Cajun Breakfast Sausage

Prep time: 10 minutes | Cook time: 15 to 20 minutes | Serves 8

1½ pounds (680 g) 85% lean ground turkey	1 teaspoon Creole seasoning
3 cloves garlic, finely chopped	1 teaspoon dried thyme
¼ onion, grated	½ teaspoon paprika
1 teaspoon Tabasco sauce	½ teaspoon cayenne

1. Preheat the air fryer to 370°F (188°C). 2. In a large bowl, combine the turkey, garlic, onion, Tabasco, Creole seasoning, thyme, paprika, and cayenne. Mix with clean hands until thoroughly combined. Shape into 16 patties, about ½ inch thick. (Wet your hands slightly if you find the sausage too sticky to handle.) 3. Working in batches if necessary, arrange the patties in a single layer in the air fryer basket. Pausing halfway through the cooking time to flip the patties, air fry for 15 to 20 minutes until a thermometer inserted into the thickest portion registers 165°F (74°C).

Turkey Sausage Breakfast Pizza

Prep time: 15 minutes | Cook time: 24 minutes | Serves 2

4 large eggs, divided	½ cup shredded provolone cheese
1 tablespoon water	
½ teaspoon garlic powder	1 link cooked turkey sausage, chopped (about 2 ounces / 57 g)
½ teaspoon onion powder	
½ teaspoon dried oregano	2 sun-dried tomatoes, finely chopped
2 tablespoons coconut flour	
3 tablespoons grated Parmesan cheese	2 scallions, thinly sliced

1. Preheat the air fryer to 400°F (204°C). Line a cake pan with parchment paper and lightly coat the paper with olive oil. 2. In a large bowl, whisk 2 of the eggs with the water, garlic powder, onion powder, and dried oregano. Add the coconut flour, breaking up any lumps with your hands as you add it to the bowl. Stir the coconut flour into the egg mixture, mixing until smooth. Stir in the Parmesan cheese. Allow the mixture to rest for a few minutes until thick and dough-like. 3. Transfer the mixture to the prepared pan. Use a spatula to spread it evenly and slightly up the sides of the pan. Air fry until the crust is set but still light in color, about 10 minutes. Top with the cheeses, sausage, and sun-dried tomatoes. 4. Break the remaining 2 eggs into a small bowl, then slide them onto the pizza. Return the pizza to the air fryer. Air fry 10 to 14 minutes until the egg whites are set and the yolks are the desired doneness. Top with the scallions and allow to rest for 5 minutes before serving.

Hearty Cheddar Biscuits

Prep time: 10 minutes | Cook time: 22 minutes | Makes 8 biscuits

2⅓ cups self-rising flour	plus more to melt on top
2 tablespoons sugar	1⅓ cups buttermilk
½ cup butter (1 stick), frozen for 15 minutes	1 cup all-purpose flour, for shaping
½ cup grated Cheddar cheese,	1 tablespoon butter, melted

1. Line a buttered 7-inch metal cake pan with parchment paper or a silicone liner. 2. Combine the flour and sugar in a large mixing bowl. Grate the butter into the flour. Add the grated cheese and stir to coat the cheese and butter with flour. Then add the buttermilk and stir just until you can no longer see streaks of flour. The dough should be quite wet. 3. Spread the all-purpose (not self-rising) flour out on a small cookie sheet. With a spoon, scoop 8 evenly sized balls of dough into the flour, making sure they don't touch each other. With floured hands, coat each dough ball with flour and toss them gently from hand to hand to shake off any excess flour. Put each floured dough ball into the prepared pan, right up next to the other. This will help the biscuits rise, rather than spreading out. 4. Preheat the air fryer to 380°F (193°C). 5. Transfer the cake pan to the basket of the air fryer. Let the ends of the aluminum foil sling hang across the cake pan before returning the basket to the air fryer. 6. Air fry for 20 minutes. Check the biscuits twice to make sure they are not getting too brown on top. If they are, re-arrange the aluminum foil strips to cover any brown parts. After 20 minutes, check the biscuits by inserting a toothpick into the center of the biscuits. It should come out clean. If it needs a little more time, continue to air fry for two extra minutes. Brush the tops of the biscuits with some melted butter and sprinkle a little more grated cheese on top if desired. Pop the basket back into the air fryer for another 2 minutes. 7. Remove the cake pan from the air fryer. Let the biscuits cool for just a minute or two and then turn them out onto a plate and pull apart. Serve immediately.

New York Strip Steaks with Eggs

Prep time: 8 minutes | Cook time: 14 minutes per batch | Serves 4

Cooking oil spray	1 teaspoon salt, divided
4 (4-ounce / 113-g) New York strip steaks	1 teaspoon freshly ground black pepper, divided
1 teaspoon granulated garlic, divided	4 eggs
	½ teaspoon paprika

1. Insert the crisper plate into the basket and the basket into the unit. Preheat the unit by selecting AIR FRY, setting the temperature to 360°F (182°C), and setting the time to 3 minutes. Select START/STOP to begin. 2. Once the unit is preheated, spray the crisper plate with cooking oil. Place 2 steaks into the basket; do not oil or season them at this time. 3. Select AIR FRY, set the temperature to 360°F (182°C), and set the time to 9 minutes. Select START/STOP to begin. 4. After 5 minutes, open the unit and flip the steaks. Sprinkle each with ¼ teaspoon of granulated garlic, ¼ teaspoon of salt, and ¼ teaspoon of pepper. Resume cooking until the steaks register at least 145°F (63°C) on a food thermometer. 5. When the cooking is complete, transfer the steaks to a plate and tent with aluminum foil to keep warm. Repeat steps 2, 3, and 4 with the remaining steaks.

6. Spray 4 ramekins with olive oil. Crack 1 egg into each ramekin. Sprinkle the eggs with the paprika and remaining ½ teaspoon each of salt and pepper. Working in batches, place 2 ramekins into the basket. 7. Select BAKE, set the temperature to 330°F (166°C), and set the time to 5 minutes. Select START/STOP to begin. 8. When the cooking is complete and the eggs are cooked to 160°F (71°C), remove the ramekins and repeat step 7 with the remaining 2 ramekins. 9. Serve the eggs with the steaks.

Breakfast Meatballs

Prep time: 10 minutes | Cook time: 15 minutes | Makes 18 meatballs

1 pound (454 g) ground pork breakfast sausage	½ cup shredded sharp Cheddar cheese
½ teaspoon salt	1 ounce (28 g) cream cheese, softened
¼ teaspoon ground black pepper	1 large egg, whisked

1. Combine all ingredients in a large bowl. Form mixture into eighteen 1-inch meatballs. 2. Place meatballs into ungreased air fryer basket. Adjust the temperature to 400°F (204°C) and air fry for 15 minutes, shaking basket three times during cooking. Meatballs will be browned on the outside and have an internal temperature of at least 145°F (63°C) when completely cooked. Serve warm.

Parmesan Ranch Risotto

Prep time: 10 minutes | Cook time: 30 minutes | Serves 2

1 tablespoon olive oil	¾ cup Arborio rice
1 clove garlic, minced	2 cups chicken stock, boiling
1 tablespoon unsalted butter	½ cup Parmesan cheese, grated
1 onion, diced	

1. Preheat the air fryer to 390°F (199°C). 2. Grease a round baking tin with olive oil and stir in the garlic, butter, and onion. 3. Transfer the tin to the air fryer and bake for 4 minutes. Add the rice and bake for 4 more minutes. 4. Turn the air fryer to 320°F (160°C) and pour in the chicken stock. Cover and bake for 22 minutes. 5. Scatter with cheese and serve.

Egg White Cups

Prep time: 10 minutes | Cook time: 15 minutes | Serves 4

2 cups 100% liquid egg whites	½ medium Roma tomato, cored and diced
3 tablespoons salted butter, melted	½ cup chopped fresh spinach leaves
¼ teaspoon salt	
¼ teaspoon onion powder	

1. In a large bowl, whisk egg whites with butter, salt, and onion powder. Stir in tomato and spinach, then pour evenly into four ramekins greased with cooking spray. 2. Place ramekins into air fryer basket. Adjust the temperature to 300°F (149°C) and bake for 15 minutes. Eggs will be fully cooked and firm in the center when done. Serve warm.

All-in-One Toast

Prep time: 10 minutes | Cook time: 10 minutes | Serves 1

1 strip bacon, diced
1 slice 1-inch thick bread
1 egg

Salt and freshly ground black pepper, to taste
¼ cup grated Colby cheese

1. Preheat the air fryer to 400°F (204°C). 2. Air fry the bacon for 3 minutes, shaking the basket once or twice while it cooks. Remove the bacon to a paper towel lined plate and set aside. 3. Use a sharp paring knife to score a large circle in the middle of the slice of bread, cutting halfway through, but not all the way through to the cutting board. Press down on the circle in the center of the bread slice to create an indentation. 4. Transfer the slice of bread, hole side up, to the air fryer basket. Crack the egg into the center of the bread, and season with salt and pepper. 5. Adjust the air fryer temperature to 380°F (193°C) and air fry for 5 minutes. Sprinkle the grated cheese around the edges of the bread, leaving the center of the yolk uncovered, and top with the cooked bacon. Press the cheese and bacon into the bread lightly to help anchor it to the bread and prevent it from blowing around in the air fryer. 6. Air fry for one or two more minutes, just to melt the cheese and finish cooking the egg. Serve immediately.

Egg Muffins

Prep time: 10 minutes | Cook time: 11 to 13 minutes | Serves 4

4 eggs
Salt and pepper, to taste
Olive oil

4 English muffins, split
1 cup shredded Colby Jack cheese
4 slices ham or Canadian bacon

1. Preheat the air fryer to 390°F (199°C). 2. Beat together eggs and add salt and pepper to taste. Spray a baking pan lightly with oil and add eggs. Bake for 2 minutes, stir, and continue cooking for 3 or 4 minutes, stirring every minute, until eggs are scrambled to your preference. Remove pan from air fryer. 3. Place bottom halves of English muffins in air fryer basket. Take half of the shredded cheese and divide it among the muffins. Top each with a slice of ham and one-quarter of the eggs. Sprinkle remaining cheese on top of the eggs. Use a fork to press the cheese into the egg a little so it doesn't slip off before it melts. 4. Air fry at 360°F (182°C) for 1 minute. Add English muffin tops and cook for 2 to 4 minutes to heat through and toast the muffins.

Chapter 2   Family Favorites

Puffed Egg Tarts

Prep time: 10 minutes | Cook time: 42 minutes | Makes 4 tarts

Oil, for spraying	4 large eggs
All-purpose flour, for dusting	2 teaspoons chopped fresh
1 (12-ounce / 340-g) sheet	parsley
frozen puff pastry, thawed	Salt and freshly ground black
¾ cup shredded Cheddar	pepper, to taste
cheese, divided	

1. Preheat the air fryer to 390ºF (199ºC). Line the air fryer basket with parchment and spray lightly with oil. 2. Lightly dust your work surface with flour. Unfold the puff pastry and cut it into 4 equal squares. Place 2 squares in the prepared basket. 3. Cook for 10 minutes. 4. Remove the basket. Press the center of each tart shell with a spoon to make an indentation. 5. Sprinkle 3 tablespoons of cheese into each indentation and crack 1 egg into the center of each tart shell. 6. Cook for another 7 to 11 minutes, or until the eggs are cooked to your desired doneness. 7. Repeat with the remaining puff pastry squares, cheese, and eggs. 8. Sprinkle evenly with the parsley, and season with salt and black pepper. Serve immediately.

Pork Burgers with Red Cabbage Salad

Prep time: 20 minutes | Cook time: 7 to 9 minutes | Serves 4

½ cup Greek yogurt	pork
2 tablespoons low-sodium	½ teaspoon paprika
mustard, divided	1 cup mixed baby lettuce greens
1 tablespoon lemon juice	2 small tomatoes, sliced
¼ cup sliced red cabbage	8 small low-sodium whole-
¼ cup grated carrots	wheat sandwich buns, cut in
1 pound (454 g) lean ground	half

1. In a small bowl, combine the yogurt, 1 tablespoon mustard, lemon juice, cabbage, and carrots; mix and refrigerate. 2. In a medium bowl, combine the pork, remaining 1 tablespoon mustard, and paprika. Form into 8 small patties. 3. Put the sliders into the air fryer basket. Air fry at 400ºF (204ºC) for 7 to 9 minutes, or until the sliders register 165ºF (74ºC) as tested with a meat thermometer. 4. Assemble the burgers by placing some of the lettuce greens on a bun bottom. Top with a tomato slice, the burgers, and the cabbage mixture. Add the bun top and serve immediately.

Pecan Rolls

Prep time: 20 minutes | Cook time: 20 to 24 minutes | Makes 12 rolls

2 cups all-purpose flour, plus	¾ cup milk, whole or 2%
more for dusting	¼ cup packed light brown
2 tablespoons granulated sugar,	sugar
plus ¼ cup, divided	½ cup chopped pecans, toasted
1 teaspoon salt	1 to 2 tablespoons oil
3 tablespoons butter, at room	¼ cup confectioners' sugar
temperature	(optional)

1. In a large bowl, whisk the flour, 2 tablespoons granulated sugar, and salt until blended. Stir in the butter and milk briefly until a sticky

dough forms. 2. In a small bowl, stir together the brown sugar and remaining ¼ cup of granulated sugar. 3. Place a piece of parchment paper on a work surface and dust it with flour. Roll the dough on the prepared surface to ¼ inch thickness. 4. Spread the sugar mixture over the dough. Sprinkle the pecans on top. Roll up the dough jelly roll-style, pinching the ends to seal. Cut the dough into 12 rolls. 5. Preheat the air fryer to 320ºF (160ºC). 6. Line the air fryer basket with parchment paper and spritz the parchment with oil. Place 6 rolls on the prepared parchment. 7. Bake for 5 minutes. Flip the rolls and bake for 5 to 7 minutes more until lightly browned. Repeat with the remaining rolls. 8. Sprinkle with confectioners' sugar (if using).

Phyllo Vegetable Triangles

Prep time: 15 minutes | Cook time: 6 to 11 minutes | Serves 6

3 tablespoons minced onion	2 tablespoons nonfat cream
2 garlic cloves, minced	cheese, at room temperature
2 tablespoons grated carrot	6 sheets frozen phyllo dough,
1 teaspoon olive oil	thawed
3 tablespoons frozen baby peas,	Olive oil spray, for coating the
thawed	dough

1. In a baking pan, combine the onion, garlic, carrot, and olive oil. Air fry at 390ºF (199ºC) for 2 to 4 minutes, or until the vegetables are crisp-tender. Transfer to a bowl. 2. Stir in the peas and cream cheese to the vegetable mixture. Let cool while you prepare the dough. 3. Lay one sheet of phyllo on a work surface and lightly spray with olive oil spray. Top with another sheet of phyllo. Repeat with the remaining 4 phyllo sheets; you'll have 3 stacks with 2 layers each. Cut each stack lengthwise into 4 strips (12 strips total). 4. Place a scant 2 teaspoons of the filling near the bottom of each strip. Bring one corner up over the filling to make a triangle; continue folding the triangles over, as you would fold a flag. Seal the edge with a bit of water. Repeat with the remaining strips and filling. 5. Air fry the triangles, in 2 batches, for 4 to 7 minutes, or until golden brown. Serve.

Pork Stuffing Meatballs

Prep time: 10 minutes | Cook time: 12 minutes | Makes 35 meatballs

Oil, for spraying	1 tablespoon dried thyme
1½ pounds (680 g) ground pork	1 teaspoon salt
1 cup bread crumbs	1 teaspoon freshly ground
½ cup milk	black pepper
¼ cup minced onion	1 teaspoon finely chopped
1 large egg	fresh parsley
1 tablespoon dried rosemary	

1. Line the air fryer basket with parchment and spray lightly with oil. 2. In a large bowl, mix together the ground pork, bread crumbs, milk, onion, egg, rosemary, thyme, salt, black pepper, and parsley. 3. Roll about 2 tablespoons of the mixture into a ball. Repeat with the rest of the mixture. You should have 30 to 35 meatballs. 4. Place the meatballs in the prepared basket in a single layer, leaving space between each one. You may need to work in batches, depending on the size of your air fryer. 5. Air fry at 390ºF (199ºC) for 10 to 12 minutes, flipping after 5 minutes, or until golden brown and the internal temperature reaches 160ºF (71ºC).

Old Bay Tilapia

Prep time: 15 minutes | Cook time: 6 minutes | Serves 4

Oil, for spraying
1 cup panko bread crumbs
2 tablespoons Old Bay seasoning
2 teaspoons granulated garlic
1 teaspoon onion powder
½ teaspoon salt
¼ teaspoon freshly ground black pepper
1 large egg
4 tilapia fillets

1. Preheat the air fryer to 400°F (204°C). Line the air fryer basket with parchment and spray lightly with oil. 2. In a shallow bowl, mix together the bread crumbs, Old Bay, garlic, onion powder, salt, and black pepper. 3. In a small bowl, whisk the egg. 4. Coat the tilapia in the egg, then dredge in the bread crumb mixture until completely coated. 5. Place the tilapia in the prepared basket. You may need to work in batches, depending on the size of your air fryer. Spray lightly with oil. 6. Cook for 4 to 6 minutes, depending on the thickness of the fillets, until the internal temperature reaches 145°F (63°C). Serve immediately.

Apple Pie Egg Rolls

Prep time: 10 minutes | Cook time: 8 minutes | Makes 6 rolls

Oil, for spraying
1 (21-ounce / 595-g) can apple pie filling
1 tablespoon all-purpose flour
½ teaspoon lemon juice
¼ teaspoon ground nutmeg
¼ teaspoon ground cinnamon
6 egg roll wrappers

1. Preheat the air fryer to 400°F (204°C). Line the air fryer basket with parchment and spray lightly with oil. 2. In a medium bowl, mix together the pie filling, flour, lemon juice, nutmeg, and cinnamon. 3. Lay out the egg roll wrappers on a work surface and spoon a dollop of pie filling in the center of each. 4. Fill a small bowl with water. Dip your finger in the water and, working one at a time, moisten the edges of the wrappers. Fold the wrapper like an envelope: First fold one corner into the center. Fold each side corner in, and then fold over the remaining corner, making sure each corner overlaps a bit and the moistened edges stay closed. Use additional water and your fingers to seal any open edges. 5. Place the rolls in the prepared basket and spray liberally with oil. You may need to work in batches, depending on the size of your air fryer. 6. Cook for 4 minutes, flip, spray with oil, and cook for another 4 minutes, or until crispy and golden brown. Serve immediately.

Elephant Ears

Prep time: 5 minutes | Cook time: 5 minutes | Serves 8

Oil, for spraying
1 (8-ounce / 227-g) can buttermilk biscuits
3 tablespoons sugar
1 tablespoon ground cinnamon
3 tablespoons unsalted butter, melted
8 scoops vanilla ice cream (optional)

1. Line the air fryer basket with parchment and spray lightly with oil. 2. Separate the dough. Using a rolling pin, roll out the biscuits into 6- to 8-inch circles. 3. Place the dough circles in the prepared basket and spray liberally with oil. You may need to work in batches,

depending on the size of your air fryer. 4. Air fry at 350°F (177°C) for 5 minutes, or until lightly browned. 5. In a small bowl, mix together the sugar and cinnamon. 6. Brush the elephant ears with the melted butter and sprinkle with the cinnamon-sugar mixture. 7. Top each serving with a scoop of ice cream (if using).

Beignets

Prep time: 30 minutes | Cook time: 6 minutes | Makes 9 beignets

Oil, for greasing and spraying
3 cups all-purpose flour, plus more for dusting
1½ teaspoons salt
1 (2¼-teaspoon) envelope active dry yeast
1 cup milk
2 tablespoons packed light brown sugar
1 tablespoon unsalted butter
1 large egg
1 cup confectioners' sugar

1. Oil a large bowl. 2. In a small bowl, mix together the flour, salt, and yeast. Set aside. 3. Pour the milk into a glass measuring cup and microwave in 1-minute intervals until it boils. 4. In a large bowl, mix together the brown sugar and butter. Pour in the hot milk and whisk until the sugar has dissolved. Let cool to room temperature. 5. Whisk the egg into the cooled milk mixture and fold in the flour mixture until a dough forms. 6. On a lightly floured work surface, knead the dough for 3 to 5 minutes. 7. Place the dough in the oiled bowl and cover with a clean kitchen towel. Let rise in a warm place for about 1 hour, or until doubled in size. 8. Roll the dough out on a lightly floured work surface until it's about ¼ inch thick. Cut the dough into 3-inch squares and place them on a lightly floured baking sheet. Cover loosely with a kitchen towel and let rise again until doubled in size, about 30 minutes. 9. Line the air fryer basket with parchment and spray lightly with oil. 10. Place the dough squares in the prepared basket and spray lightly with oil. You may need to work in batches, depending on the size of your air fryer. 11. Air fry at 390°F (199°C) for 3 minutes, flip, spray with oil, and cook for another 3 minutes, until crispy. 12. Dust with the confectioners' sugar before serving.

Meringue Cookies

Prep time: 15 minutes | Cook time: 1 hour 30 minutes | Makes 20 cookies

Oil, for spraying
4 large egg whites
1 cup sugar
Pinch cream of tartar

1. Preheat the air fryer to 140°F (60°C). Line the air fryer basket with parchment and spray lightly with oil. 2. In a small heatproof bowl, whisk together the egg whites and sugar. Fill a small saucepan halfway with water, place it over medium heat, and bring to a light simmer. Place the bowl with the egg whites on the saucepan, making sure the bottom of the bowl does not touch the water. Whisk the mixture until the sugar is dissolved. 3. Transfer the mixture to a large bowl and add the cream of tartar. Using an electric mixer, beat the mixture on high until it is glossy and stiff peaks form. Transfer the mixture to a piping bag or a zip-top plastic bag with a corner cut off. 4. Pipe rounds into the prepared basket. You may need to work in batches, depending on the size of your air fryer. 5. Cook for 1 hour 30 minutes. 6. Turn off the air fryer and let the meringues cool completely inside. The residual heat will continue to dry them out.

Cajun Shrimp

Prep time: 15 minutes | Cook time: 9 minutes | Serves 4

Oil, for spraying
1 pound (454 g) jumbo raw shrimp, peeled and deveined
1 tablespoon Cajun seasoning
6 ounces (170 g) cooked kielbasa, cut into thick slices
½ medium zucchini, cut into ¼-inch-thick slices
½ medium yellow squash, cut into ¼-inch-thick slices
1 green bell pepper, seeded and cut into 1-inch pieces
2 tablespoons olive oil
½ teaspoon salt

1. Preheat the air fryer to 400°F (204°C). Line the air fryer basket with parchment and spray lightly with oil. 2. In a large bowl, toss together the shrimp and Cajun seasoning. Add the kielbasa, zucchini, squash, bell pepper, olive oil, and salt and mix well. 3. Transfer the mixture to the prepared basket, taking care not to overcrowd. You may need to work in batches, depending on the size of your air fryer. 4. Cook for 9 minutes, shaking and stirring every 3 minutes. Serve immediately.

Mixed Berry Crumble

Prep time: 10 minutes | Cook time: 11 to 16 minutes | Serves 4

½ cup chopped fresh strawberries
½ cup fresh blueberries
⅓ cup frozen raspberries
1 tablespoon freshly squeezed lemon juice
1 tablespoon honey
⅔ cup whole-wheat pastry flour
3 tablespoons packed brown sugar
2 tablespoons unsalted butter, melted

1. In a baking pan, combine the strawberries, blueberries, and raspberries. Drizzle with the lemon juice and honey. 2. In a small bowl, mix the pastry flour and brown sugar. 3. Stir in the butter and mix until crumbly. Sprinkle this mixture over the fruit. 4. Bake at 380°F (193°C) for 11 to 16 minutes, or until the fruit is tender and bubbly and the topping is golden brown. Serve warm.

Meatball Subs

Prep time: 15 minutes | Cook time: 19 minutes | Serves 6

Oil, for spraying
1 pound (454 g) 85% lean ground beef
½ cup Italian bread crumbs
1 tablespoon dried minced onion
1 tablespoon minced garlic
1 large egg
1 teaspoon salt
1 teaspoon freshly ground black pepper
6 hoagie rolls
1 (18-ounce / 510-g) jar marinara sauce
1½ cups shredded Mozzarella cheese

1. Line the air fryer basket with parchment and spray lightly with oil. 2. In a large bowl, mix together the ground beef, bread crumbs, onion, garlic, egg, salt, and black pepper. Roll the mixture into 18 meatballs. 3. Place the meatballs in the prepared basket. 4. Air fry at 390°F (199°C) for 15 minutes. 5. Place 3 meatballs in each hoagie roll. Top with marinara and Mozzarella cheese. 6. Place the loaded rolls in the air fryer and cook for 3 to 4 minutes, or until the cheese is melted. You may need to work in batches, depending on the size of your air fryer. Serve immediately.

Steak Tips and Potatoes

Prep time: 10 minutes | Cook time: 20 minutes | Serves 4

Oil, for spraying
8 ounces (227 g) baby gold potatoes, cut in half
½ teaspoon salt
1 pound (454 g) steak, cut into ½-inch pieces
1 teaspoon Worcestershire sauce
1 teaspoon granulated garlic
½ teaspoon salt
½ teaspoon freshly ground black pepper

1. Line the air fryer basket with parchment and spray lightly with oil. 2. In a microwave-safe bowl, combine the potatoes and salt, then pour in about ½ inch of water. Microwave for 7 minutes, or until the potatoes are nearly tender. Drain. 3. In a large bowl, gently mix together the steak, potatoes, Worcestershire sauce, garlic, salt, and black pepper. Spread the mixture in an even layer in the prepared basket. 4. Air fry at 400°F (204°C) for 12 to 17 minutes, stirring after 5 to 6 minutes. The cooking time will depend on the thickness of the meat and preferred doneness.

Bacon-Wrapped Hot Dogs

Prep time: 5 minutes | Cook time: 10 minutes | Serves 4

Oil, for spraying
4 bacon slices
4 all-beef hot dogs
4 hot dog buns
Toppings of choice

1. Line the air fryer basket with parchment and spray lightly with oil. 2. Wrap a strip of bacon tightly around each hot dog, taking care to cover the tips so they don't get too crispy. Secure with a toothpick at each end to keep the bacon from shrinking. 3. Place the hot dogs in the prepared basket. 4. Air fry at 380°F (193°C) for 8 to 9 minutes, depending on how crispy you like the bacon. For extra-crispy, cook the hot dogs at 400°F (204°C) for 6 to 8 minutes. 5. Place the hot dogs in the buns, return them to the air fryer, and cook for another 1 to 2 minutes, or until the buns are warm. Add your desired toppings and serve.

Buffalo Cauliflower

Prep time: 15 minutes | Cook time: 5 minutes | Serves 6

1 large head cauliflower, separated into small florets
1 tablespoon olive oil
½ teaspoon garlic powder
⅓ cup low-sodium hot wing sauce
⅔ cup nonfat Greek yogurt
½ teaspoons Tabasco sauce
1 celery stalk, chopped
1 tablespoon crumbled blue cheese

1. In a large bowl, toss the cauliflower florets with the olive oil. Sprinkle with the garlic powder and toss again to coat. Put half of the cauliflower in the air fryer basket. Air fry at 380°F (193°C) for 5 to 7 minutes, until the cauliflower is browned, shaking the basket once during cooking. 2. Transfer to a serving bowl and toss with half of the wing sauce. Repeat with the remaining cauliflower and wing sauce. 3. In a small bowl, stir together the yogurt, Tabasco sauce, celery, and blue cheese. Serve with the cauliflower for dipping.

Fish and Vegetable Tacos

Prep time: 15 minutes | Cook time: 9 to 12 minutes | Serves 4

1 pound (454 g) white fish fillets, such as sole or cod	1 large carrot, grated
2 teaspoons olive oil	½ cup low-sodium salsa
3 tablespoons freshly squeezed lemon juice, divided	⅓ cup low-fat Greek yogurt
1½ cups chopped red cabbage	4 soft low-sodium whole-wheat tortillas

1. Brush the fish with the olive oil and sprinkle with 1 tablespoon of lemon juice. Air fry in the air fryer basket at 390°F (199°C) for 9 to 12 minutes, or until the fish just flakes when tested with a fork. 2. Meanwhile, in a medium bowl, stir together the remaining 2 tablespoons of lemon juice, the red cabbage, carrot, salsa, and yogurt. 3. When the fish is cooked, remove it from the air fryer basket and break it up into large pieces. 4. Offer the fish, tortillas, and the cabbage mixture, and let each person assemble a taco.

Berry Cheesecake

Prep time: 5 minutes | Cook time: 10 minutes | Serves 4

Oil, for spraying	1 large egg
8 ounces (227 g) cream cheese	½ teaspoon vanilla extract
6 tablespoons sugar	¼ teaspoon lemon juice
1 tablespoon sour cream	½ cup fresh mixed berries

1. Preheat the air fryer to 350°F (177°C). Line the air fryer basket with parchment and spray lightly with oil. 2. In a blender, combine the cream cheese, sugar, sour cream, egg, vanilla, and lemon juice and blend until smooth. Pour the mixture into a 4-inch springform pan. 3. Place the pan in the prepared basket. 4. Cook for 8 to 10 minutes, or until only the very center jiggles slightly when the pan is moved. 5. Refrigerate the cheesecake in the pan for at least 2 hours. 6. Release the sides from the springform pan, top the cheesecake with the mixed berries, and serve.

Steak and Vegetable Kebabs

Prep time: 15 minutes | Cook time: 5 to 7 minutes | Serves 4

2 tablespoons balsamic vinegar	¾ pound (340 g) round steak, cut into 1-inch pieces
2 teaspoons olive oil	1 red bell pepper, sliced
½ teaspoon dried marjoram	16 button mushrooms
⅛ teaspoon freshly ground black pepper	1 cup cherry tomatoes

1. In a medium bowl, stir together the balsamic vinegar, olive oil, marjoram, and black pepper. 2. Add the steak and stir to coat. Let stand for 10 minutes at room temperature. 3. Alternating items, thread the beef, red bell pepper, mushrooms, and tomatoes onto 8 bamboo or metal skewers that fit in the air fryer. 4. Air fry at 390°F (199°C) for 5 to 7 minutes, or until the beef is browned and reaches at least 145°F (63°C) on a meat thermometer. Serve immediately.

Avocado and Egg Burrito

Prep time: 10 minutes | Cook time: 3 to 5 minutes | Serves 4

2 hard-boiled egg whites, chopped	salsa, plus additional for serving (optional)
1 hard-boiled egg, chopped	1 (1.2-ounce / 34-g) slice low-sodium, low-fat American cheese, torn into pieces
1 avocado, peeled, pitted, and chopped	
1 red bell pepper, chopped	4 low-sodium whole-wheat flour tortillas
3 tablespoons low-sodium	

1. In a medium bowl, thoroughly mix the egg whites, egg, avocado, red bell pepper, salsa, and cheese. 2. Place the tortillas on a work surface and evenly divide the filling among them. Fold in the edges and roll up. Secure the burritos with toothpicks if necessary. 3. Put the burritos in the air fryer basket. Air fry at 390°F (199°C) for 3 to 5 minutes, or until the burritos are light golden brown and crisp. Serve with more salsa (if using).

Chapter 3   Fast and Easy Everyday Favorites

Crispy Potato Chips with Lemony Cream Dip

Prep time: 20 minutes | Cook time: 15 minutes | Serves 2 to 4

2 large russet potatoes, sliced into ⅛-inch slices, rinsed	¼ teaspoon lemon juice
Sea salt and freshly ground black pepper, to taste	2 scallions, white part only, minced
Cooking spray	1 tablespoon olive oil
Lemony Cream Dip:	¼ teaspoon salt
½ cup sour cream	Freshly ground black pepper, to taste

1. Soak the potato slices in water for 10 minutes, then pat dry with paper towels. 2. Preheat the air fryer to 300°F (149°C). 3. Transfer the potato slices in the preheated air fryer. Spritz the slices with cooking spray. You may need to work in batches to avoid overcrowding. 4. Air fry for 15 minutes or until crispy and golden brown. Shake the basket periodically. Sprinkle with salt and ground black pepper in the last minute. 5. Meanwhile, combine the ingredients for the dip in a small bowl. Stir to mix well. 6. Serve the potato chips immediately with the dip.

Air Fried Butternut Squash with Chopped Hazelnuts

Prep time: 10 minutes | Cook time: 20 minutes | Makes 3 cups

2 tablespoons whole hazelnuts	¼ teaspoon freshly ground black pepper
3 cups butternut squash, peeled, deseeded, and cubed	2 teaspoons olive oil
¼ teaspoon kosher salt	Cooking spray

1. Preheat the air fryer to 300°F (149°C). Spritz the air fryer basket with cooking spray. 2. Arrange the hazelnuts in the preheated air fryer. Air fry for 3 minutes or until soft. 3. Chopped the hazelnuts roughly and transfer to a small bowl. Set aside. 4. Set the air fryer temperature to 360°F (182°C). Spritz with cooking spray. 5. Put the butternut squash in a large bowl, then sprinkle with salt and pepper and drizzle with olive oil. Toss to coat well. 6. Transfer the squash in the air fryer. Air fry for 20 minutes or until the squash is soft. Shake the basket halfway through the frying time. 7. When the frying is complete, transfer the squash onto a plate and sprinkle with chopped hazelnuts before serving.

Sweet Corn and Carrot Fritters

Prep time: 10 minutes | Cook time: 8 to 11 minutes | Serves 4

1 medium-sized carrot, grated	1 medium-sized egg, whisked
1 yellow onion, finely chopped	2 tablespoons plain milk
4 ounces (113 g) canned sweet corn kernels, drained	1 cup grated Parmesan cheese
1 teaspoon sea salt flakes	¼ cup flour
1 tablespoon chopped fresh cilantro	⅓ teaspoon baking powder
	⅓ teaspoon sugar
	Cooking spray

1. Preheat the air fryer to 350°F (177°C). 2. Place the grated carrot in a colander and press down to squeeze out any excess moisture. Dry it with a paper towel. 3. Combine the carrots with the remaining ingredients. 4. Mold 1 tablespoon of the mixture into a ball and press it down with your hand or a spoon to flatten it. Repeat until the rest of the mixture is used up. 5. Spritz the balls with cooking spray. 6. Arrange in the air fryer basket, taking care not to overlap any balls. Bake for 8 to 11 minutes, or until they're firm. 7. Serve warm.

Simple Pea Delight

Prep time: 5 minutes | Cook time: 15 minutes | Serves 2 to 4

1 cup flour	3 tablespoons pea protein
1 teaspoon baking powder	½ cup chicken or turkey strips
3 eggs	Pinch of sea salt
1 cup coconut milk	1 cup Mozzarella cheese
1 cup cream cheese	

1. Preheat the air fryer to 390°F (199°C). 2. In a large bowl, mix all ingredients together using a large wooden spoon. 3. Spoon equal amounts of the mixture into muffin cups and bake for 15 minutes. 4. Serve immediately.

Parsnip Fries with Garlic-Yogurt Dip

Prep time: 10 minutes | Cook time: 10 minutes | Serves 4

3 medium parsnips, peeled, cut into sticks	¼ cup plain Greek yogurt
¼ teaspoon kosher salt	⅛ teaspoon garlic powder
1 teaspoon olive oil	1 tablespoon sour cream
1 garlic clove, unpeeled	¼ teaspoon kosher salt
Cooking spray	Freshly ground black pepper, to taste
Dip:	

1. Preheat the air fryer to 360°F (182°C). Spritz the air fryer basket with cooking spray. 2. Put the parsnip sticks in a large bowl, then sprinkle with salt and drizzle with olive oil. 3. Transfer the parsnip into the preheated air fryer and add the garlic. 4. Air fry for 5 minutes, then remove the garlic from the air fryer and shake the basket. Air fry for 5 more minutes or until the parsnip sticks are crisp. 5. Meanwhile, peel the garlic and crush it. Combine the crushed garlic with the ingredients for the dip. Stir to mix well. 6. When the frying is complete, remove the parsnip fries from the air fryer and serve with the dipping sauce.

Air Fried Shishito Peppers

Prep time: 5 minutes | Cook time: 5 minutes | Serves 4

½ pound (227 g) shishito peppers (about 24)	Coarse sea salt, to taste
1 tablespoon olive oil	Lemon wedges, for serving
	Cooking spray

1. Preheat the air fryer to 400°F (204°C). Spritz the air fryer basket with cooking spray. 2. Toss the peppers with olive oil in a large bowl to coat well. 3. Arrange the peppers in the preheated air fryer. 4. Air fryer for 5 minutes or until blistered and lightly charred. Shake the basket and sprinkle the peppers with salt halfway through the cooking time. 5. Transfer the peppers onto a plate and squeeze the lemon wedges on top before serving.

Air Fried Broccoli

Prep time: 5 minutes | Cook time: 6 minutes | Serves 1

4 egg yolks	Salt and pepper, to taste
¼ cup butter, melted	2 cups broccoli florets
2 cups coconut flower	

1. Preheat the air fryer to 400°F (204°C). 2. In a bowl, whisk the egg yolks and melted butter together. Throw in the coconut flour, salt and pepper, then stir again to combine well. 3. Dip each broccoli floret into the mixture and place in the air fryer basket. Air fry for 6 minutes in batches if necessary. Take care when removing them from the air fryer and serve immediately.

Beet Salad with Lemon Vinaigrette

Prep time: 10 minutes | Cook time: 12 to 15 minutes | Serves 4

6 medium red and golden beets, peeled and sliced	Cooking spray
1 teaspoon olive oil	Vinaigrette:
¼ teaspoon kosher salt	2 teaspoons olive oil
½ cup crumbled feta cheese	2 tablespoons chopped fresh chives
8 cups mixed greens	Juice of 1 lemon

1. Preheat the air fryer to 360°F (182°C). 2. In a large bowl, toss the beets, olive oil, and kosher salt. 3. Spray the air fryer basket with cooking spray, then place the beets in the basket and air fry for 12 to 15 minutes or until tender. 4. While the beets cook, make the vinaigrette in a large bowl by whisking together the olive oil, lemon juice, and chives. 5. Remove the beets from the air fryer, toss in the vinaigrette, and allow to cool for 5 minutes. Add the feta and serve on top of the mixed greens.

Easy Cinnamon Toast

Prep time: 5 minutes | Cook time: 20 minutes | Serves 6

1½ teaspoons cinnamon	pepper
1½ teaspoons vanilla extract	2 tablespoons melted coconut oil
½ cup sugar	
2 teaspoons ground black	12 slices whole wheat bread

1. Preheat the air fryer to 400°F (204°C). 2. Combine all the ingredients, except for the bread, in a large bowl. Stir to mix well. 3. Dunk the bread in the bowl of mixture gently to coat and infuse well. Shake the excess off. 4. Arrange the bread slices in the preheated air fryer. Air fry for 5 minutes or until golden brown. Flip the bread halfway through. You may need to cook in batches to avoid overcrowding. 5. Remove the bread slices from the air fryer and slice to serve.

Frico

Prep time: 5 minutes | Cook time: 5 minutes | Serves 2

1 cup shredded aged Manchego cheese	½ teaspoon cumin seeds
1 teaspoon all-purpose flour	¼ teaspoon cracked black pepper

1. Preheat the air fryer to 375°F (191°C). Line the air fryer basket with parchment paper. 2. Combine the cheese and flour in a bowl. Stir to mix well. Spread the mixture in the basket into a 4-inch round. 3. Combine the cumin and black pepper in a small bowl. Stir to mix well. Sprinkle the cumin mixture over the cheese round. 4. Air fry 5 minutes or until the cheese is lightly browned and frothy. 5. Use tongs to transfer the cheese wafer onto a plate and slice to serve.

Peppery Brown Rice Fritters

Prep time: 10 minutes | Cook time: 8 to 10 minutes | Serves 4

1 (10-ounce / 284-g) bag frozen cooked brown rice, thawed	2 tablespoons minced fresh basil
1 egg	3 tablespoons grated Parmesan cheese
3 tablespoons brown rice flour	
⅓ cup finely grated carrots	2 teaspoons olive oil
⅓ cup minced red bell pepper	

1. Preheat the air fryer to 380°F (193°C). 2. In a small bowl, combine the thawed rice, egg, and flour and mix to blend. 3. Stir in the carrots, bell pepper, basil, and Parmesan cheese. 4. Form the mixture into 8 fritters and drizzle with the olive oil. 5. Put the fritters carefully into the air fryer basket. Air fry for 8 to 10 minutes, or until the fritters are golden brown and cooked through. 6. Serve immediately.

Spicy Air Fried Old Bay Shrimp

Prep time: 7 minutes | Cook time: 10 minutes | Makes 2 cups

½ teaspoon Old Bay Seasoning	⅛ teaspoon salt
1 teaspoon ground cayenne pepper	½ pound (227 g) shrimps, peeled and deveined
½ teaspoon paprika	Juice of half a lemon
1 tablespoon olive oil	

1. Preheat the air fryer to 390°F (199°C). 2. Combine the Old Bay Seasoning, cayenne pepper, paprika, olive oil, and salt in a large bowl, then add the shrimps and toss to coat well. 3. Put the shrimps in the preheated air fryer. Air fry for 10 minutes or until opaque. Flip the shrimps halfway through. 4. Serve the shrimps with lemon juice on top.

Easy Air Fried Edamame

Prep time: 5 minutes | Cook time: 7 minutes | Serves 6

1½ pounds (680 g) unshelled edamame	2 tablespoons olive oil
	1 teaspoon sea salt

1. Preheat the air fryer to 400°F (204°C). 2. Place the edamame in a large bowl, then drizzle with olive oil. Toss to coat well. 3. Transfer the edamame to the preheated air fryer. Cook for 7 minutes or until tender and warmed through. Shake the basket at least three times during the cooking. 4. Transfer the cooked edamame onto a plate and sprinkle with salt. Toss to combine well and set aside for 3 minutes to infuse before serving.

Southwest Corn and Bell Pepper Roast

Prep time: 10 minutes | Cook time: 10 minutes | Serves 4

For the Corn:	1 teaspoon ground cumin
1½ cups thawed frozen corn kernels	½ teaspoon kosher salt
	Cooking spray
1 cup mixed diced bell peppers	For Serving:
1 jalapeño, diced	¼ cup feta cheese
1 cup diced yellow onion	¼ cup chopped fresh cilantro
½ teaspoon ancho chile powder	1 tablespoon fresh lemon juice
1 tablespoon fresh lemon juice	

1. Preheat the air fryer to 375ºF (191ºC). Spritz the air fryer with cooking spray. 2. Combine the ingredients for the corn in a large bowl. Stir to mix well. 3. Pout the mixture into the air fryer. Air fry for 10 minutes or until the corn and bell peppers are soft. Shake the basket halfway through the cooking time. 4. Transfer them onto a large plate, then spread with feta cheese and cilantro. Drizzle with lemon juice and serve.

Baked Chorizo Scotch Eggs

Prep time: 5 minutes | Cook time: 15 to 20 minutes | Makes 4 eggs

1 pound (454 g) Mexican chorizo or other seasoned sausage meat	1 tablespoon water
	½ cup all-purpose flour
	1 cup panko bread crumbs
4 soft-boiled eggs plus 1 raw egg	Cooking spray

1. Divide the chorizo into 4 equal portions. Flatten each portion into a disc. Place a soft-boiled egg in the center of each disc. Wrap the chorizo around the egg, encasing it completely. Place the encased eggs on a plate and chill for at least 30 minutes. 2. Preheat the air fryer to 360ºF (182ºC). 3. Beat the raw egg with 1 tablespoon of water. Place the flour on a small plate and the panko on a second plate. Working with 1 egg at a time, roll the encased egg in the flour, then dip it in the egg mixture. Dredge the egg in the panko and place on a plate. Repeat with the remaining eggs. 4. Spray the eggs with oil and place in the air fryer basket. Bake for 10 minutes. Turn and bake for an additional 5 to 10 minutes, or until browned and crisp on all sides. 5. Serve immediately.

Rosemary and Orange Roasted Chickpeas

Prep time: 5 minutes | Cook time: 10 to 12 minutes | Makes 4 cups

4 cups cooked chickpeas	1 teaspoon paprika
2 tablespoons vegetable oil	Zest of 1 orange
1 teaspoon kosher salt	1 tablespoon chopped fresh rosemary
1 teaspoon cumin	

1. Preheat the air fryer to 400ºF (204ºC). 2. Make sure the chickpeas are completely dry prior to roasting. In a medium bowl, toss the chickpeas with oil, salt, cumin, and paprika. 3. Working in batches, spread the chickpeas in a single layer in the air fryer basket. Air fry for 10 to 12 minutes until crisp, shaking once halfway through. 4. Return the warm chickpeas to the bowl and toss with the orange zest

and rosemary. Allow to cool completely. 5. Serve.

Easy Devils on Horseback

Prep time: 5 minutes | Cook time: 7 minutes | Serves 12

24 petite pitted prunes (4½ ounces / 128 g)	divided
¼ cup crumbled blue cheese,	8 slices center-cut bacon, cut crosswise into thirds

1. Preheat the air fryer to 400ºF (204ºC). 2. Halve the prunes lengthwise, but don't cut them all the way through. Place ½ teaspoon of cheese in the center of each prune. Wrap a piece of bacon around each prune and secure the bacon with a toothpick. 3. Working in batches, arrange a single layer of the prunes in the air fryer basket. Air fry for about 7 minutes, flipping halfway, until the bacon is cooked through and crisp. 4. Let cool slightly and serve warm.

Garlicky Zoodles

Prep time: 10 minutes | Cook time: 10 minutes | Serves 4

2 large zucchini, peeled and spiralized	½ teaspoon kosher salt
	1 garlic clove, whole
2 large yellow summer squash, peeled and spiralized	2 tablespoons fresh basil, chopped
1 tablespoon olive oil, divided	Cooking spray

1. Preheat the air fryer to 360ºF (182ºC). Spritz the air fryer basket with cooking spray. 2. Combine the zucchini and summer squash with 1 teaspoon olive oil and salt in a large bowl. Toss to coat well. 3. Transfer the zucchini and summer squash in the preheated air fryer and add the garlic. 4. Air fry for 10 minutes or until tender and fragrant. Toss the spiralized zucchini and summer squash halfway through the cooking time. 5. Transfer the cooked zucchini and summer squash onto a plate and set aside. 6. Remove the garlic from the air fryer and allow to cool for a few minutes. Mince the garlic and combine with remaining olive oil in a small bowl. Stir to mix well. 7. Drizzle the spiralized zucchini and summer squash with garlic oil and sprinkle with basil. Toss to serve.

Simple Cheesy Shrimps

Prep time: 10 minutes | Cook time: 16 minutes | Serves 4 to 6

⅔ cup grated Parmesan cheese	2 tablespoons olive oil
4 minced garlic cloves	2 pounds (907 g) cooked large shrimps, peeled and deveined
1 teaspoon onion powder	
½ teaspoon oregano	Lemon wedges, for topping
1 teaspoon basil	Cooking spray
1 teaspoon ground black pepper	

1. Preheat the air fryer to 350ºF (177ºC). Spritz the air fryer basket with cooking spray. 2. Combine all the ingredients, except for the shrimps, in a large bowl. Stir to mix well. 3. Dunk the shrimps in the mixture and toss to coat well. Shake the excess off. 4. Arrange the shrimps in the preheated air fryer. Air fry for 8 minutes or until opaque. Flip the shrimps halfway through. You may need to work in batches to avoid overcrowding. 5. Transfer the cooked shrimps on a

large plate and squeeze the lemon wedges over before serving.

Cheesy Baked Grits

Prep time: 10 minutes | Cook time: 12 minutes | Serves 6

¾ cup hot water	2 cloves garlic, minced
2 (1-ounce / 28-g) packages instant grits	½ to 1 teaspoon red pepper flakes
1 large egg, beaten	1 cup shredded Cheddar cheese or jalapeño Jack cheese
1 tablespoon butter, melted	

1. Preheat the air fryer to 400°F (204°C). 2. In a baking pan, combine the water, grits, egg, butter, garlic, and red pepper flakes. Stir until well combined. Stir in the shredded cheese. 3. Place the pan in the air fryer basket and air fry for 12 minutes, or until the grits have cooked through and a knife inserted near the center comes out clean. 4. Let stand for 5 minutes before serving.

Golden Salmon and Carrot Croquettes

Prep time: 15 minutes | Cook time: 10 minutes | Serves 6

2 egg whites	2 tablespoons minced garlic cloves
1 cup almond flour	
1 cup panko breadcrumbs	½ cup chopped onion
1 pound (454 g) chopped salmon fillet	2 tablespoons chopped chives
⅔ cup grated carrots	Cooking spray

1. Preheat the air fryer to 350°F (177°C). Spritz the air fryer basket with cooking spray. 2. Whisk the egg whites in a bowl. Put the flour in a second bowl. Pour the breadcrumbs in a third bowl. Set aside. 3. Combine the salmon, carrots, garlic, onion, and chives in a large bowl. Stir to mix well. 4. Form the mixture into balls with your hands. Dredge the balls into the flour, then egg, and then breadcrumbs to coat well. 5. Arrange the salmon balls in the preheated air fryer and spritz with cooking spray. 6. Air fry for 10 minutes or until crispy and browned. Shake the basket halfway through. 7. Serve immediately.

Beef Bratwursts

Prep time: 5 minutes | Cook time: 15 minutes | Serves 4

4 (3-ounce / 85-g) beef bratwursts

1. Preheat the air fryer to 375°F (191°C). 2. Place the beef bratwursts in the air fryer basket and air fry for 15 minutes, turning once halfway through. 3. Serve hot.

South Carolina Shrimp and Corn Bake

Prep time: 10 minutes | Cook time: 18 minutes | Serves 2

1 ear corn, husk and silk removed, cut into 2-inch rounds	unpeeled, cut into 1-inch pieces
	2 teaspoons Old Bay Seasoning, divided
8 ounces (227 g) red potatoes,	2 teaspoons vegetable oil,

divided
¼ teaspoon ground black pepper
8 ounces (227 g) large shrimps (about 12 shrimps), deveined
6 ounces (170 g) andouille or
chorizo sausage, cut into 1-inch pieces
2 garlic cloves, minced
1 tablespoon chopped fresh parsley

1. Preheat the air fryer to 400°F (204°C). 2. Put the corn rounds and potatoes in a large bowl. Sprinkle with 1 teaspoon of Old Bay seasoning and drizzle with vegetable oil. Toss to coat well. 3. Transfer the corn rounds and potatoes on a baking sheet, then put in the preheated air fryer. 4. Bake for 12 minutes or until soft and browned. Shake the basket halfway through the cooking time. 5. Meanwhile, cut slits into the shrimps but be careful not to cut them through. Combine the shrimps, sausage, remaining Old Bay seasoning, and remaining vegetable oil in the large bowl. Toss to coat well. 6. When the baking of the potatoes and corn rounds is complete, add the shrimps and sausage and bake for 6 more minutes or until the shrimps are opaque. Shake the basket halfway through the cooking time. 7. When the baking is finished, serve them on a plate and spread with parsley before serving.

Simple Air Fried Crispy Brussels Sprouts

Prep time: 5 minutes | Cook time: 20 minutes | Serves 4

¼ teaspoon salt	oil
⅛ teaspoon ground black pepper	1 pound (454 g) Brussels sprouts, trimmed and halved
1 tablespoon extra-virgin olive	Lemon wedges, for garnish

1. Preheat the air fryer to 350°F (177°C). 2. Combine the salt, black pepper, and olive oil in a large bowl. Stir to mix well. 3. Add the Brussels sprouts to the bowl of mixture and toss to coat well. 4. Arrange the Brussels sprouts in the preheated air fryer. Air fry for 20 minutes or until lightly browned and wilted. Shake the basket two times during the air frying. 5. Transfer the cooked Brussels sprouts to a large plate and squeeze the lemon wedges on top to serve.

Beery and Crunchy Onion Rings

Prep time: 10 minutes | Cook time: 16 minutes | Serves 2 to 4

⅔ cup all-purpose flour	¾ cup beer
1 teaspoon paprika	1½ cups breadcrumbs
½ teaspoon baking soda	1 tablespoons olive oil
1 teaspoon salt	1 large Vidalia onion, peeled
½ teaspoon freshly ground black pepper	and sliced into ½-inch rings
1 egg, beaten	Cooking spray

1. Preheat the air fryer to 360°F (182°C). Spritz the air fryer basket with cooking spray. 2. Combine the flour, paprika, baking soda, salt, and ground black pepper in a bowl. Stir to mix well. 3. Combine the egg and beer in a separate bowl. Stir to mix well. 4. Make a well in the center of the flour mixture, then pour the egg mixture in the well. Stir to mix everything well. 5. Pour the breadcrumbs and olive oil in a shallow plate. Stir to mix well. 6. Dredge the onion rings gently into the flour and egg mixture, then shake the excess off and put into the plate of breadcrumbs. Flip to coat the both sides well. 7. Arrange

the onion rings in the preheated air fryer. Air fry in batches for 16 minutes or until golden brown and crunchy. Flip the rings and put the bottom rings to the top halfway through. 8. Serve immediately.

Garlicky Knots with Parsley

Prep time: 10 minutes | Cook time: 10 minutes | Makes 8 knots

1 teaspoon dried parsley	1 (11-ounce / 312-g) tube
¼ cup melted butter	refrigerated French bread
2 teaspoons garlic powder	dough, cut into 8 slices

1. Preheat the air fryer to 350°F (177°C). 2. Combine the parsley, butter, and garlic powder in a bowl. Stir to mix well. 3. Place the French bread dough slices on a clean work surface, then roll each slice into a 6-inch long rope. Tie the ropes into knots and arrange them on a plate. Brush the knots with butter mixture. 4. Transfer the knots into the air fryer. You need to work in batches to avoid overcrowding. 5. Air fry for 5 minutes or until the knots are golden brown. Flip the knots halfway through the cooking time. 6. Serve immediately.

Buttery Sweet Potatoes

Prep time: 5 minutes | Cook time: 10 minutes | Serves 4

2 tablespoons butter, melted	cut into ½-inch cubes
1 tablespoon light brown sugar	Cooking spray
2 sweet potatoes, peeled and	

1. Preheat the air fryer to 400°F (204°C). Line the air fryer basket with parchment paper. 2. In a medium bowl, stir together the melted butter and brown sugar until blended. Toss the sweet potatoes in the butter mixture until coated. 3. Place the sweet potatoes on the parchment and spritz with oil. 4. Air fry for 5 minutes. Shake the basket, spritz the sweet potatoes with oil, and air fry for 5 minutes more until they're soft enough to cut with a fork. 5. Serve immediately.

Baked Cheese Sandwich

Prep time: 5 minutes | Cook time: 8 minutes | Serves 2

2 tablespoons mayonnaise	4 thick slices Brie cheese
4 thick slices sourdough bread	8 slices hot capicola

1. Preheat the air fryer to 350°F (177°C). 2. Spread the mayonnaise on one side of each slice of bread. Place 2 slices of bread in the air fryer basket, mayonnaise-side down. 3. Place the slices of Brie and capicola on the bread and cover with the remaining two slices of bread, mayonnaise-side up. 4. Bake for 8 minutes, or until the cheese has melted. 5. Serve immediately.

Crispy Green Tomatoes Slices

Prep time: 10 minutes | Cook time: 8 minutes | Makes 12 slices

½ cup all-purpose flour	¼-inch-thick slices, patted dry
1 egg	½ teaspoon salt
½ cup buttermilk	½ teaspoon ground black
1 cup cornmeal	pepper
1 cup panko	Cooking spray
2 green tomatoes, cut into	

1. Preheat the air fryer to 400°F (204°C). Line the air fryer basket with parchment paper. 2. Pour the flour in a bowl. Whisk the egg and buttermilk in a second bowl. Combine the cornmeal and panko in a third bowl. 3. Dredge the tomato slices in the bowl of flour first, then into the egg mixture, and then dunk the slices into the cornmeal mixture. Shake the excess off. 4. Transfer the well-coated tomato slices in the preheated air fryer and sprinkle with salt and ground black pepper. 5. Spritz the tomato slices with cooking spray. Air fry for 8 minutes or until crispy and lightly browned. Flip the slices halfway through the cooking time. 6. Serve immediately.

Chapter 4   Poultry

Chipotle Drumsticks

Prep time: 5 minutes | Cook time: 25 minutes | Serves 4

1 tablespoon tomato paste	8 chicken drumsticks
½ teaspoon chipotle powder	½ teaspoon salt
¼ teaspoon apple cider vinegar	⅛ teaspoon ground black
¼ teaspoon garlic powder	pepper

1. In a small bowl, combine tomato paste, chipotle powder, vinegar, and garlic powder. 2. Sprinkle drumsticks with salt and pepper, then place into a large bowl and pour in tomato paste mixture. Toss or stir to evenly coat all drumsticks in mixture. 3. Place drumsticks into ungreased air fryer basket. Adjust the temperature to 400°F (204°C) and air fry for 25 minutes, turning drumsticks halfway through cooking. Drumsticks will be dark red with an internal temperature of at least 165°F (74°C) when done. Serve warm.

Spanish Chicken and Mini Sweet Pepper Baguette

Prep time: 10 minutes | Cook time: 20 minutes | Serves 2

1¼ pounds (567 g) assorted small chicken parts, breasts cut into halves	½ pound (227 g) mini sweet peppers
¼ teaspoon salt	¼ cup light mayonnaise
¼ teaspoon ground black pepper	¼ teaspoon smoked paprika
2 teaspoons olive oil	½ clove garlic, crushed
	Baguette, for serving
	Cooking spray

1. Preheat air fryer to 375°F (191°C). Spritz the air fryer basket with cooking spray. 2. Toss the chicken with salt, ground black pepper, and olive oil in a large bowl. 3. Arrange the sweet peppers and chicken in the preheated air fryer and air fry for 10 minutes, then transfer the peppers on a plate. 4. Flip the chicken and air fry for 10 more minutes or until well browned. 5. Meanwhile, combine the mayo, paprika, and garlic in a small bowl. Stir to mix well. 6. Assemble the baguette with chicken and sweet pepper, then spread with mayo mixture and serve.

Chicken Rochambeau

Prep time: 15 minutes | Cook time: 20 minutes | Serves 4

1 tablespoon butter	Sauce:
4 chicken tenders, cut in half crosswise	2 tablespoons butter
Salt and pepper, to taste	½ cup chopped green onions
¼ cup flour	½ cup chopped mushrooms
Oil for misting	2 tablespoons flour
4 slices ham, ¼- to ⅜-inches thick and large enough to cover an English muffin	1 cup chicken broth
	¼ teaspoon garlic powder
2 English muffins, split	1½ teaspoons Worcestershire sauce

1. Place 1 tablespoon of butter in a baking pan and air fry at 390°F (199°C) for 2 minutes to melt. 2. Sprinkle chicken tenders with salt and pepper to taste, then roll in the ¼ cup of flour. 3. Place chicken in baking pan, turning pieces to coat with melted butter. 4. Air fry at 390°F (199°C) for 5 minutes. Turn chicken pieces over, and spray tops lightly with olive oil. Cook 5 minutes longer or until juices run clear. The chicken will not brown. 5. While chicken is cooking, make the sauce: In a medium saucepan, melt the 2 tablespoons of butter. 6. Add onions and mushrooms and sauté until tender, about 3 minutes. 7. Stir in the flour. Gradually add broth, stirring constantly until you have a smooth gravy. 8. Add garlic powder and Worcestershire sauce and simmer on low heat until sauce thickens, about 5 minutes. 9. When chicken is cooked, remove baking pan from air fryer and set aside. 10. Place ham slices directly into air fryer basket and air fry at 390°F (199°C) for 5 minutes or until hot and beginning to sizzle a little. Remove and set aside on top of the chicken for now. 11. Place the English muffin halves in air fryer basket and air fry at 390°F (199°C) for 1 minute. 12. Open air fryer and place a ham slice on top of each English muffin half. Stack 2 pieces of chicken on top of each ham slice. Air fry for 1 to 2 minutes to heat through. 13. Place each English muffin stack on a serving plate and top with plenty of sauce.

Almond-Crusted Chicken

Prep time: 15 minutes | Cook time: 25 minutes | Serves 4

¼ cup slivered almonds	2 tablespoons full-fat mayonnaise
2 (6-ounce / 170-g) boneless, skinless chicken breasts	1 tablespoon Dijon mustard

1. Pulse the almonds in a food processor or chop until finely chopped. Place almonds evenly on a plate and set aside. 2. Completely slice each chicken breast in half lengthwise. 3. Mix the mayonnaise and mustard in a small bowl and then coat chicken with the mixture. 4. Lay each piece of chicken in the chopped almonds to fully coat. Carefully move the pieces into the air fryer basket. 5. Adjust the temperature to 350°F (177°C) and air fry for 25 minutes. 6. Chicken will be done when it has reached an internal temperature of 165°F (74°C) or more. Serve warm.

Fried Chicken Breasts

Prep time: 30 minutes | Cook time: 12 to 14 minutes | Serves 4

1 pound (454 g) boneless, skinless chicken breasts	cheese
	½ teaspoon sea salt
¾ cup dill pickle juice	½ teaspoon freshly ground black pepper
¾ cup finely ground blanched almond flour	2 large eggs
¾ cup finely grated Parmesan	Avocado oil spray

1. Place the chicken breasts in a zip-top bag or between two pieces of plastic wrap. Using a meat mallet or heavy skillet, pound the chicken to a uniform ½-inch thickness. 2. Place the chicken in a large bowl with the pickle juice. Cover and allow to brine in the refrigerator for up to 2 hours. 3. In a shallow dish, combine the almond flour, Parmesan cheese, salt, and pepper. In a separate, shallow bowl, beat the eggs. 4. Drain the chicken and pat it dry with paper towels. Dip in the eggs and then in the flour mixture, making sure to press the coating into the chicken. Spray both sides of the coated breasts with oil. 5. Spray the air fryer basket with oil and put the chicken inside. Set the temperature to 400°F (204°C) and air fry for 6 to 7 minutes. 6. Carefully flip the breasts with a spatula. Spray the breasts again with oil and continue cooking for 6 to 7 minutes more, until golden and crispy.

Classic Whole Chicken

Prep time: 5 minutes | Cook time: 50 minutes | Serves 4

Oil, for spraying	½ teaspoon salt
1 (4-pound / 1.8-kg) whole	½ teaspoon freshly ground
chicken, giblets removed	black pepper
1 tablespoon olive oil	¼ teaspoon finely chopped
1 teaspoon paprika	fresh parsley, for garnish
½ teaspoon granulated garlic	

1. Line the air fryer basket with parchment and spray lightly with oil. 2. Pat the chicken dry with paper towels. Rub it with the olive oil until evenly coated. 3. In a small bowl, mix together the paprika, garlic, salt, and black pepper and sprinkle it evenly over the chicken. 4. Place the chicken in the prepared basket, breast-side down. 5. Air fry at 360°F (182°C) for 30 minutes, flip, and cook for another 20 minutes, or until the internal temperature reaches 165°F (74°C) and the juices run clear. 6. Sprinkle with the parsley before serving.

Barbecue Chicken

Prep time: 10 minutes | Cook time: 18 to 20 minutes | Serves 4

⅓ cup no-salt-added tomato	2 garlic cloves, minced
sauce	1 jalapeño pepper, minced
2 tablespoons low-sodium	3 tablespoons minced onion
grainy mustard	4 (5-ounce / 142-g) low-sodium
2 tablespoons apple cider	boneless, skinless chicken
vinegar	breasts
1 tablespoon honey	

1. Preheat the air fryer to 370°F (188°C). 2. In a small bowl, stir together the tomato sauce, mustard, cider vinegar, honey, garlic, jalapeño, and onion. 3. Brush the chicken breasts with some sauce and air fry for 10 minutes. 4. Remove the air fryer basket and turn the chicken; brush with more sauce. Air fry for 5 minutes more. 5. Remove the air fryer basket and turn the chicken again; brush with more sauce. Air fry for 3 to 5 minutes more, or until the chicken reaches an internal temperature of 165°F (74°C) on a meat thermometer. Discard any remaining sauce. Serve immediately.

Teriyaki Chicken Thighs with Lemony Snow Peas

Prep time: 30 minutes | Cook time: 34 minutes | Serves 4

¼ cup chicken broth	1 tablespoon sugar
½ teaspoon grated fresh ginger	6 ounces (170 g) snow peas,
⅛ teaspoon red pepper flakes	strings removed
1½ tablespoons soy sauce	⅛ teaspoon lemon zest
4 (5-ounce / 142-g) bone-in	1 garlic clove, minced
chicken thighs, trimmed	¼ teaspoon salt
1 tablespoon mirin	Ground black pepper, to taste
½ teaspoon cornstarch	½ teaspoon lemon juice

1. Combine the broth, ginger, pepper flakes, and soy sauce in a large bowl. Stir to mix well. 2. Pierce 10 to 15 holes into the chicken skin. Put the chicken in the broth mixture and toss to coat well. Let sit for 10 minutes to marinate. 3. Preheat the air fryer to 400°F (205°C). 4. Transfer the marinated chicken on a plate and pat dry with paper towels. 5. Scoop 2 tablespoons of marinade in a microwave-safe bowl and combine with mirin, cornstarch and sugar. Stir to mix well. Microwave for 1 minute or until frothy and has a thick consistency. Set aside. 6. Arrange the chicken in the preheated air fryer, skin side up, and air fry for 25 minutes or until the internal temperature of the chicken reaches at least 165°F (74°C). Gently turn the chicken over halfway through. 7. When the frying is complete, brush the chicken skin with marinade mixture. Air fryer the chicken for 5 more minutes or until glazed. 8. Remove the chicken from the air fryer and reserve ½ teaspoon of chicken fat remains in the air fryer. Allow the chicken to cool for 10 minutes. 9. Meanwhile, combine the reserved chicken fat, snow peas, lemon zest, garlic, salt, and ground black pepper in a small bowl. Toss to coat well. 10. Transfer the snow peas in the air fryer and air fry for 3 minutes or until soft. Remove the peas from the air fryer and toss with lemon juice. 11. Serve the chicken with lemony snow peas.

Chicken with Lettuce

Prep time: 15 minutes | Cook time: 14 minutes | Serves 4

1 pound (454 g) chicken breast	and thinly sliced
tenders, chopped into bite-size	1 tablespoon olive oil
pieces	1 tablespoon fajita seasoning
½ onion, thinly sliced	1 teaspoon kosher salt
½ red bell pepper, seeded and	Juice of ½ lime
thinly sliced	8 large lettuce leaves
½ green bell pepper, seeded	1 cup prepared guacamole

1. Preheat the air fryer to 400°F (204°C). 2. In a large bowl, combine the chicken, onion, and peppers. Drizzle with the olive oil and toss until thoroughly coated. Add the fajita seasoning and salt and toss again. 3. Working in batches if necessary, arrange the chicken and vegetables in a single layer in the air fryer basket. Pausing halfway through the cooking time to shake the basket, air fry for 14 minutes, or until the vegetables are tender and a thermometer inserted into the thickest piece of chicken registers 165°F (74°C). 4. Transfer the mixture to a serving platter and drizzle with the fresh lime juice. Serve with the lettuce leaves and top with the guacamole.

One-Dish Chicken and Rice

Prep time: 10 minutes | Cook time: 40 minutes | Serves 4

1 cup long-grain white rice,	3 cloves garlic, minced
rinsed and drained	1 tablespoon toasted sesame oil
1 cup cut frozen green beans	1 teaspoon kosher salt
(do not thaw)	1 teaspoon black pepper
1 tablespoon minced fresh	1 pound (454 g) chicken wings,
ginger	preferably drumettes

1. In a baking pan, combine the rice, green beans, ginger, garlic, sesame oil, salt, and pepper. Stir to combine. Place the chicken wings on top of the rice mixture. 2. Cover the pan with foil. Make a long slash in the foil to allow the pan to vent steam. Place the pan in the air fryer basket. Set the air fryer to 375°F (191°C) for 30 minutes. 3. Remove the foil. Set the air fryer to 400°F (204°C) for 10 minutes, or until the wings have browned and rendered fat into the rice and vegetables, turning the wings halfway through the cooking time.

African Piri-Piri Chicken Drumsticks

Prep time: 30 minutes | Cook time: 20 minutes | Serves 2

Chicken:	1 teaspoon smoked paprika
1 tablespoon chopped fresh	½ teaspoon kosher salt
thyme leaves	½ teaspoon black pepper
1 tablespoon minced fresh	4 chicken drumsticks
ginger	Glaze:
1 small shallot, finely chopped	2 tablespoons butter or ghee
2 garlic cloves, minced	1 teaspoon chopped fresh
⅓ cup piri-piri sauce or hot	thyme leaves
sauce	1 garlic clove, minced
3 tablespoons extra-virgin olive	1 tablespoon piri-piri sauce
oil	1 tablespoon fresh lemon juice
Zest and juice of 1 lemon	

1. For the chicken: In a small bowl, stir together all the ingredients except the chicken. Place the chicken and the marinade in a gallon-size resealable plastic bag. Seal the bag and massage to coat. Refrigerate for at least 2 hours or up to 24 hours, turning the bag occasionally. 2. Place the chicken legs in the air fryer basket. Set the air fryer to 400ºF (204ºC) for 20 minutes, turning the chicken halfway through the cooking time. 3. Meanwhile, for the glaze: Melt the butter in a small saucepan over medium-high heat. Add the thyme and garlic. Cook, stirring, until the garlic just begins to brown, 1 to 2 minutes. Add the piri-piri sauce and lemon juice. Reduce the heat to medium-low and simmer for 1 to 2 minutes. 4. Transfer the chicken to a serving platter. Pour the glaze over the chicken. Serve immediately.

Jalapeño Chicken Balls

Prep time: 10 minutes | Cook time: 25 minutes | Serves 4

1 medium red onion, minced	1 egg
2 garlic cloves, minced	1 teaspoon dried thyme
1 jalapeño pepper, minced	1 pound (454 g) ground
2 teaspoons extra-virgin olive	chicken breast
oil	Cooking oil spray
3 tablespoons ground almonds	

1. Insert the crisper plate into the basket and the basket into the unit. Preheat the unit by selecting BAKE, setting the temperature to 400ºF (204ºC), and setting the time to 3 minutes. Select START/STOP to begin. 2. In a 6-by-2-inch round pan, combine the red onion, garlic, jalapeño, and olive oil. 3. Once the unit is preheated, place the pan into the basket. 4. Select BAKE, set the temperature to 400ºF (204ºC), and set the time to 4 minutes. Select START/STOP to begin. 5. When the cooking is complete, the vegetables should be crisp-tender. Transfer to a medium bowl. 6. Mix the almonds, egg, and thyme into the vegetable mixture. Add the chicken and mix until just combined. Form the chicken mixture into about 24 (1-inch) balls. 7. Insert the crisper plate into the basket and the basket into the unit. Preheat the unit by selecting BAKE, setting the temperature to 400ºF (204ºC), and setting the time to 3 minutes. Select START/STOP to begin. 8. Once the unit is preheated, spray the crisper plate with cooking oil. Working in batches, place half the meatballs in a single layer, not touching, into the basket. 9. Select BAKE, set the temperature to 400ºF (204ºC), and set the time to 10 minutes.

Select START/STOP to begin. 10. When the cooking is complete, a food thermometer inserted into the meatballs should register at least 165ºF (74ºC). 11. Repeat steps 8 and 9 with the remaining meatballs. Serve warm.

Pickle Brined Fried Chicken

Prep time: 30 minutes | Cook time: 47 minutes | Serves 4

4 bone-in, skin-on chicken legs,	1 cup fine bread crumbs
cut into drumsticks and thighs	1 teaspoon salt
(about 3½ pounds / 1.6 kg)	1 teaspoon freshly ground
Pickle juice from 1 (24-ounce /	black pepper
680-g) jar kosher dill pickles	½ teaspoon ground paprika
½ cup flour	⅛ teaspoon ground cayenne
Salt and freshly ground black	pepper
pepper, to taste	Vegetable or canola oil
2 eggs	

1. Place the chicken in a shallow dish and pour the pickle juice over the top. Cover and transfer the chicken to the refrigerator to brine in the pickle juice for 3 to 8 hours. 2. When you are ready to cook, remove the chicken from the refrigerator to let it come to room temperature while you set up a dredging station. Place the flour in a shallow dish and season well with salt and freshly ground black pepper. Whisk the eggs in a second shallow dish. In a third shallow dish, combine the bread crumbs, salt, pepper, paprika and cayenne pepper. 3. Preheat the air fryer to 370ºF (188ºC). 4. Remove the chicken from the pickle brine and gently dry it with a clean kitchen towel. Dredge each piece of chicken in the flour, then dip it into the egg mixture, and finally press it into the bread crumb mixture to coat all sides of the chicken. Place the breaded chicken on a plate or baking sheet and spray each piece all over with vegetable oil. 5. Air fry the chicken in two batches. Place two chicken thighs and two drumsticks into the air fryer basket. Air fry for 10 minutes. Then, gently turn the chicken pieces over and air fry for another 10 minutes. Remove the chicken pieces and let them rest on plate, do not cover. Repeat with the second batch of chicken, air frying for 20 minutes, turning the chicken over halfway through. 6. Lower the temperature of the air fryer to 340ºF (171ºC). Place the first batch of chicken on top of the second batch already in the basket and air fry for an additional 7 minutes. Serve warm and enjoy.

Honey-Glazed Chicken Thighs

Prep time: 5 minutes | Cook time: 14 minutes | Serves 4

Oil, for spraying	1 tablespoon balsamic vinegar
4 boneless, skinless chicken	2 teaspoons honey
thighs, fat trimmed	2 teaspoons minced garlic
3 tablespoons soy sauce	1 teaspoon ground ginger

1. Preheat the air fryer to 400ºF (204ºC). Line the air fryer basket with parchment and spray lightly with oil. 2. Place the chicken in the prepared basket. 3. Cook for 7 minutes, flip, and cook for another 7 minutes, or until the internal temperature reaches 165ºF (74ºC) and the juices run clear. 4. In a small saucepan, combine the soy sauce, balsamic vinegar, honey, garlic, and ginger and cook over low heat for 1 to 2 minutes, until warmed through. 5. Transfer the chicken to a serving plate and drizzle with the sauce just before serving.

Personal Cauliflower Pizzas

Prep time: 10 minutes | Cook time: 25 minutes | Serves 2

1 (12-ounce / 340-g) bag frozen riced cauliflower	4 tablespoons no-sugar-added marinara sauce, divided
⅓ cup shredded Mozzarella cheese	4 ounces (113 g) fresh Mozzarella, chopped, divided
¼ cup almond flour	1 cup cooked chicken breast, chopped, divided
¼ grated Parmesan cheese	½ cup chopped cherry tomatoes, divided
1 large egg	
½ teaspoon salt	¼ cup fresh baby arugula, divided
1 teaspoon garlic powder	
1 teaspoon dried oregano	

1. Preheat the air fryer to 400°F (204°C). Cut 4 sheets of parchment paper to fit the basket of the air fryer. Brush with olive oil and set aside. 2. In a large glass bowl, microwave the cauliflower according to package directions. Place the cauliflower on a clean towel, draw up the sides, and squeeze tightly over a sink to remove the excess moisture. Return the cauliflower to the bowl and add the shredded Mozzarella along with the almond flour, Parmesan, egg, salt, garlic powder, and oregano. Stir until thoroughly combined. 3. Divide the dough into two equal portions. Place one piece of dough on the prepared parchment paper and pat gently into a thin, flat disk 7 to 8 inches in diameter. Air fry for 15 minutes until the crust begins to brown. Let cool for 5 minutes. 4. Transfer the parchment paper with the crust on top to a baking sheet. Place a second sheet of parchment paper over the crust. While holding the edges of both sheets together, carefully lift the crust off the baking sheet, flip it, and place it back in the air fryer basket. The new sheet of parchment paper is now on the bottom. Remove the top piece of paper and air fry the crust for another 15 minutes until the top begins to brown. Remove the basket from the air fryer. 5. Spread 2 tablespoons of the marinara sauce on top of the crust, followed by half the fresh Mozzarella, chicken, cherry tomatoes, and arugula. Air fry for 5 to 10 minutes longer, until the cheese is melted and beginning to brown. Remove the pizza from the oven and let it sit for 10 minutes before serving. Repeat with the remaining ingredients to make a second pizza.

Broccoli Cheese Chicken

Prep time: 10 minutes | Cook time: 19 to 24 minutes | Serves 6

1 tablespoon avocado oil	additional for seasoning, divided
¼ cup chopped onion	
½ cup finely chopped broccoli	¼ freshly ground black pepper, plus additional for seasoning, divided
4 ounces (113 g) cream cheese, at room temperature	
2 ounces (57 g) Cheddar cheese, shredded	2 pounds (907 g) boneless, skinless chicken breasts
1 teaspoon garlic powder	1 teaspoon smoked paprika
½ teaspoon sea salt, plus	

1. Heat a medium skillet over medium-high heat and pour in the avocado oil. Add the onion and broccoli and cook, stirring occasionally, for 5 to 8 minutes, until the onion is tender. 2. Transfer to a large bowl and stir in the cream cheese, Cheddar cheese, and garlic powder, and season to taste with salt and pepper. 3. Hold

a sharp knife parallel to the chicken breast and cut a long pocket into one side. Stuff the chicken pockets with the broccoli mixture, using toothpicks to secure the pockets around the filling. 4. In a small dish, combine the paprika, ½ teaspoon salt, and ¼ teaspoon pepper. Sprinkle this over the outside of the chicken. 5. Set the air fryer to 400°F (204°C). Place the chicken in a single layer in the air fryer basket, cooking in batches if necessary, and cook for 14 to 16 minutes, until an instant-read thermometer reads 160°F (71°C). Place the chicken on a plate and tent a piece of aluminum foil over the chicken. Allow to rest for 5 to 10 minutes before serving.

Easy Chicken Fingers

Prep time: 20 minutes | Cook time: 30 minutes | Makes 12 chicken fingers

½ cup all-purpose flour	breasts, each cut into 4 strips
2 cups panko breadcrumbs	Kosher salt and freshly ground black pepper, to taste
2 tablespoons canola oil	
1 large egg	Cooking spray
3 boneless and skinless chicken	

1. Preheat the air fryer to 360°F (182°C). Spritz the air fryer basket with cooking spray. 2. Pour the flour in a large bowl. Combine the panko and canola oil on a shallow dish. Whisk the egg in a separate bowl. 3. Rub the chicken strips with salt and ground black pepper on a clean work surface, then dip the chicken in the bowl of flour. Shake the excess off and dunk the chicken strips in the bowl of whisked egg, then roll the strips over the panko to coat well. 4. Arrange 4 strips in the air fryer basket each time and air fry for 10 minutes or until crunchy and lightly browned. Flip the strips halfway through. Repeat with remaining ingredients. 5. Serve immediately.

Sesame Chicken

Prep time: 10 minutes | Cook time: 18 minutes | Serves 6

Oil, for spraying	brown sugar
2 (6-ounce / 170-g) boneless, skinless chicken breasts, cut into bite-size pieces	2 tablespoons pineapple juice
	1 tablespoon molasses
	½ teaspoon ground ginger
½ cup cornstarch, plus 1 tablespoon	1 tablespoon water
	2 teaspoons sesame seeds
¼ cup soy sauce	
2 tablespoons packed light	

1. Line the air fryer basket with parchment and spray lightly with oil. 2. Place the chicken and ½ cup of cornstarch in a zip-top plastic bag, seal, and shake well until evenly coated. 3. Place the chicken in an even layer in the prepared basket and spray liberally with oil. You may need to work in batches, depending on the size of your fryer. 4. Air fry at 390°F (199°C) for 9 minutes, flip, spray with more oil, and cook for another 8 to 9 minutes, or until the internal temperature reaches 165°F (74°C). 5. In a small saucepan, combine the soy sauce, brown sugar, pineapple juice, molasses, and ginger over medium heat and cook, stirring frequently, until the brown sugar has dissolved. 6. In a small bowl, mix together the water and remaining 1 tablespoon of cornstarch. Pour it into the soy sauce mixture. 7. Bring the mixture to a boil, stirring frequently, until the sauce thickens. Remove from the heat. 8. Transfer the chicken to a large bowl, add the sauce, and toss until evenly coated. Sprinkle with the sesame seeds and serve.

Barbecued Chicken with Creamy Coleslaw

Prep time: 10 minutes | Cook time: 20 minutes | Serves 2

3 cups shredded coleslaw mix	2 tablespoons mayonnaise
Salt and pepper	2 tablespoons sour cream
2 (12-ounce / 340-g) bone-in split chicken breasts, trimmed	1 teaspoon distilled white vinegar, plus extra for seasoning
1 teaspoon vegetable oil	¼ teaspoon sugar
2 tablespoons barbecue sauce, plus extra for serving	

1. Preheat the air fryer to 350°F (177°C). 2. Toss coleslaw mix and ¼ teaspoon salt in a colander set over bowl. Let sit until wilted slightly, about 30 minutes. Rinse, drain, and dry well with a dish towel. 3. Meanwhile, pat chicken dry with paper towels, rub with oil, and season with salt and pepper. Arrange breasts skin-side down in air fryer basket, spaced evenly apart, alternating ends. Bake for 10 minutes. Flip breasts and brush skin side with barbecue sauce. Return basket to air fryer and bake until well browned and chicken registers 160°F (71°C), 10 to 15 minutes. 4. Transfer chicken to serving platter, tent loosely with aluminum foil, and let rest for 5 minutes. While chicken rests, whisk mayonnaise, sour cream, vinegar, sugar, and pinch pepper together in a large bowl. Stir in coleslaw mix and season with salt, pepper, and additional vinegar to taste. Serve chicken with coleslaw, passing extra barbecue sauce separately.

Teriyaki Chicken Legs

Prep time: 12 minutes | Cook time: 18 to 20 minutes | Serves 2

4 tablespoons teriyaki sauce	4 chicken legs
1 tablespoon orange juice	Cooking spray
1 teaspoon smoked paprika	

1. Mix together the teriyaki sauce, orange juice, and smoked paprika. Brush on all sides of chicken legs. 2. Spray the air fryer basket with nonstick cooking spray and place chicken in basket. 3. Air fry at 360°F (182°C) for 6 minutes. Turn and baste with sauce. Cook for 6 more minutes, turn and baste. Cook for 6 to 8 minutes more, until juices run clear when chicken is pierced with a fork.

Chicken Patties

Prep time: 15 minutes | Cook time: 12 minutes | Serves 4

1 pound (454 g) ground chicken thigh meat	½ teaspoon garlic powder
½ cup shredded Mozzarella cheese	¼ teaspoon onion powder
	1 large egg
1 teaspoon dried parsley	2 ounces (57 g) pork rinds, finely ground

1. In a large bowl, mix ground chicken, Mozzarella, parsley, garlic powder, and onion powder. Form into four patties. 2. Place patties in the freezer for 15 to 20 minutes until they begin to firm up. 3. Whisk egg in a medium bowl. Place the ground pork rinds into a large bowl. 4. Dip each chicken patty into the egg and then press into pork rinds to fully coat. Place patties into the air fryer basket. 5. Adjust the temperature to 360°F (182°C) and air fry for 12 minutes. 6. Patties will be firm and cooked to an internal temperature of 165°F (74°C) when done. Serve immediately.

Cilantro Lime Chicken Thighs

Prep time: 15 minutes | Cook time: 22 minutes | Serves 4

4 bone-in, skin-on chicken thighs	2 teaspoons chili powder
1 teaspoon baking powder	1 teaspoon cumin
½ teaspoon garlic powder	2 medium limes
	¼ cup chopped fresh cilantro

1. Pat chicken thighs dry and sprinkle with baking powder. 2. In a small bowl, mix garlic powder, chili powder, and cumin and sprinkle evenly over thighs, gently rubbing on and under chicken skin. 3. Cut one lime in half and squeeze juice over thighs. Place chicken into the air fryer basket. 4. Adjust the temperature to 380°F (193°C) and roast for 22 minutes. 5. Cut other lime into four wedges for serving and garnish cooked chicken with wedges and cilantro.

Lemon-Basil Turkey Breasts

Prep time: 30 minutes | Cook time: 58 minutes | Serves 4

2 tablespoons olive oil	1 teaspoon fresh basil leaves, chopped
2 pounds (907 g) turkey breasts, bone-in, skin-on	2 tablespoons lemon zest, grated
Coarse sea salt and ground black pepper, to taste	

1. Rub olive oil on all sides of the turkey breasts; sprinkle with salt, pepper, basil, and lemon zest. 2. Place the turkey breasts skin side up on the parchment-lined air fryer basket. 3. Cook in the preheated air fryer at 330°F (166°C) for 30 minutes. Now, turn them over and cook an additional 28 minutes. 4. Serve with lemon wedges, if desired. Bon appétit!

Pork Rind Fried Chicken

Prep time: 30 minutes | Cook time: 20 minutes | Serves 4

¼ cup buffalo sauce	¼ teaspoon ground black pepper
4 (4-ounce / 113-g) boneless, skinless chicken breasts	2 ounces (57 g) plain pork rinds, finely crushed
½ teaspoon paprika	
½ teaspoon garlic powder	

1. Pour buffalo sauce into a large sealable bowl or bag. Add chicken and toss to coat. Place sealed bowl or bag into refrigerator and let marinate at least 30 minutes up to overnight. 2. Remove chicken from marinade but do not shake excess sauce off chicken. Sprinkle both sides of thighs with paprika, garlic powder, and pepper. 3. Place pork rinds into a large bowl and press each chicken breast into pork rinds to coat evenly on both sides. 4. Place chicken into ungreased air fryer basket. Adjust the temperature to 400°F (204°C) and roast for 20 minutes, turning chicken halfway through cooking. Chicken will be golden and have an internal temperature of at least 165°F (74°C) when done. Serve warm.

French Garlic Chicken

Prep time: 30 minutes | Cook time: 27 minutes | Serves 4

2 tablespoon extra-virgin olive oil	1 teaspoon black pepper
1 tablespoon Dijon mustard	1 pound (454 g) boneless, skinless chicken thighs, halved crosswise
1 tablespoon apple cider vinegar	
3 cloves garlic, minced	2 tablespoons butter
2 teaspoons herbes de Provence	8 cloves garlic, chopped
½ teaspoon kosher salt	¼ cup heavy whipping cream

1. In a small bowl, combine the olive oil, mustard, vinegar, minced garlic, herbes de Provence, salt, and pepper. Use a wire whisk to emulsify the mixture. 2. Pierce the chicken all over with a fork to allow the marinade to penetrate better. Place the chicken in a resealable plastic bag, pour the marinade over, and seal. Massage until the chicken is well coated. Marinate at room temperature for 30 minutes or in the refrigerator for up to 24 hours. 3. When you are ready to cook, place the butter and chopped garlic in a baking pan and place it in the air fryer basket. Set the air fryer to 400°F (204°C) for 5 minutes, or until the butter has melted and the garlic is sizzling. 4. Add the chicken and the marinade to the seasoned butter. Set the air fryer to 350°F (177°C) for 15 minutes. Use a meat thermometer to ensure the chicken has reached an internal temperature of 165°F (74°C). Transfer the chicken to a plate and cover lightly with foil to keep warm. 5. Add the cream to the pan, stirring to combine with the garlic, butter, and cooking juices. Place the pan in the air fryer basket. Set the air fryer to 350°F (177°C) for 7 minutes. 6. Pour the thickened sauce over the chicken and serve.

Tex-Mex Chicken Breasts

Prep time: 10 minutes | Cook time: 17 to 20 minutes | Serves 4

1 pound (454 g) low-sodium boneless, skinless chicken breasts, cut into 1-inch cubes	2 teaspoons olive oil
	⅔ cup canned low-sodium black beans, rinsed and drained
1 medium onion, chopped	½ cup low-sodium salsa
1 red bell pepper, chopped	2 teaspoons chili powder
1 jalapeño pepper, minced	

1. Preheat the air fryer to 400°F (204°C). 2. In a medium metal bowl, mix the chicken, onion, bell pepper, jalapeño, and olive oil. Roast for 10 minutes, stirring once during cooking. 3. Add the black beans, salsa, and chili powder. Roast for 7 to 10 minutes more, stirring once, until the chicken reaches an internal temperature of 165°F (74°C) on a meat thermometer. Serve immediately.

Barbecue Chicken and Coleslaw Tostadas

Prep time: 15 minutes | Cook time: 40 minutes | Makes 4 tostadas

Coleslaw:	½ tablespoon white vinegar
¼ cup sour cream	½ teaspoon garlic powder
¼ small green cabbage, finely chopped	½ teaspoon salt
	¼ teaspoon ground black pepper
Tostadas:	4 corn tortillas
2 cups pulled rotisserie chicken	½ cup shredded Mozzarella cheese
½ cup barbecue sauce	Cooking spray

Make the Coleslaw: 1. Combine the ingredients for the coleslaw in a large bowl. Toss to mix well. 2. Refrigerate until ready to serve. Make the Tostadas: 1. Preheat the air fryer to 370°F (188°C). Spritz the air fryer basket with cooking spray. 2. Toss the chicken with barbecue sauce in a separate large bowl to combine well. Set aside. 3. Place one tortilla in the preheated air fryer and spritz with cooking spray. Work in batches to avoid overcrowding. 4. Air fry the tortilla for 5 minutes or until lightly browned, then spread a quarter of the barbecue chicken and cheese over. 5. Air fry for another 5 minutes or until the cheese melts. Repeat with remaining tortillas, chicken, and cheese. 6. Serve the tostadas with coleslaw on top.

Ginger Turmeric Chicken Thighs

Prep time: 5 minutes | Cook time: 25 minutes | Serves 4

4 (4-ounce / 113-g) boneless, skin-on chicken thighs	½ teaspoon salt
	½ teaspoon garlic powder
2 tablespoons coconut oil, melted	½ teaspoon ground ginger
	¼ teaspoon ground black pepper
½ teaspoon ground turmeric	

1. Place chicken thighs in a large bowl and drizzle with coconut oil. Sprinkle with remaining ingredients and toss to coat both sides of thighs. 2. Place thighs skin side up into ungreased air fryer basket. Adjust the temperature to 400°F (204°C) and air fry for 25 minutes. After 10 minutes, turn thighs. When 5 minutes remain, flip thighs once more. Chicken will be done when skin is golden brown and the internal temperature is at least 165°F (74°C). Serve warm.

Chicken and Vegetable Fajitas

Prep time: 15 minutes | Cook time: 23 minutes | Serves 6

Chicken:	lengthwise
1 pound (454 g) boneless, skinless chicken thighs, cut crosswise into thirds	1 tablespoon vegetable oil
	½ teaspoon kosher salt
	½ teaspoon ground cumin
1 tablespoon vegetable oil	For Serving:
4½ teaspoons taco seasoning	Tortillas
Vegetables:	Sour cream
1 cup sliced onion	Shredded cheese
1 cup sliced bell pepper	Guacamole
1 or 2 jalapeños, quartered	Salsa

1. For the chicken: In a medium bowl, toss together the chicken, vegetable oil, and taco seasoning to coat. 2. For the vegetables: In a separate bowl, toss together the onion, bell pepper, jalapeño(s), vegetable oil, salt, and cumin to coat. 3. Place the chicken in the air fryer basket. Set the air fryer to 375°F (191°C) for 10 minutes. Add the vegetables to the basket, toss everything together to blend the seasonings, and set the air fryer for 13 minutes more. Use a meat thermometer to ensure the chicken has reached an internal temperature of 165°F (74°C). 4. Transfer the chicken and vegetables to a serving platter. Serve with tortillas and the desired fajita fixings.

Yakitori

Prep time: 10 minutes | Cook time: 15 minutes | Serves 4

½ cup mirin	4 medium scallions, trimmed,
¼ cup dry white wine	cut into 1½-inch pieces
½ cup soy sauce	Cooking spray
1 tablespoon light brown sugar	Special Equipment:
1½ pounds (680 g) boneless,	4 (4-inch) bamboo skewers,
skinless chicken thighs, cut into	soaked in water for at least 30
1½-inch pieces, fat trimmed	minutes

1. Combine the mirin, dry white wine, soy sauce, and brown sugar in a saucepan. Bring to a boil over medium heat. Keep stirring. 2. Boil for another 2 minutes or until it has a thick consistency. Turn off the heat. 3. Preheat the air fryer to 400ºF (204ºC). Spritz the air fryer basket with cooking spray. 4. Run the bamboo skewers through the chicken pieces and scallions alternatively. 5. Arrange the skewers in the preheated air fryer, then brush with mirin mixture on both sides. Spritz with cooking spray. 6. Air fry for 10 minutes or until the chicken and scallions are glossy. Flip the skewers halfway through. 7. Serve immediately.

Fajita Chicken Strips

Prep time: 10 minutes | Cook time: 15 minutes | Serves 4

1 pound (454 g) boneless,	1 onion, cut into chunks
skinless chicken tenderloins,	1 tablespoon olive oil
cut into strips	1 tablespoon fajita seasoning
3 bell peppers, any color, cut	mix
into chunks	Cooking spray

1. Preheat the air fryer to 370ºF (188ºC). 2. In a large bowl, mix together the chicken, bell peppers, onion, olive oil, and fajita seasoning mix until completely coated. 3. Spray the air fryer basket lightly with cooking spray. 4. Place the chicken and vegetables in the air fryer basket and lightly spray with cooking spray. 5. Air fry for 7 minutes. Shake the basket and air fry for an additional 5 to 8 minutes, until the chicken is cooked through and the veggies are starting to char. 6. Serve warm.

Chicken Hand Pies

Prep time: 30 minutes | Cook time: 10 minutes per batch | Makes 8 pies

¾ cup chicken broth	Salt and pepper, to taste
¾ cup frozen mixed peas and	1 (8-count) can organic flaky
carrots	biscuits
1 cup cooked chicken, chopped	Oil for misting or cooking
1 tablespoon cornstarch	spray
1 tablespoon milk	

1. In a medium saucepan, bring chicken broth to a boil. Stir in the frozen peas and carrots and cook for 5 minutes over medium heat. Stir in chicken. 2. Mix the cornstarch into the milk until it dissolves. Stir it into the simmering chicken broth mixture and cook just until thickened. 3. Remove from heat, add salt and pepper to taste, and let cool slightly. 4. Lay biscuits out on wax paper. Peel each biscuit apart in the middle to make 2 rounds so you have 16 rounds total. Using your hands or a rolling pin, flatten each biscuit round slightly to make it larger and thinner. 5. Divide chicken filling among 8 of the biscuit rounds. Place remaining biscuit rounds on top and press edges all around. Use the tines of a fork to crimp biscuit edges and make sure they are sealed well. 6. Spray both sides lightly with oil or cooking spray. 7. Cook in a single layer, 4 at a time, at 330ºF (166ºC) for 10 minutes or until biscuit dough is cooked through and golden brown.

Italian Chicken with Sauce

Prep time: 15 minutes | Cook time: 20 minutes | Serves 4

2 large skinless chicken breasts	1 egg, lightly beaten
(about 1¼ pounds / 567 g)	1 tablespoon olive oil
Salt and freshly ground black	1 cup no-sugar-added marinara
pepper	sauce
½ cup almond meal	4 slices Mozzarella cheese or ½
½ cup grated Parmesan cheese	cup shredded Mozzarella
2 teaspoons Italian seasoning	

1. Preheat the air fryer to 360ºF (182ºC). 2. Slice the chicken breasts in half horizontally to create 4 thinner chicken breasts. Working with one piece at a time, place the chicken between two pieces of parchment paper and pound with a meat mallet or rolling pin to flatten to an even thickness. Season both sides with salt and freshly ground black pepper. 3. In a large shallow bowl, combine the almond meal, Parmesan, and Italian seasoning; stir until thoroughly combined. Place the egg in another large shallow bowl. 4. Dip the chicken in the egg, followed by the almond meal mixture, pressing the mixture firmly into the chicken to create an even coating. 5. Working in batches if necessary, arrange the chicken breasts in a single layer in the air fryer basket and coat both sides lightly with olive oil. Pausing halfway through the cooking time to flip the chicken, air fry for 15 minutes, or until a thermometer inserted into the thickest part registers 165ºF (74ºC). 6. Spoon the marinara sauce over each piece of chicken and top with the Mozzarella cheese. Air fry for an additional 3 to 5 minutes until the cheese is melted.

Peachy Chicken Chunks with Cherries

Prep time: 8 minutes | Cook time: 14 to 16 minutes | Serves 4

⅓ cup peach preserves	chicken breasts, cut in 1½-inch
1 teaspoon ground rosemary	chunks
½ teaspoon black pepper	Oil for misting or cooking
½ teaspoon salt	spray
½ teaspoon marjoram	1 (10-ounce / 283-g) package
1 teaspoon light olive oil	frozen unsweetened dark
1 pound (454 g) boneless	cherries, thawed and drained

1. In a medium bowl, mix together peach preserves, rosemary, pepper, salt, marjoram, and olive oil. 2. Stir in chicken chunks and toss to coat well with the preserve mixture. 3. Spray the air fryer basket with oil or cooking spray and lay chicken chunks in basket. 4. Air fry at 390ºF (199ºC) for 7 minutes. Stir. Cook for 6 to 8 more minutes or until chicken juices run clear. 5. When chicken has cooked through, scatter the cherries over and cook for additional minute to heat cherries.

Chicken Chimichangas

Prep time: 20 minutes | Cook time: 8 to 10 minutes | Serves 4

2 cups cooked chicken, shredded	Oil for misting or cooking spray
2 tablespoons chopped green chiles	Chimichanga Sauce:
½ teaspoon oregano	2 tablespoons butter
½ teaspoon cumin	2 tablespoons flour
½ teaspoon onion powder	1 cup chicken broth
¼ teaspoon garlic powder	¼ cup light sour cream
Salt and pepper, to taste	¼ teaspoon salt
8 flour tortillas (6- or 7-inch diameter)	2 ounces (57 g) Pepper Jack or Monterey Jack cheese, shredded

1. Make the sauce by melting butter in a saucepan over medium-low heat. Stir in flour until smooth and slightly bubbly. Gradually add broth, stirring constantly until smooth. Cook and stir 1 minute, until the mixture slightly thickens. Remove from heat and stir in sour cream and salt. Set aside. 2. In a medium bowl, mix together the chicken, chiles, oregano, cumin, onion powder, garlic, salt, and pepper. Stir in 3 to 4 tablespoons of the sauce, using just enough to make the filling moist but not soupy. 3. Divide filling among the 8 tortillas. Place filling down the center of tortilla, stopping about 1 inch from edges. Fold one side of tortilla over filling, fold the two sides in, and then roll up. Mist all sides with oil or cooking spray. 4. Place chimichangas in air fryer basket seam side down. To fit more into the basket, you can stand them on their sides with the seams against the sides of the basket. 5. Air fry at 360ºF (182ºC) for 8 to 10 minutes or until heated through and crispy brown outside. 6. Add the shredded cheese to the remaining sauce. Stir over low heat, warming just until the cheese melts. Don't boil or sour cream may curdle. 7. Drizzle the sauce over the chimichangas.

Ranch Chicken Wings

Prep time: 10 minutes | Cook time: 40 minutes | Serves 4

2 tablespoons water	1 (1-ounce / 28-g) envelope ranch salad dressing mix
2 tablespoons hot pepper sauce	1 teaspoon paprika
2 tablespoons unsalted butter, melted	4 pounds (1.8 kg) chicken wings, tips removed
2 tablespoons apple cider vinegar	Cooking oil spray

1. In a large bowl, whisk the water, hot pepper sauce, melted butter, vinegar, salad dressing mix, and paprika until combined. 2. Add the wings and toss to coat. At this point, you can cover the bowl and marinate the wings in the refrigerator for 4 to 24 hours for best results. However, you can just let the wings stand for 30 minutes in the refrigerator. 3. Insert the crisper plate into the basket and the basket into the unit. Preheat the unit by selecting AIR FRY, setting the temperature to 400ºF (204ºC), and setting the time to 3 minutes. Select START/STOP to begin. 4. Once the unit is preheated, spray the crisper plate with cooking oil. Working in batches, put half the wings into the basket; it is okay to stack them. Refrigerate the remaining wings. 5. Select AIR FRY, set the temperature to 400ºF (204ºC), and set the time to 20 minutes. Select START/STOP to begin. 6. After 5 minutes, remove the basket and shake it. Reinsert the basket to resume cooking. Remove and shake the basket every 5 minutes, three more times, until the chicken is browned and glazed and a food thermometer inserted into the wings registers 165ºF (74ºC). 7. Repeat steps 4, 5, and 6 with the remaining wings. 8. When the cooking is complete, serve warm.

Sweet Chili Spiced Chicken

Prep time: 10 minutes | Cook time: 43 minutes | Serves 4

Spice Rub:	kosher salt
2 tablespoons brown sugar	2 teaspoons coarsely ground black pepper
2 tablespoons paprika	
1 teaspoon dry mustard powder	1 tablespoon vegetable oil
1 teaspoon chili powder	1 (3½-pound / 1.6-kg) chicken, cut into 8 pieces
2 tablespoons coarse sea salt or	

1. Prepare the spice rub by combining the brown sugar, paprika, mustard powder, chili powder, salt and pepper. Rub the oil all over the chicken pieces and then rub the spice mix onto the chicken, covering completely. This is done very easily in a zipper sealable bag. You can do this ahead of time and let the chicken marinate in the refrigerator, or just proceed with cooking right away. 2. Preheat the air fryer to 370ºF (188ºC). 3. Air fry the chicken in two batches. Place the two chicken thighs and two drumsticks into the air fryer basket. Air fry at 370ºF (188ºC) for 10 minutes. Then, gently turn the chicken pieces over and air fry for another 10 minutes. Remove the chicken pieces and let them rest on a plate while you cook the chicken breasts. Air fry the chicken breasts, skin side down for 8 minutes. Turn the chicken breasts over and air fry for another 12 minutes. 4. Lower the temperature of the air fryer to 340ºF (171ºC). Place the first batch of chicken on top of the second batch already in the basket and air fry for a final 3 minutes. 5. Let the chicken rest for 5 minutes and serve warm with some mashed potatoes and a green salad or vegetables.

Buffalo Chicken Wings

Prep time: 10 minutes | Cook time: 20 to 25 minutes | Serves 4

2 tablespoons baking powder	½ cup Buffalo hot sauce, such as Frank's RedHot
1 teaspoon smoked paprika	
Sea salt and freshly ground black pepper, to taste	¼ cup (4 tablespoons) unsalted butter
2 pounds (907 g) chicken wings or chicken drumettes	2 tablespoons apple cider vinegar
Avocado oil spray	1 teaspoon minced garlic
⅓ cup avocado oil	

1. In a large bowl, stir together the baking powder, smoked paprika, and salt and pepper to taste. Add the chicken wings and toss to coat. 2. Set the air fryer to 400ºF (204ºC). Spray the wings with oil. 3. Place the wings in the basket in a single layer, working in batches, and air fry for 20 to 25 minutes. Check with an instant-read thermometer and remove when they reach 155ºF (68ºC). Let rest until they reach 165ºF (74ºC). 4. While the wings are cooking, whisk together the avocado oil, hot sauce, butter, vinegar, and garlic in a small saucepan over medium-low heat until warm. 5. When the wings are done cooking, toss them with the Buffalo sauce. Serve warm.

Gochujang Chicken Wings

Prep time: 15 minutes | Cook time: 25 minutes | Serves 4

Wings:	1 tablespoon toasted sesame oil
2 pounds (907 g) chicken wings	1 tablespoon minced fresh ginger
1 teaspoon kosher salt	1 tablespoon minced garlic
1 teaspoon black pepper or gochugaru (Korean red pepper)	1 teaspoon sugar
Sauce:	1 teaspoon agave nectar or honey
2 tablespoons gochujang (Korean chile paste)	For Serving
1 tablespoon mayonnaise	1 teaspoon sesame seeds
	¼ cup chopped scallions

1. For the wings: Season the wings with the salt and pepper and place in the air fryer basket. Set the air fryer to 400°F (204°C) for 20 minutes, turning the wings halfway through the cooking time. 2. Meanwhile, for the sauce: In a small bowl, combine the gochujang, mayonnaise, sesame oil, ginger, garlic, sugar, and agave; set aside. 3. As you near the 20-minute mark, use a meat thermometer to check the meat. When the wings reach 160°F (71°C), transfer them to a large bowl. Pour about half the sauce on the wings; toss to coat (serve the remaining sauce as a dip). 4. Return the wings to the air fryer basket and cook for 5 minutes, until the sauce has glazed. 5. Transfer the wings to a serving platter. Sprinkle with the sesame seeds and scallions. Serve with the reserved sauce on the side for dipping.

Quick Chicken Fajitas

Prep time: 10 minutes | Cook time: 15 minutes | Serves 2

10 ounces (283 g) boneless, skinless chicken breast, sliced into ¼-inch strips	½ teaspoon garlic powder
	¼ medium onion, peeled and sliced
2 tablespoons coconut oil, melted	½ medium green bell pepper, seeded and sliced
1 tablespoon chili powder	½ medium red bell pepper, seeded and sliced
½ teaspoon cumin	
½ teaspoon paprika	

1. Place chicken and coconut oil into a large bowl and sprinkle with chili powder, cumin, paprika, and garlic powder. Toss chicken until well coated with seasoning. Place chicken into the air fryer basket. 2. Adjust the temperature to 350°F (177°C) and air fry for 15 minutes. 3. Add onion and peppers into the basket when the cooking time has 7 minutes remaining. 4. Toss the chicken two or three times during cooking. Vegetables should be tender and chicken fully cooked to at least 165°F (74°C) internal temperature when finished. Serve warm.

Chicken Schnitzel

Prep time: 15 minutes | Cook time: 5 minutes | Serves 4

½ cup all-purpose flour	½ teaspoon salt
1 teaspoon marjoram	1 egg
½ teaspoon thyme	1 teaspoon lemon juice
1 teaspoon dried parsley flakes	1 teaspoon water
1 cup breadcrumbs	thin, cut in half lengthwise
4 chicken tenders, pounded	Cooking spray

1. Preheat the air fryer to 390°F (199°C) and spritz with cooking spray. 2. Combine the flour, marjoram, thyme, parsley, and salt in a shallow dish. Stir to mix well. 3. Whisk the egg with lemon juice and water in a large bowl. Pour the breadcrumbs in a separate shallow dish. 4. Roll the chicken halves in the flour mixture first, then in the egg mixture, and then roll over the breadcrumbs to coat well. Shake the excess off. 5. Arrange the chicken halves in the preheated air fryer and spritz with cooking spray on both sides. 6. Air fry for 5 minutes or until the chicken halves are golden brown and crispy. Flip the halves halfway through. 7. Serve immediately.

Thanksgiving Turkey Breast

Prep time: 5 minutes | Cook time: 30 minutes | Serves 4

1½ teaspoons fine sea salt	1 teaspoon chopped fresh thyme leaves
1 teaspoon ground black pepper	
1 teaspoon chopped fresh rosemary leaves	1 (2-pound / 907-g) turkey breast
1 teaspoon chopped fresh sage	3 tablespoons ghee or unsalted butter, melted
1 teaspoon chopped fresh tarragon	3 tablespoons Dijon mustard

1. Spray the air fryer with avocado oil. Preheat the air fryer to 390°F (199°C). 2. In a small bowl, stir together the salt, pepper, and herbs until well combined. Season the turkey breast generously on all sides with the seasoning. 3. In another small bowl, stir together the ghee and Dijon. Brush the ghee mixture on all sides of the turkey breast. 4. Place the turkey breast in the air fryer basket and air fry for 30 minutes, or until the internal temperature reaches 165°F (74°C). Transfer the breast to a cutting board and allow it to rest for 10 minutes before cutting it into ½-inch-thick slices. 5. Store leftovers in an airtight container in the refrigerator for up to 4 days or in the freezer for up to a month. Reheat in a preheated 350°F (177°C) air fryer for 4 minutes, or until warmed through.

Gold Livers

Prep time: 10 minutes | Cook time: 20 minutes | Serves 4

2 eggs	½ teaspoon ground black pepper
2 tablespoons water	
¾ cup flour	20 ounces (567 g) chicken livers
2 cups panko breadcrumbs	
1 teaspoon salt	Cooking spray

1. Preheat the air fryer to 390°F (199°C). Spritz the air fryer basket with cooking spray. 2. Whisk the eggs with water in a large bowl. Pour the flour in a separate bowl. Pour the panko on a shallow dish and sprinkle with salt and pepper. 3. Dredge the chicken livers in the flour. Shake the excess off, then dunk the livers in the whisked eggs, and then roll the livers over the panko to coat well. 4. Arrange the livers in the preheated air fryer and spritz with cooking spray. Work in batches to avoid overcrowding. 5. Air fry for 10 minutes or until the livers are golden and crispy. Flip the livers halfway through. Repeat with remaining livers. 6. Serve immediately.

Bacon Lovers' Stuffed Chicken

Prep time: 10 minutes | Cook time: 20 minutes | Serves 4

4 (5-ounce / 142-g) boneless, skinless chicken breasts, pounded to ¼ inch thick	spread, softened, for dairy-free)
	8 slices thin-cut bacon or beef bacon
2 (5.2-ounce / 147-g) packages Boursin cheese (or Kite Hill brand chive cream cheese style	Sprig of fresh cilantro, for garnish (optional)

1. Spray the air fryer basket with avocado oil. Preheat the air fryer to 400°F (204°C). 2. Place one of the chicken breasts on a cutting board. With a sharp knife held parallel to the cutting board, make a 1-inch-wide incision at the top of the breast. Carefully cut into the breast to form a large pocket, leaving a ½-inch border along the sides and bottom. Repeat with the other 3 chicken breasts. 3. Snip the corner of a large resealable plastic bag to form a ¾-inch hole. Place the Boursin cheese in the bag and pipe the cheese into the pockets in the chicken breasts, dividing the cheese evenly among them. 4. Wrap 2 slices of bacon around each chicken breast and secure the ends with toothpicks. Place the bacon-wrapped chicken in the air fryer basket and air fry until the bacon is crisp and the chicken's internal temperature reaches 165°F (74°C), about 18 to 20 minutes, flipping after 10 minutes. Garnish with a sprig of cilantro before serving, if desired. 5. Store leftovers in an airtight container in the refrigerator for up to 4 days. Reheat in a preheated 400°F (204°C) air fryer for 5 minutes, or until warmed through.

Korean Honey Wings

Prep time: 10 minutes | Cook time: 25 minutes per batch | Serves 4

¼ cup gochujang, or red pepper paste	2 teaspoons ground ginger
¼ cup mayonnaise	3 pounds (1.4 kg) whole chicken wings
2 tablespoons honey	Olive oil spray
1 tablespoon sesame oil	1 teaspoon salt
2 teaspoons minced garlic	½ teaspoon freshly ground black pepper
1 tablespoon sugar	

1. In a large bowl, whisk the gochujang, mayonnaise, honey, sesame oil, garlic, sugar, and ginger. Set aside. 2. Insert the crisper plate into the basket and the basket into the unit. Preheat the unit by selecting AIR FRY, setting the temperature to 400°F (204°C), and setting the time to 3 minutes. Select START/STOP to begin. 3. To prepare the chicken wings, cut the wings in half. The meatier part is the drumette. Cut off and discard the wing tip from the flat part (or save the wing tips in the freezer to make chicken stock). 4. Once the unit is preheated, spray the crisper plate with olive oil. Working in batches, place half the chicken wings into the basket, spray them with olive oil, and sprinkle with the salt and pepper. 5. Select AIR FRY, set the temperature to 400°F (204°C), and set the time to 20 minutes. Select START/STOP to begin. 6. After 10 minutes, remove the basket, flip the wings, and spray them with more olive oil. Reinsert the basket to resume cooking. 7. Cook the wings to an internal temperature of 165°F (74°C), then transfer them to the bowl with the prepared sauce and toss to coat. 8. Repeat steps 4, 5, 6, and 7 for the remaining chicken wings. 9. Return the coated wings to the basket and air fry for 4 to 6 minutes more until the sauce has glazed the wings and the

chicken is crisp. After 3 minutes, check the wings to make sure they aren't burning. Serve hot.

Brazilian Tempero Baiano Chicken Drumsticks

Prep time: 30 minutes | Cook time: 20 minutes | Serves 4

1 teaspoon cumin seeds	½ teaspoon black peppercorns
1 teaspoon dried oregano	½ teaspoon cayenne pepper
1 teaspoon dried parsley	¼ cup fresh lime juice
1 teaspoon ground turmeric	2 tablespoons olive oil
½ teaspoon coriander seeds	1½ pounds (680 g) chicken drumsticks
1 teaspoon kosher salt	

1. In a clean coffee grinder or spice mill, combine the cumin, oregano, parsley, turmeric, coriander seeds, salt, peppercorns, and cayenne. Process until finely ground. 2. In a small bowl, combine the ground spices with the lime juice and oil. Place the chicken in a resealable plastic bag. Add the marinade, seal, and massage until the chicken is well coated. Marinate at room temperature for 30 minutes or in the refrigerator for up to 24 hours. 3. When you are ready to cook, place the drumsticks skin side up in the air fryer basket. Set the air fryer to 400°F (204°C) for 20 to 25 minutes, turning the legs halfway through the cooking time. Use a meat thermometer to ensure that the chicken has reached an internal temperature of 165°F (74°C). 4. Serve with plenty of napkins.

Buffalo Chicken Cheese Sticks

Prep time: 5 minutes | Cook time: 8 minutes | Serves 2

1 cup shredded cooked chicken	cheese
¼ cup buffalo sauce	1 large egg
1 cup shredded Mozzarella	¼ cup crumbled feta

1. In a large bowl, mix all ingredients except the feta. Cut a piece of parchment to fit your air fryer basket and press the mixture into a ½-inch-thick circle. 2. Sprinkle the mixture with feta and place into the air fryer basket. 3. Adjust the temperature to 400°F (204°C) and air fry for 8 minutes. 4. After 5 minutes, flip over the cheese mixture. 5. Allow to cool 5 minutes before cutting into sticks. Serve warm.

Chicken Enchiladas

Prep time: 10 minutes | Cook time: 8 minutes | Serves 4

Oil, for spraying	rinsed and drained
3 cups shredded cooked chicken	1 (4-ounce / 113-g) can diced green chiles, drained
1 package taco seasoning	1 (10-ounce / 283-g) can red or green enchilada sauce
8 flour tortillas, at room temperature	1 cup shredded Cheddar cheese
½ cup canned black beans,	

1. Line the air fryer basket with parchment and spray lightly with oil. (Do not skip the step of lining the basket; the parchment will keep the sauce and cheese from dripping through the holes.) 2. In a small bowl, mix together the chicken and taco seasoning. 3. Divide the mixture among the tortillas. Top with the black beans and green chiles. Carefully roll up each tortilla. 4. Place the enchiladas, seam-

side down, in the prepared basket. You may need to work in batches, depending on the size of your air fryer. 5. Spoon the enchilada sauce over the enchiladas. Use just enough sauce to keep them from drying out. You can add more sauce when serving. Sprinkle the cheese on top. 6. Air fry at 360ºF (182ºC) for 5 to 8 minutes, or until heated through and the cheese is melted. 7. Place 2 enchiladas on each plate and top with more enchilada sauce, if desired.

Chapter 5   Beef, Pork, and Lamb

Greek Stuffed Tenderloin

Prep time: 10 minutes | Cook time: 10 minutes | Serves 4

1½ pounds (680 g) venison or beef tenderloin, pounded to ¼ inch thick	¼ cup finely chopped onions
3 teaspoons fine sea salt	2 cloves garlic, minced
1 teaspoon ground black pepper	For Garnish/Serving (Optional):
2 ounces (57 g) creamy goat cheese	Prepared yellow mustard
½ cup crumbled feta cheese (about 2 ounces / 57 g)	Halved cherry tomatoes
	Extra-virgin olive oil
	Sprigs of fresh rosemary
	Lavender flowers

1. Spray the air fryer basket with avocado oil. Preheat the air fryer to 400°F (204°C). 2. Season the tenderloin on all sides with the salt and pepper. 3. In a medium-sized mixing bowl, combine the goat cheese, feta, onions, and garlic. Place the mixture in the center of the tenderloin. Starting at the end closest to you, tightly roll the tenderloin like a jelly roll. Tie the rolled tenderloin tightly with kitchen twine. 4. Place the meat in the air fryer basket and air fry for 5 minutes. Flip the meat over and cook for another 5 minutes, or until the internal temperature reaches 135°F (57°C) for medium-rare. 5. To serve, smear a line of prepared yellow mustard on a platter, then place the meat next to it and add halved cherry tomatoes on the side, if desired. Drizzle with olive oil and garnish with rosemary sprigs and lavender flowers, if desired. 6. Best served fresh. Store leftovers in an airtight container in the fridge for 3 days. Reheat in a preheated 350°F (177°C) air fryer for 4 minutes, or until heated through.

Beef Empanadas

Prep time: 15 minutes | Cook time: 25 minutes | Serves 5

2 garlic cloves, chopped	pepper, to taste
⅓ cup chopped green bell pepper	15 empanada wrappers
⅓ medium onion, chopped	1 cup shredded Mozzarella cheese
8 ounces (227 g) 93% lean ground beef	1 cup shredded pepper Jack cheese
1 teaspoon hamburger seasoning	1 tablespoon butter
Salt and freshly ground black	Cooking oil spray

1. Spray a skillet with the cooking oil and place it over medium-high heat. Add the garlic, green bell pepper, and onion. Cook until fragrant, about 2 minutes. 2. Add the ground beef to the skillet. Season it with the hamburger seasoning, salt, and pepper. Using a spatula or spoon, break up the beef into small pieces. Cook the beef for about 5 minutes until browned. Drain any excess fat. 3. Lay the empanada wrappers on a work surface. 4. Dip a basting brush in water. Glaze each wrapper along the edges with the wet brush. This will soften the crust and make it easier to roll. You can also dip your fingers in water to moisten the edges. 5. Scoop 2 to 3 tablespoons of the ground beef mixture onto each empanada wrapper. Sprinkle the Mozzarella and pepper Jack cheeses over the beef. 6. Close the empanadas by folding the empanada wrapper in half over the filling. Using the back of a fork, press along the edges to seal. 7. Insert the crisper plate into the basket and the basket into the unit. Preheat the unit by selecting AIR FRY, setting the temperature to 400°F (204°C), and setting the time to 3 minutes. Select START/STOP to begin. 8. Once the unit is preheated, spray the crisper plate with cooking oil. Working in batches, place 7 or 8 empanadas into the basket. Spray each with cooking oil. 9. Select AIR FRY, set the temperature to 400°F (204°C), and set the time to 12 minutes. Select START/STOP to begin. 10. After 8 minutes, flip the empanadas and spray them with more cooking oil. Resume cooking. 11. When the cooking is complete, transfer the empanadas to a plate. For added flavor, top each hot empanada with a bit of butter and let melt. Repeat steps 8, 9, and 10 for the remaining empanadas. 12. Cool for 5 minutes before serving.

Mustard Lamb Chops

Prep time: 5 minutes | Cook time: 14 minutes | Serves 4

Oil, for spraying	¼ teaspoon freshly ground black pepper
1 tablespoon Dijon mustard	
2 teaspoons lemon juice	4 (1¼-inch-thick) loin lamb chops
½ teaspoon dried tarragon	
¼ teaspoon salt	

1. Preheat the air fryer to 390°F (199°C). Line the air fryer basket with parchment and spray lightly with oil. 2. In a small bowl, mix together the mustard, lemon juice, tarragon, salt, and black pepper. 3. Pat dry the lamb chops with a paper towel. Brush the chops on both sides with the mustard mixture. 4. Place the chops in the prepared basket. You may need to work in batches, depending on the size of your air fryer. 5. Cook for 8 minutes, flip, and cook for another 6 minutes, or until the internal temperature reaches 125°F (52°C) for rare, 145°F (63°C) for medium-rare, or 155°F (68°C) for medium.

Meat and Rice Stuffed Bell Peppers

Prep time: 20 minutes | Cook time: 18 minutes | Serves 4

¾ pound (340 g) lean ground beef	1 teaspoon honey
4 ounces (113 g) lean ground pork	½ teaspoon dried basil
¼ cup onion, minced	½ cup cooked brown rice
1 (15-ounce / 425-g) can crushed tomatoes	½ teaspoon garlic powder
1 teaspoon Worcestershire sauce	½ teaspoon oregano
1 teaspoon barbecue seasoning	½ teaspoon salt
	2 small bell peppers, cut in half, stems removed, deseeded
	Cooking spray

1. Preheat the air fryer to 360°F (182°C) and spritz a baking pan with cooking spray. 2. Arrange the beef, pork, and onion in the baking pan and bake in the preheated air fryer for 8 minutes. Break the ground meat into chunks halfway through the cooking. 3. Meanwhile, combine the tomatoes, Worcestershire sauce, barbecue seasoning, honey, and basil in a saucepan. Stir to mix well. 4. Transfer the cooked meat mixture to a large bowl and add the cooked rice, garlic powder, oregano, salt, and ¼ cup of the tomato mixture. Stir to mix well. 5. Stuff the pepper halves with the mixture, then arrange the pepper halves in the air fryer and air fry for 10 minutes or until the peppers are lightly charred. 6. Serve the stuffed peppers with the remaining tomato sauce on top.

Sausage and Peppers

Prep time: 7 minutes | Cook time: 35 minutes | Serves 4

Oil, for spraying	1 tablespoon olive oil
2 pounds (907 g) hot or sweet Italian sausage links, cut into thick slices	1 tablespoon chopped fresh parsley
4 large bell peppers of any color, seeded and cut into slices	1 teaspoon dried oregano
1 onion, thinly sliced	1 teaspoon dried basil
	1 teaspoon balsamic vinegar

1. Line the air fryer basket with parchment and spray lightly with oil. 2. In a large bowl, combine the sausage, bell peppers, and onion. 3. In a small bowl, whisk together the olive oil, parsley, oregano, basil, and balsamic vinegar. Pour the mixture over the sausage and peppers and toss until evenly coated. 4. Using a slotted spoon, transfer the mixture to the prepared basket, taking care to drain out as much excess liquid as possible. 5. Air fry at 350°F (177°C) for 20 minutes, stir, and cook for another 15 minutes, or until the sausage is browned and the juices run clear.

Air Fried Crispy Venison

Prep time: 10 minutes | Cook time: 20 minutes | Serves 4

2 eggs	pepper
¼ cup milk	1 pound (454 g) venison backstrap, sliced
1 cup whole wheat flour	Cooking spray
½ teaspoon salt	
¼ teaspoon ground black	

1. Preheat the air fryer to 360°F (182°C) and spritz with cooking spray. 2. Whisk the eggs with milk in a large bowl. Combine the flour with salt and ground black pepper in a shallow dish. 3. Dredge the venison in the flour first, then into the egg mixture. Shake the excess off and roll the venison back over the flour to coat well. 4. Arrange half of the venison in the preheated air fryer and spritz with cooking spray. 5. Air fry for 10 minutes or until the internal temperature of the venison reaches at least 145°F (63°C) for medium rare. Flip the venison halfway through. Repeat with remaining venison. 6. Serve immediately.

Bacon, Cheese and Pear Stuffed Pork

Prep time: 10 minutes | Cook time: 24 minutes | Serves 3

4 slices bacon, chopped	⅛ teaspoon black pepper
1 tablespoon butter	1 pear, finely diced
½ cup finely diced onion	⅓ cup crumbled blue cheese
⅓ cup chicken stock	3 boneless center-cut pork chops (2-inch thick)
1½ cups seasoned stuffing cubes	Olive oil
1 egg, beaten	Salt and freshly ground black pepper, to taste
½ teaspoon dried thyme	
½ teaspoon salt	

1. Preheat the air fryer to 400°F (204°C). 2. Place the bacon into the air fryer basket and air fry for 6 minutes, stirring halfway through the cooking time. Remove the bacon and set it aside on a paper towel. Pour out the grease from the bottom of the air fryer. 3. Make the stuffing: Melt the butter in a medium saucepan over medium heat on the stovetop. Add the onion and sauté for a few minutes, until it starts to soften. Add the chicken stock and simmer for 1 minute. Remove the pan from the heat and add the stuffing cubes. Stir until the stock has been absorbed. Add the egg, dried thyme, salt and freshly ground black pepper, and stir until combined. Fold in the diced pear and crumbled blue cheese. 4. Place the pork chops on a cutting board. Using the palm of your hand to hold the chop flat and steady, slice into the side of the pork chop to make a pocket in the center of the chop. Leave about an inch of chop uncut and make sure you don't cut all the way through the pork chop. Brush both sides of the pork chops with olive oil and season with salt and freshly ground black pepper. Stuff each pork chop with a third of the stuffing, packing the stuffing tightly inside the pocket. 5. Preheat the air fryer to 360°F (182°C). 6. Spray or brush the sides of the air fryer basket with oil. Place the pork chops in the air fryer basket with the open stuffed edge of the pork chop facing the outside edges of the basket. 7. Air fry the pork chops for 18 minutes, turning the pork chops over halfway through the cooking time. When the chops are done, let them rest for 5 minutes and then transfer to a serving platter.

Mediterranean Beef Steaks

Prep time: 20 minutes | Cook time: 20 minutes | Serves 4

2 tablespoons coconut aminos	pepper
3 heaping tablespoons fresh chives	½ teaspoon dried basil
2 tablespoons olive oil	½ teaspoon dried rosemary
3 tablespoons dry white wine	1 teaspoon freshly ground black pepper
4 small-sized beef steaks	1 teaspoon sea salt, or more to taste
2 teaspoons smoked cayenne	

1. Firstly, coat the steaks with the cayenne pepper, black pepper, salt, basil, and rosemary. 2. Drizzle the steaks with olive oil, white wine, and coconut aminos. 3. Finally, roast in the air fryer for 20 minutes at 340°F (171°C). Serve garnished with fresh chives. Bon appétit!

Crescent Dogs

Prep time: 15 minutes | Cook time: 8 minutes | Makes 24 crescent dogs

Oil, for spraying	24 cocktail sausages or 8 (6-inch) hot dogs, cut into thirds
1 (8-ounce / 227-g) can refrigerated crescent rolls	2 tablespoons unsalted butter, melted
8 slices Cheddar cheese, cut into thirds	1 tablespoon sea salt flakes

1. Line the air fryer basket with parchment and spray lightly with oil. 2. Separate the dough into 8 triangles. Cut each triangle into 3 narrow triangles so you have 24 total triangles. 3. Top each triangle with 1 piece of cheese and 1 cocktail sausage. 4. Roll up each piece of dough, starting at the wide end and rolling toward the point. 5. Place the rolls in the prepared basket in a single layer. You may need to cook in batches, depending on the size of your air fryer. 6. Air fry at 325°F (163°C) for 3 to 4 minutes, flip, and cook for another 3 to 4 minutes, or until golden brown. 7. Brush with the melted butter and sprinkle with the sea salt flakes before serving.

Bulgogi Burgers

Prep time: 30 minutes | Cook time: 10 minutes | Serves 4

Burgers:
1 pound (454 g) 85% lean ground beef
¼ cup chopped scallions
2 tablespoons gochujang (Korean red chile paste)
1 tablespoon dark soy sauce
2 teaspoons minced garlic
2 teaspoons minced fresh ginger
2 teaspoons sugar

1 tablespoon toasted sesame oil
½ teaspoon kosher salt
Gochujang Mayonnaise:
¼ cup mayonnaise
¼ cup chopped scallions
1 tablespoon gochujang (Korean red chile paste)
1 tablespoon toasted sesame oil
2 teaspoons sesame seeds
4 hamburger buns

1. For the burgers: In a large bowl, mix the ground beef, scallions, gochujang, soy sauce, garlic, ginger, sugar, sesame oil, and salt. Marinate at room temperature for 30 minutes, or cover and refrigerate for up to 24 hours. 2. Divide the meat into four portions and form them into round patties. Make a slight depression in the middle of each patty with your thumb to prevent them from puffing up into a dome shape while cooking. 3. Place the patties in a single layer in the air fryer basket. Set the air fryer to 350ºF (177ºC) for 10 minutes. 4. Meanwhile, for the gochujang mayonnaise: Stir together the mayonnaise, scallions, gochujang, sesame oil, and sesame seeds. 5. At the end of the cooking time, use a meat thermometer to ensure the burgers have reached an internal temperature of 160ºF / 71ºC (medium). 6. To serve, place the burgers on the buns and top with the mayonnaise.

Italian Steak Rolls

Prep time: 30 minutes | Cook time: 9 minutes | Serves 4

1 tablespoon vegetable oil
2 cloves garlic, minced
2 teaspoons dried Italian seasoning
1 teaspoon kosher salt
1 teaspoon black pepper
1 pound (454 g) flank or skirt steak, ¼ to ½ inch thick

1 (10-ounce / 283-g) package frozen spinach, thawed and squeezed dry
½ cup diced jarred roasted red pepper
1 cup shredded Mozzarella cheese

1. In a large bowl, combine the oil, garlic, Italian seasoning, salt, and pepper. Whisk to combine. Add the steak to the bowl, turning to ensure the entire steak is covered with the seasonings. Cover and marinate at room temperature for 30 minutes or in the refrigerator for up to 24 hours. 2. Lay the steak on a flat surface. Spread the spinach evenly over the steak, leaving a ¼-inch border at the edge. Evenly top each steak with the red pepper and cheese. 3. Starting at a long end, roll up the steak as tightly as possible, ending seam side down. Use 2 or 3 wooden toothpicks to hold the roll together. Using a sharp knife, cut the roll in half so that it better fits in the air fryer basket. 4. Place the steak roll, seam side down, in the air fryer basket. Set the air fryer to 400ºF (204ºC) for 9 minutes. Use a meat thermometer to ensure the steak has reached an internal temperature of 145ºF (63ºC). (It is critical to not overcook flank steak, so as to not toughen the meat.) 5. Let the steak rest for 10 minutes before cutting into slices to serve.

Bone-in Pork Chops

Prep time: 5 minutes | Cook time: 10 to 12 minutes | Serves 2

1 pound (454 g) bone-in pork chops
1 tablespoon avocado oil
1 teaspoon smoked paprika

½ teaspoon onion powder
¼ teaspoon cayenne pepper
Sea salt and freshly ground black pepper, to taste

1. Brush the pork chops with the avocado oil. In a small dish, mix together the smoked paprika, onion powder, cayenne pepper, and salt and black pepper to taste. Sprinkle the seasonings over both sides of the pork chops. 2. Set the air fryer to 400ºF (204ºC). Place the chops in the air fryer basket in a single layer, working in batches if necessary. Air fry for 10 to 12 minutes, until an instant-read thermometer reads 145ºF (63ºC) at the chops' thickest point. 3. Remove the chops from the air fryer and allow them to rest for 5 minutes before serving.

Cube Steak Roll-Ups

Prep time: 30 minutes | Cook time: 8 to 10 minutes | Serves 4

4 cube steaks (6 ounces / 170 g each)
1 (16-ounce / 454-g) bottle Italian dressing
1 teaspoon salt
½ teaspoon freshly ground black pepper

½ cup finely chopped yellow onion
½ cup finely chopped green bell pepper
½ cup finely chopped mushrooms
1 to 2 tablespoons oil

1. In a large resealable bag or airtight storage container, combine the steaks and Italian dressing. Seal the bag and refrigerate to marinate for 2 hours. 2. Remove the steaks from the marinade and place them on a cutting board. Discard the marinade. Evenly season the steaks with salt and pepper. 3. In a small bowl, stir together the onion, bell pepper, and mushrooms. Sprinkle the onion mixture evenly over the steaks. Roll up the steaks, jelly roll-style, and secure with toothpicks. 4. Preheat the air fryer to 400ºF (204ºC). 5. Place the steaks in the air fryer basket. 6. Cook for 4 minutes. Flip the steaks and spritz them with oil. Cook for 4 to 6 minutes more until the internal temperature reaches 145ºF (63ºC). Let rest for 5 minutes before serving.

Almond and Caraway Crust Steak

Prep time: 16 minutes | Cook time: 10 minutes | Serves 4

⅓ cup almond flour
2 eggs
2 teaspoons caraway seeds
4 beef steaks

2 teaspoons garlic powder
1 tablespoon melted butter
Fine sea salt and cayenne pepper, to taste

1. Generously coat steaks with garlic powder, caraway seeds, salt, and cayenne pepper. 2. In a mixing dish, thoroughly combine melted butter with seasoned crumbs. In another bowl, beat the eggs until they're well whisked. 3. First, coat steaks with the beaten egg; then, coat beef steaks with the buttered crumb mixture. Place the steaks in the air fryer basket; cook for 10 minutes at 355ºF (179ºC). Bon appétit!

Air Fried London Broil

Prep time: 8 hours 5 minutes | Cook time: 25 minutes | Serves 6

2 tablespoons Worcestershire sauce	½ teaspoon paprika
2 tablespoons minced onion	¼ cup olive oil
¼ cup honey	1 teaspoon salt
⅔ cup ketchup	1 teaspoon freshly ground black pepper
2 tablespoons apple cider vinegar	2 pounds (907 g) London broil, top round (about 1-inch thick)

1. Combine all the ingredients, except for the London broil, in a large bowl. Stir to mix well. 2. Pierce the meat with a fork generously on both sides, then dunk the meat in the mixture and press to coat well. 3. Wrap the bowl in plastic and refrigerate to marinate for at least 8 hours. 4. Preheat the air fryer to 400°F (204°C). 5. Discard the marinade and transfer the London broil to the preheated air fryer basket. 6. Air fry for 25 minutes or until the meat reaches your desired doneness. Flip the meat halfway through the cooking time. 7. Transfer the cooked London broil on a plate and allow to cool for 5 minutes before slicing to serve.

Roast Beef with Horseradish Cream

Prep time: 5 minutes | Cook time: 35 to 45 minutes | Serves 6

2 pounds (907 g) beef roast top round or eye of round	Horseradish Cream:
1 tablespoon salt	⅓ cup heavy cream
2 teaspoons garlic powder	⅓ cup sour cream
1 teaspoon freshly ground black pepper	⅓ cup prepared horseradish
	2 teaspoons fresh lemon juice
1 teaspoon dried thyme	Salt and freshly ground black pepper, to taste

1. Preheat the air fryer to 400°F (204°C). 2. Season the beef with the salt, garlic powder, black pepper, and thyme. Place the beef fat-side down in the basket of the air fryer and lightly coat with olive oil. Pausing halfway through the cooking time to turn the meat, air fry for 35 to 45 minutes, until a thermometer inserted into the thickest part indicates the desired doneness, 125°F (52°C) (rare) to 150°F (66°C) (medium). Let the beef rest for 10 minutes before slicing. 3. To make the horseradish cream: In a small bowl, combine the heavy cream, sour cream, horseradish, and lemon juice. Whisk until thoroughly combined. Season to taste with salt and freshly ground black pepper. Serve alongside the beef.

Super Bacon with Meat

Prep time: 5 minutes | Cook time: 1 hour | Serves 4

30 slices thick-cut bacon	10 ounces (283 g) pork sausage
4 ounces (113 g) Cheddar cheese, shredded	Salt and ground black pepper, to taste
12 ounces (340 g) steak	

1. Preheat the air fryer to 400°F (204°C). 2. Lay out 30 slices of bacon in a woven pattern and bake for 20 minutes until crisp. Put the cheese in the center of the bacon. 3. Combine the steak and sausage to form a meaty mixture. 4. Lay out the meat in a rectangle of similar size to the bacon strips. Season with salt and pepper. 5. Roll the meat into a tight roll and refrigerate. 6. Preheat the air fryer to 400°F (204°C). 7. Make a 7×7 bacon weave and roll the bacon weave over the meat, diagonally. 8. Bake for 60 minutes or until the internal temperature reaches at least 165°F (74°C). 9. Let rest for 5 minutes before serving.

Herbed Lamb Steaks

Prep time: 30 minutes | Cook time: 15 minutes | Serves 4

½ medium onion	1 teaspoon cayenne pepper
2 tablespoons minced garlic	1 teaspoon salt
2 teaspoons ground ginger	4 (6-ounce / 170-g) boneless lamb sirloin steaks
1 teaspoon ground cinnamon	
1 teaspoon onion powder	Oil, for spraying

1. In a blender, combine the onion, garlic, ginger, cinnamon, onion powder, cayenne pepper, and salt and pulse until the onion is minced. 2. Place the lamb steaks in a large bowl or zip-top plastic bag and sprinkle the onion mixture over the top. Turn the steaks until they are evenly coated. Cover with plastic wrap or seal the bag and refrigerate for 30 minutes. 3. Preheat the air fryer to 330°F (166°C). Line the air fryer basket with parchment and spray lightly with oil. 4. Place the lamb steaks in a single layer in the prepared basket, making sure they don't overlap. You may need to work in batches, depending on the size of your air fryer. 5. Cook for 8 minutes, flip, and cook for another 7 minutes, or until the internal temperature reaches 155°F (68°C).

Kheema Burgers

Prep time: 15 minutes | Cook time: 12 minutes | Serves 4

Burgers:	⅛ teaspoon ground cardamom
1 pound (454 g) 85% lean ground beef or ground lamb	1 teaspoon kosher salt
2 large eggs, lightly beaten	1 teaspoon cayenne pepper
1 medium yellow onion, diced	Raita Sauce:
¼ cup chopped fresh cilantro	1 cup grated cucumber
1 tablespoon minced fresh ginger	½ cup sour cream
3 cloves garlic, minced	¼ teaspoon kosher salt
2 teaspoons garam masala	¼ teaspoon black pepper
1 teaspoon ground turmeric	For Serving:
½ teaspoon ground cinnamon	4 lettuce leaves, hamburger buns, or naan breads

1. For the burgers: In a large bowl, combine the ground beef, eggs, onion, cilantro, ginger, garlic, garam masala, turmeric, cinnamon, cardamom, salt, and cayenne. Gently mix until ingredients are thoroughly combined. 2. Divide the meat into four portions and form into round patties. Make a slight depression in the middle of each patty with your thumb to prevent them from puffing up into a dome shape while cooking. 3. Place the patties in the air fryer basket. Set the air fryer to 350°F (177°C) for 12 minutes. Use a meat thermometer to ensure the burgers have reached an internal temperature of 160°F / 71°C (for medium). 4. Meanwhile, for the sauce: In a small bowl, combine the cucumber, sour cream, salt, and pepper. 5. To serve: Place the burgers on the lettuce, buns, or naan and top with the sauce.

Bacon-Wrapped Cheese Pork

Prep time: 10 minutes | Cook time: 20 minutes | Serves 4

4 (1-inch-thick) boneless pork chops	Boursin cheese
2 (5.2-ounce / 147-g) packages	8 slices thin-cut bacon

1. Spray the air fryer basket with avocado oil. Preheat the air fryer to 400°F (204°C). 2. Place one of the chops on a cutting board. With a sharp knife held parallel to the cutting board, make a 1-inch-wide incision on the top edge of the chop. Carefully cut into the chop to form a large pocket, leaving a ½-inch border along the sides and bottom. Repeat with the other 3 chops. 3. Snip the corner of a large resealable plastic bag to form a ¾-inch hole. Place the Boursin cheese in the bag and pipe the cheese into the pockets in the chops, dividing the cheese evenly among them. 4. Wrap 2 slices of bacon around each chop and secure the ends with toothpicks. Place the bacon-wrapped chops in the air fryer basket and cook for 10 minutes, then flip the chops and cook for another 8 to 10 minutes, until the bacon is crisp, the chops are cooked through, and the internal temperature reaches 145°F (63°C). 5. Store leftovers in an airtight container in the refrigerator for up to 3 days. Reheat in a preheated 400°F (204°C) air fryer for 5 minutes, or until warmed through.

Pork Bulgogi

Prep time: 30 minutes | Cook time: 15 minutes | Serves 4

1 onion, thinly sliced	1 teaspoon sugar
2 tablespoons gochujang (Korean red chile paste)	¼ to 1 teaspoon cayenne pepper or gochugaru (Korean ground red pepper)
1 tablespoon minced fresh ginger	1 pound (454 g) boneless pork shoulder, cut into ½-inch-thick slices
1 tablespoon minced garlic	
1 tablespoon soy sauce	
1 tablespoon Shaoxing wine (rice cooking wine)	1 tablespoon sesame seeds
1 tablespoon toasted sesame oil	¼ cup sliced scallions

1. In a large bowl, combine the onion, gochujang, ginger, garlic, soy sauce, wine, sesame oil, sugar, and cayenne. Add the pork and toss to coat. Marinate at room temperature for 30 minutes, or cover and refrigerate for up to 24 hours. 2. Arrange the pork and onion slices in the air fryer basket; discard the marinade. Set the air fryer to 400°F (204°C) for 15 minutes, turning the pork halfway through the cooking time. 3. Arrange the pork on a serving platter. Sprinkle with the sesame seeds and scallions and serve.

Spinach and Provolone Steak Rolls

Prep time: 10 minutes | Cook time: 12 minutes | Makes 8 rolls

1 (1-pound / 454-g) flank steak, butterflied	1 cup fresh spinach leaves
	½ teaspoon salt
8 (1-ounce / 28-g, ¼-inch-thick) deli slices provolone cheese	¼ teaspoon ground black pepper

1. Place steak on a large plate. Place provolone slices to cover steak, leaving 1-inch at the edges. Lay spinach leaves over cheese. Gently roll steak and tie with kitchen twine or secure with toothpicks. Carefully slice into eight pieces. Sprinkle each with salt and pepper. 2. Place rolls into ungreased air fryer basket, cut side up. Adjust the temperature to 400°F (204°C) and air fry for 12 minutes. Steak rolls will be browned and cheese will be melted when done and have an internal temperature of at least 150°F (66°C) for medium steak and 180°F (82°C) for well-done steak. Serve warm.

Spaghetti Zoodles and Meatballs

Prep time: 30 minutes | Cook time: 11 to 13 minutes | Serves 6

1 pound (454 g) ground beef	Freshly ground black pepper, to taste
1½ teaspoons sea salt, plus more for seasoning	Avocado oil spray
1 large egg, beaten	Keto-friendly marinara sauce, for serving
1 teaspoon gelatin	6 ounces (170 g) zucchini noodles, made using a
¾ cup Parmesan cheese	
2 teaspoons minced garlic	spiralizer or store-bought
1 teaspoon Italian seasoning	

1. Place the ground beef in a large bowl, and season with the salt. 2. Place the egg in a separate bowl and sprinkle with the gelatin. Allow to sit for 5 minutes. 3. Stir the gelatin mixture, then pour it over the ground beef. Add the Parmesan, garlic, and Italian seasoning. Season with salt and pepper. 4. Form the mixture into 1½-inch meatballs and place them on a plate; cover with plastic wrap and refrigerate for at least 1 hour or overnight. 5. Spray the meatballs with oil. Set the air fryer to 400°F (204°C) and arrange the meatballs in a single layer in the air fryer basket. Air fry for 4 minutes. Flip the meatballs and spray them with more oil. Air fry for 4 minutes more, until an instant-read thermometer reads 160°F (71°C). Transfer the meatballs to a plate and allow them to rest. 6. While the meatballs are resting, heat the marinara in a saucepan on the stove over medium heat. 7. Place the zucchini noodles in the air fryer, and cook at 400°F (204°C) for 3 to 5 minutes. 8. To serve, place the zucchini noodles in serving bowls. Top with meatballs and warm marinara.

Honey-Baked Pork Loin

Prep time: 30 minutes | Cook time: 22 to 25 minutes | Serves 6

¼ cup honey	1 teaspoon garlic powder
¼ cup freshly squeezed lemon juice	1 (2-pound / 907-g) pork loin
2 tablespoons soy sauce	2 tablespoons vegetable oil

1. In a medium bowl, whisk together the honey, lemon juice, soy sauce, and garlic powder. Reserve half of the mixture for basting during cooking. 2. Cut 5 slits in the pork loin and transfer it to a resealable bag. Add the remaining honey mixture. Seal the bag and refrigerate to marinate for at least 2 hours. 3. Preheat the air fryer to 400°F (204°C). Line the air fryer basket with parchment paper. 4. Remove the pork from the marinade, and place it on the parchment. Spritz with oil, then baste with the reserved marinade. 5. Cook for 15 minutes. Flip the pork, baste with more marinade and spritz with oil again. Cook for 7 to 10 minutes more until the internal temperature reaches 145°F (63°C). Let rest for 5 minutes before serving.

Asian Glazed Meatballs

Prep time: 15 minutes | Cook time: 10 minutes per batch | Serves 4 to 6

1 large shallot, finely chopped	Freshly ground black pepper,
2 cloves garlic, minced	to taste
1 tablespoon grated fresh	1 pound (454 g) ground beef
ginger	½ pound (227 g) ground pork
2 teaspoons fresh thyme, finely	3 egg yolks
chopped	1 cup Thai sweet chili sauce
1½ cups brown mushrooms,	(spring roll sauce)
very finely chopped (a food	¼ cup toasted sesame seeds
processor works well here)	2 scallions, sliced
2 tablespoons soy sauce	

1. Combine the shallot, garlic, ginger, thyme, mushrooms, soy sauce, freshly ground black pepper, ground beef and pork, and egg yolks in a bowl and mix the ingredients together. Gently shape the mixture into 24 balls, about the size of a golf ball. 2. Preheat the air fryer to 380°F (193°C). 3. Working in batches, air fry the meatballs for 8 minutes, turning the meatballs over halfway through the cooking time. Drizzle some of the Thai sweet chili sauce on top of each meatball and return the basket to the air fryer, air frying for another 2 minutes. Reserve the remaining Thai sweet chili sauce for serving. 4. As soon as the meatballs are done, sprinkle with toasted sesame seeds and transfer them to a serving platter. Scatter the scallions around and serve warm.

Lemony Pork Loin Chop Schnitzel

Prep time: 15 minutes | Cook time: 15 minutes | Serves 4

4 thin boneless pork loin chops	1 cup panko breadcrumbs
2 tablespoons lemon juice	2 eggs
½ cup flour	Lemon wedges, for serving
¼ teaspoon marjoram	Cooking spray
1 teaspoon salt	

1. Preheat the air fryer to 390°F (199°C) and spritz with cooking spray. 2. On a clean work surface, drizzle the pork chops with lemon juice on both sides. 3. Combine the flour with marjoram and salt on a shallow plate. Pour the breadcrumbs on a separate shallow dish. Beat the eggs in a large bowl. 4. Dredge the pork chops in the flour, then dunk in the beaten eggs to coat well. Shake the excess off and roll over the breadcrumbs. 5. Arrange the chops in the preheated air fryer and spritz with cooking spray. Air fry for 15 minutes or until the chops are golden and crispy. Flip the chops halfway through. Squeeze the lemon wedges over the fried chops and serve immediately.

Cajun Bacon Pork Loin Fillet

Prep time: 30 minutes | Cook time: 20 minutes | Serves 6

1½ pounds (680 g) pork loin	Salt, to taste
fillet or pork tenderloin	6 slices bacon
3 tablespoons olive oil	Olive oil spray
2 tablespoons Cajun spice mix	

1. Cut the pork in half so that it will fit in the air fryer basket. 2. Place both pieces of meat in a resealable plastic bag. Add the oil, Cajun seasoning, and salt to taste, if using. Seal the bag and massage to coat all of the meat with the oil and seasonings. Marinate in the refrigerator for at least 1 hour or up to 24 hours. 3. Remove the pork from the bag and wrap 3 bacon slices around each piece. Spray the air fryer basket with olive oil spray. Place the meat in the air fryer. Set the air fryer to 350°F (177°C) for 15 minutes. Increase the temperature to 400°F (204°C) for 5 minutes. Use a meat thermometer to ensure the meat has reached an internal temperature of 145°F (63°C). 4. Let the meat rest for 10 minutes. Slice into 6 medallions and serve.

Italian Sausages with Peppers and Onions

Prep time: 5 minutes | Cook time: 28 minutes | Serves 3

1 medium onion, thinly sliced	coconut oil
1 yellow or orange bell pepper,	1 teaspoon fine sea salt
thinly sliced	6 Italian sausages
1 red bell pepper, thinly sliced	Dijon mustard, for serving
¼ cup avocado oil or melted	(optional)

1. Preheat the air fryer to 400°F (204°C). 2. Place the onion and peppers in a large bowl. Drizzle with the oil and toss well to coat the veggies. Season with the salt. 3. Place the onion and peppers in a pie pan and cook in the air fryer for 8 minutes, stirring halfway through. Remove from the air fryer and set aside. 4. Spray the air fryer basket with avocado oil. Place the sausages in the air fryer basket and air fry for 20 minutes, or until crispy and golden brown. During the last minute or two of cooking, add the onion and peppers to the basket with the sausages to warm them through. 5. Place the onion and peppers on a serving platter and arrange the sausages on top. Serve Dijon mustard on the side, if desired. 6. Store leftovers in an airtight container in the fridge for up to 7 days or in the freezer for up to a month. Reheat in a preheated 390°F (199°C) air fryer for 3 minutes, or until heated through.

Sumptuous Pizza Tortilla Rolls

Prep time: 10 minutes | Cook time: 6 minutes | Serves 4

1 teaspoon butter	8 flour tortillas
½ medium onion, slivered	8 thin slices deli ham
½ red or green bell pepper,	24 pepperoni slices
julienned	1 cup shredded Mozzarella
4 ounces (113 g) fresh white	cheese
mushrooms, chopped	Cooking spray
½ cup pizza sauce	

1. Preheat the air fryer to 390°F (199°C). 2. Put butter, onions, bell pepper, and mushrooms in a baking pan. Bake in the preheated air fryer for 3 minutes. Stir and cook 3 to 4 minutes longer until just crisp and tender. Remove pan and set aside. 3. To assemble rolls, spread about 2 teaspoons of pizza sauce on one half of each tortilla. Top with a slice of ham and 3 slices of pepperoni. Divide sautéed vegetables among tortillas and top with cheese. 4. Roll up tortillas, secure with toothpicks if needed, and spray with oil. 5. Put 4 rolls in air fryer basket and air fry for 4 minutes. Turn and air fry 4 minutes, until heated through and lightly browned. 6. Repeat step 4 to air fry remaining pizza rolls. 7. Serve immediately.

Savory Sausage Cobbler

Prep time: 15 minutes | Cook time: 34 minutes | Serves 4

Filling:
1 pound (454 g) ground Italian sausage
1 cup sliced mushrooms
1 teaspoon fine sea salt
2 cups marinara sauce
Biscuits:
3 large egg whites

¾ cup blanched almond flour
1 teaspoon baking powder
¼ teaspoon fine sea salt
2½ tablespoons very cold unsalted butter, cut into ¼-inch pieces
Fresh basil leaves, for garnish

1. Preheat the air fryer to 400°F (204°C). 2. Place the sausage in a pie pan (or a pan that fits into your air fryer). Use your hands to break up the sausage and spread it evenly on the bottom of the pan. Place the pan in the air fryer and air fry for 5 minutes. 3. Remove the pan from the air fryer and use a fork or metal spatula to crumble the sausage more. Season the mushrooms with the salt and add them to the pie pan. Stir to combine the mushrooms and sausage, then return the pan to the air fryer and air fry for 4 minutes, or until the mushrooms are soft and the sausage is cooked through. 4. Remove the pan from the air fryer. Add the marinara sauce and stir well. Set aside. 5. Make the biscuits: Place the egg whites in a large mixing bowl or the bowl of a stand mixer. Using a hand mixer or stand mixer, whip the egg whites until stiff peaks form. 6. In a medium-sized bowl, whisk together the almond flour, baking powder, and salt, then cut in the butter. Gently fold the flour mixture into the egg whites with a rubber spatula. 7. Using a large spoon or ice cream scoop, spoon one-quarter of the dough on top of the sausage mixture, making sure the butter stays in separate clumps. Repeat with the remaining dough, spacing the biscuits about 1 inch apart. 8. Place the pan in the air fryer and cook for 5 minutes, then lower the heat to 325°F (163°C) and bake for another 15 to 20 minutes, until the biscuits are golden brown. Serve garnished with fresh basil leaves. 9. Store leftovers in an airtight container in the refrigerator for up to 3 days. Reheat in a preheated 350°F (177°C) air fryer for 5 minutes, or until warmed through.

Lamb Chops with Horseradish Sauce

Prep time: 30 minutes | Cook time: 13 minutes | Serves 4

Lamb:
4 lamb loin chops
2 tablespoons vegetable oil
1 clove garlic, minced
½ teaspoon kosher salt
½ teaspoon black pepper
Horseradish Cream Sauce:

½ cup mayonnaise
1 tablespoon Dijon mustard
1 to 1½ tablespoons prepared horseradish
2 teaspoons sugar
Vegetable oil spray

1. For the lamb: Brush the lamb chops with the oil, rub with the garlic, and sprinkle with the salt and pepper. Marinate at room temperature for 30 minutes. 2. Meanwhile, for the sauce: In a medium bowl, combine the mayonnaise, mustard, horseradish, and sugar. Stir until well combined. Set aside half of the sauce for serving. 3. Spray the air fryer basket with vegetable oil spray and place the chops in the basket. Set the air fryer to 325°F (163°C) for 10 minutes, turning the chops halfway through the cooking time. 4. Remove the chops from the air fryer and add to the bowl with the horseradish sauce, turning to coat with the sauce. Place the chops back in the air fryer

basket. Set the air fryer to 400°F (204°C) for 3 minutes. Use a meat thermometer to ensure the meat has reached an internal temperature of 145°F (63°C) (for medium-rare). 5. Serve the chops with the reserved horseradish sauce.

Short Ribs with Chimichurri

Prep time: 30 minutes | Cook time: 13 minutes | Serves 4

1 pound (454 g) boneless short ribs
1½ teaspoons sea salt, divided
½ teaspoon freshly ground black pepper, divided
½ cup fresh parsley leaves
½ cup fresh cilantro leaves
1 teaspoon minced garlic

1 tablespoon freshly squeezed lemon juice
½ teaspoon ground cumin
¼ teaspoon red pepper flakes
2 tablespoons extra-virgin olive oil
Avocado oil spray

1. Pat the short ribs dry with paper towels. Sprinkle the ribs all over with 1 teaspoon salt and ¼ teaspoon black pepper. Let sit at room temperature for 45 minutes. 2. Meanwhile, place the parsley, cilantro, garlic, lemon juice, cumin, red pepper flakes, the remaining ½ teaspoon salt, and the remaining ¼ teaspoon black pepper in a blender or food processor. With the blender running, slowly drizzle in the olive oil. Blend for about 1 minute, until the mixture is smooth and well combined. 3. Set the air fryer to 400°F (204°C). Spray both sides of the ribs with oil. Place in the basket and air fry for 8 minutes. Flip and cook for another 5 minutes, until an instant-read thermometer reads 125°F (52°C) for medium-rare (or to your desired doneness). 4. Allow the meat to rest for 5 to 10 minutes, then slice. Serve warm with the chimichurri sauce.

Hoisin BBQ Pork Chops

Prep time: 5 minutes | Cook time: 22 minutes | Serves 2 to 3

3 tablespoons hoisin sauce
¼ cup honey
1 tablespoon soy sauce
3 tablespoons rice vinegar
2 tablespoons brown sugar
1½ teaspoons grated fresh ginger

1 to 2 teaspoons Sriracha sauce, to taste
2 to 3 bone-in center cut pork chops, 1-inch thick (about 1¼ pounds / 567 g)
Chopped scallions, for garnish

1. Combine the hoisin sauce, honey, soy sauce, rice vinegar, brown sugar, ginger, and Sriracha sauce in a small saucepan. Whisk the ingredients together and bring the mixture to a boil over medium-high heat on the stovetop. Reduce the heat and simmer the sauce until it has reduced in volume and thickened slightly, about 10 minutes. 2. Preheat the air fryer to 400°F (204°C). 3. Place the pork chops into the air fryer basket and pour half the hoisin BBQ sauce over the top. Air fry for 6 minutes. Then, flip the chops over, pour the remaining hoisin BBQ sauce on top and air fry for 5 to 6 more minutes, depending on the thickness of the pork chops. The internal temperature of the pork chops should be 155°F (68°C) when tested with an instant read thermometer. 4. Let the pork chops rest for 5 minutes before serving. You can spoon a little of the sauce from the bottom drawer of the air fryer over the top if desired. Sprinkle with chopped scallions and serve.

Pigs in a Blanket

Prep time: 10 minutes | Cook time: 7 minutes | Serves 2

½ cup shredded Mozzarella cheese
2 tablespoons blanched finely ground almond flour
1 ounce (28 g) full-fat cream

cheese
2 (2-ounce / 57-g) beef smoked sausages
½ teaspoon sesame seeds

1. Place Mozzarella, almond flour, and cream cheese in a large microwave-safe bowl. Microwave for 45 seconds and stir until smooth. Roll dough into a ball and cut in half. 2. Press each half out into a 4 × 5-inch rectangle. Roll one sausage up in each dough half and press seams closed. Sprinkle the top with sesame seeds. 3. Place each wrapped sausage into the air fryer basket. 4. Adjust the temperature to 400°F (204°C) and air fry for 7 minutes. 5. The outside will be golden when completely cooked. Serve immediately.

Carne Asada

Prep time: 5 minutes | Cook time: 15 minutes | Serves 4

3 chipotle peppers in adobo, chopped
⅓ cup chopped fresh oregano
⅓ cup chopped fresh parsley
4 cloves garlic, minced
Juice of 2 limes

1 teaspoon ground cumin seeds
⅓ cup olive oil
1 to 1½ pounds (454 g to 680 g) flank steak
Salt, to taste

1. Combine the chipotle, oregano, parsley, garlic, lime juice, cumin, and olive oil in a large bowl. Stir to mix well. 2. Dunk the flank steak in the mixture and press to coat well. Wrap the bowl in plastic and marinate under room temperature for at least 30 minutes. 3. Preheat the air fryer to 390°F (199°C). 4. Discard the marinade and place the steak in the preheated air fryer. Sprinkle with salt. 5. Air fry for 15 minutes or until the steak is medium-rare or it reaches your desired doneness. Flip the steak halfway through the cooking time. 6. Remove the steak from the air fryer and slice to serve.

Easy Beef Satay

Prep time: 30 minutes | Cook time: 8 minutes | Serves 4

1 pound (454 g) beef flank steak, thinly sliced into long strips
2 tablespoons vegetable oil
1 tablespoon fish sauce
1 tablespoon soy sauce
1 tablespoon minced fresh ginger

1 tablespoon minced garlic
1 tablespoon sugar
1 teaspoon Sriracha or other hot sauce
1 teaspoon ground coriander
½ cup chopped fresh cilantro
¼ cup chopped roasted peanuts

1. Place the beef strips in a large bowl or resealable plastic bag. Add the vegetable oil, fish sauce, soy sauce, ginger, garlic, sugar, Sriracha, coriander, and ¼ cup of the cilantro to the bag. Seal and massage the bag to thoroughly coat and combine. Marinate at room temperature for 30 minutes, or cover and refrigerate for up to 24 hours. 2. Using tongs, remove the beef strips from the bag and lay them flat in the air fryer basket, minimizing overlap as much as possible; discard the marinade. Set the air fryer to 400°F (204°C) for 8 minutes, turning the beef strips halfway through the cooking time.

3. Transfer the meat to a serving platter. Sprinkle with the remaining ¼ cup cilantro and the peanuts. Serve.

Beef Loin with Thyme and Parsley

Prep time: 5 minutes | Cook time: 15 minutes | Serves 4

1 tablespoon butter, melted
¼ dried thyme
1 teaspoon garlic salt

¼ teaspoon dried parsley
1 pound (454 g) beef loin

1. Preheat the air fryer to 400°F (204°C). 2. In a bowl, combine the melted butter, thyme, garlic salt, and parsley. 3. Cut the beef loin into slices and generously apply the seasoned butter using a brush. Transfer to the air fryer basket. 4. Air fry the beef for 15 minutes. 5. Take care when removing it and serve hot.

Baby Back Ribs

Prep time: 5 minutes | Cook time: 25 minutes | Serves 4

2 pounds (907 g) baby back ribs
2 teaspoons chili powder
1 teaspoon paprika
½ teaspoon onion powder

½ teaspoon garlic powder
¼ teaspoon ground cayenne pepper
½ cup low-carb, sugar-free barbecue sauce

1. Rub ribs with all ingredients except barbecue sauce. Place into the air fryer basket. 2. Adjust the temperature to 400°F (204°C) and roast for 25 minutes. 3. When done, ribs will be dark and charred with an internal temperature of at least 185°F (85°C). Brush ribs with barbecue sauce and serve warm.

Spicy Sirloin Tip Steak

Prep time: 25 minutes | Cook time: 12 to 18 minutes | Serves 4

2 tablespoons salsa
1 tablespoon minced chipotle pepper
1 tablespoon apple cider vinegar
1 teaspoon ground cumin
⅛ teaspoon freshly ground

black pepper
⅛ teaspoon red pepper flakes
12 ounces (340 g) sirloin tip steak, cut into 4 pieces and gently pounded to about ⅓ inch thick
Cooking oil spray

1. In a small bowl, thoroughly mix the salsa, chipotle pepper, vinegar, cumin, black pepper, and red pepper flakes. Rub this mixture into both sides of each steak piece. Let stand for 15 minutes at room temperature. 2. Insert the crisper plate into the basket and place the basket into the unit. Preheat the unit by selecting AIR FRY, setting the temperature to 390°F (199°C), and setting the time to 3 minutes. Select START/STOP to begin. 3. Once the unit is preheated, spray the crisper plate with cooking oil. Working in batches, place 2 steaks into the basket. 4. Select AIR FRY, set the temperature to 390°F (199°C), and set the time to 9 minutes. Select START/STOP to begin. 5. After about 6 minutes, check the steaks. If a food thermometer inserted into the meat registers at least 145°F (63°C), they are done. If not, resume cooking. 6. When the cooking is done, transfer the steaks to a clean plate and cover with aluminum foil to keep warm. Repeat steps 3, 4, and 5 with the remaining steaks. 7. Thinly slice the steaks against the grain and serve.

Spicy Tomato Beef Meatballs

Prep time: 10 minutes | Cook time: 15 minutes | Serves 4

3 scallions, minced	1 pound (454 g) 95% lean
1 garlic clove, minced	ground beef
1 egg yolk	Olive oil spray
¼ cup saltine cracker crumbs	1¼ cups any tomato pasta
Pinch salt	sauce (from a 16-ounce / 454-g
Freshly ground black pepper,	jar)
to taste	2 tablespoons Dijon mustard

1. In a large bowl, combine the scallions, garlic, egg yolk, cracker crumbs, salt, and pepper and mix well. 2. Add the ground beef and gently but thoroughly mix with your hands until combined. Form the meat mixture into 1½-inch round meatballs. 3. Insert the crisper plate into the basket and the basket into the unit. Preheat the unit by selecting BAKE, setting the temperature to 400°F (204°C), and setting the time to 3 minutes. Select START/STOP to begin. 4. Once the unit is preheated, spray the crisper plate with olive oil. Working in batches, spray the meatballs with olive oil and place them into the basket in a single layer, without touching. 5. Select BAKE, set the temperature to 400°F (204°C), and set the time to 11 minutes. Select START/STOP to begin. 6. When the cooking is complete, a food thermometer inserted into the meatballs should register 165°F (74°C). Transfer the meatballs to a 6-inch metal bowl. 7. Repeat steps 4, 5, and 6 with the remaining meatballs. 8. Top the meatballs with the pasta sauce and Dijon mustard, and mix gently. Place the bowl into the basket. 9. Select BAKE, set the temperature to 400°F (204°C), and set the time to 4 minutes. Select START/STOP to begin. 10. When the cooking is complete, serve hot.

Ritzy Skirt Steak Fajitas

Prep time: 15 minutes | Cook time: 30 minutes | Serves 4

2 tablespoons olive oil	1 green pepper, sliced
¼ cup lime juice	Salt and freshly ground black
1 clove garlic, minced	pepper, to taste
½ teaspoon ground cumin	8 flour tortillas
½ teaspoon hot sauce	Toppings:
½ teaspoon salt	Shredded lettuce
2 tablespoons chopped fresh	Crumbled Queso Fresco (or
cilantro	grated Cheddar cheese)
1 pound (454 g) skirt steak	Sliced black olives
1 onion, sliced	Diced tomatoes
1 teaspoon chili powder	Sour cream
1 red pepper, sliced	Guacamole

1. Combine the olive oil, lime juice, garlic, cumin, hot sauce, salt and cilantro in a shallow dish. Add the skirt steak and turn it over several times to coat all sides. Pierce the steak with a needle-style meat tenderizer or paring knife. Marinate the steak in the refrigerator for at least 3 hours, or overnight. When you are ready to cook, remove the steak from the refrigerator and let it sit at room temperature for 30 minutes. 2. Preheat the air fryer to 400°F (204°C). 3. Toss the onion slices with the chili powder and a little olive oil and transfer them to the air fryer basket. Air fry for 5 minutes. Add the red and green peppers to the air fryer basket with the onions, season with salt and pepper and air fry for 8 more minutes, until the onions and peppers are soft. Transfer the vegetables to a dish and cover with aluminum foil to keep warm. 4. Put the skirt steak in the air fryer basket and pour the marinade over the top. Air fry at 400°F (204°C) for 12 minutes. Flip the steak over and air fry for an additional 5 minutes. Transfer the cooked steak to a cutting board and let the steak rest for a few minutes. If the peppers and onions need to be heated, return them to the air fryer for just 1 to 2 minutes. 5. Thinly slice the steak at an angle, cutting against the grain of the steak. Serve the steak with the onions and peppers, the warm tortillas and the fajita toppings on the side.

Bacon-Wrapped Pork Tenderloin

Prep time: 30 minutes | Cook time: 22 to 25 minutes | Serves 6

½ cup minced onion	¼ teaspoon freshly ground
½ cup hard apple cider, or	black pepper
apple juice	2 pounds (907 g) pork
¼ cup honey	tenderloin
1 tablespoon minced garlic	1 to 2 tablespoons oil
¼ teaspoon salt	8 uncooked bacon slices

1. In a medium bowl, stir together the onion, hard cider, honey, garlic, salt, and pepper. Transfer to a large resealable bag or airtight container and add the pork. Seal the bag. Refrigerate to marinate for at least 2 hours. 2. Preheat the air fryer to 400°F (204°C). Line the air fryer basket with parchment paper. 3. Remove the pork from the marinade and place it on the parchment. Spritz with oil. 4. Cook for 15 minutes. 5. Wrap the bacon slices around the pork and secure them with toothpicks. Turn the pork roast and spritz with oil. Cook for 7 to 10 minutes more until the internal temperature reaches 145°F (63°C), depending on how well-done you like pork loin. It will continue cooking after it's removed from the fryer, so let it sit for 5 minutes before serving.

Fajita Meatball Lettuce Wraps

Prep time: 10 minutes | Cook time: 10 minutes | Serves 4

1 pound (454 g) ground beef	1 teaspoon fine sea salt
(85% lean)	½ teaspoon chili powder
½ cup salsa, plus more for	½ teaspoon ground cumin
serving if desired	1 clove garlic, minced
¼ cup chopped onions	For Serving (Optional):
¼ cup diced green or red bell	8 leaves Boston lettuce
peppers	Pico de gallo or salsa
1 large egg, beaten	Lime slices

1. Spray the air fryer basket with avocado oil. Preheat the air fryer to 350°F (177°C). 2. In a large bowl, mix together all the ingredients until well combined. 3. Shape the meat mixture into eight 1-inch balls. Place the meatballs in the air fryer basket, leaving a little space between them. Air fry for 10 minutes, or until cooked through and no longer pink inside and the internal temperature reaches 145°F (63°C). 4. Serve each meatball on a lettuce leaf, topped with pico de gallo or salsa, if desired. Serve with lime slices if desired. 5. Store leftovers in an airtight container in the fridge for 3 days or in the freezer for up to a month. Reheat in a preheated 350°F (177°C) air fryer for 4 minutes, or until heated through.

Cheese Crusted Chops

Prep time: 10 minutes | Cook time: 12 minutes | Serves 4 to 6

¼ teaspoon pepper	½ teaspoons onion powder
½ teaspoons salt	1 teaspoon smoked paprika
4 to 6 thick boneless pork chops	2 beaten eggs
1 cup pork rind crumbs	3 tablespoons grated Parmesan cheese
¼ teaspoon chili powder	Cooking spray

1. Preheat the air fryer to 400°F (205°C). 2. Rub the pepper and salt on both sides of pork chops. 3. In a food processor, pulse pork rinds into crumbs. Mix crumbs with chili powder, onion powder, and paprika in a bowl. 4. Beat eggs in another bowl. 5. Dip pork chops into eggs then into pork rind crumb mixture. 6. Spritz the air fryer basket with cooking spray and add pork chops to the basket. 7. Air fry for 12 minutes. 8. Serve garnished with the Parmesan cheese.

Steak with Bell Pepper

Prep time: 30 minutes | Cook time: 20 to 23 minutes | Serves 6

¼ cup avocado oil	steak or flank steak, thinly sliced against the grain
¼ cup freshly squeezed lime juice	1 red bell pepper, cored, seeded, and cut into ½-inch slices
2 teaspoons minced garlic	
1 tablespoon chili powder	
½ teaspoon ground cumin	1 green bell pepper, cored, seeded, and cut into ½-inch slices
Sea salt and freshly ground black pepper, to taste	
1 pound (454 g) top sirloin	1 large onion, sliced

1. In a small bowl or blender, combine the avocado oil, lime juice, garlic, chili powder, cumin, and salt and pepper to taste. 2. Place the sliced steak in a zip-top bag or shallow dish. Place the bell peppers and onion in a separate zip-top bag or dish. Pour half the marinade over the steak and the other half over the vegetables. Seal both bags and let the steak and vegetables marinate in the refrigerator for at least 1 hour or up to 4 hours. 3. Line the air fryer basket with an air fryer liner or aluminum foil. Remove the vegetables from their bag or dish and shake off any excess marinade. Set the air fryer to 400°F (204°C). Place the vegetables in the air fryer basket and cook for 13 minutes. 4. Remove the steak from its bag or dish and shake off any excess marinade. Place the steak on top of the vegetables in the air fryer, and cook for 7 to 10 minutes or until an instant-read thermometer reads 120°F (49°C) for medium-rare (or cook to your desired doneness). 5. Serve with desired fixings, such as keto tortillas, lettuce, sour cream, avocado slices, shredded Cheddar cheese, and cilantro.

TParmesan-Crusted Steak

Prep time: 30 minutes | Cook time: 12 minutes | Serves 6

½ cup (1 stick) unsalted butter, at room temperature	¼ cup finely ground blanched almond flour
1 cup finely grated Parmesan cheese	1½ pounds (680 g) New York strip steak

Sea salt and freshly ground black pepper, to taste

1. Place the butter, Parmesan cheese, and almond flour in a food processor. Process until smooth. Transfer to a sheet of parchment paper and form into a log. Wrap tightly in plastic wrap. Freeze for 45 minutes or refrigerate for at least 4 hours. 2. While the butter is chilling, season the steak liberally with salt and pepper. Let the steak rest at room temperature for about 45 minutes. 3. Place the grill pan or basket in your air fryer, set it to 400°F (204°C), and let it preheat for 5 minutes. 4. Working in batches, if necessary, place the steak on the grill pan and air fry for 4 minutes. Flip and cook for 3 minutes more, until the steak is brown on both sides. 5. Remove the steak from the air fryer and arrange an equal amount of the Parmesan butter on top of each steak. Return the steak to the air fryer and continue cooking for another 5 minutes, until an instant-read thermometer reads 120°F (49°C) for medium-rare and the crust is golden brown (or to your desired doneness). 6. Transfer the cooked steak to a plate; let rest for 10 minutes before serving.

Teriyaki Rump Steak with Broccoli and Capsicum

Prep time: 5 minutes | Cook time: 13 minutes | Serves 4

½ pound (227 g) rump steak	2 red capsicums, sliced
⅓ cup teriyaki marinade	Fine sea salt and ground black pepper, to taste
1½ teaspoons sesame oil	
½ head broccoli, cut into florets	Cooking spray

1. Toss the rump steak in a large bowl with teriyaki marinade. Wrap the bowl in plastic and refrigerate to marinate for at least an hour. 2. Preheat the air fryer to 400°F (204°C) and spritz with cooking spray. 3. Discard the marinade and transfer the steak in the preheated air fryer. Spritz with cooking spray. 4. Air fry for 13 minutes or until well browned. Flip the steak halfway through. 5. Meanwhile, heat the sesame oil in a nonstick skillet over medium heat. Add the broccoli and capsicum. Sprinkle with salt and ground black pepper. Sauté for 5 minutes or until the broccoli is tender. 6. Transfer the air fried rump steak on a plate and top with the sautéed broccoli and capsicum. Serve hot.

enderloin with Crispy Shallots

Prep time: 30 minutes | Cook time: 18 to 20 minutes | Serves 6

1½ pounds (680 g) beef tenderloin steaks	4 medium shallots
Sea salt and freshly ground black pepper, to taste	1 teaspoon olive oil or avocado oil

1. Season both sides of the steaks with salt and pepper, and let them sit at room temperature for 45 minutes. 2. Set the air fryer to 400°F (204°C) and let it preheat for 5 minutes. 3. Working in batches if necessary, place the steaks in the air fryer basket in a single layer and air fry for 5 minutes. Flip and cook for 5 minutes longer, until an instant-read thermometer inserted in the center of the steaks registers 120°F (49°C) for medium-rare (or as desired). Remove the steaks and tent with aluminum foil to rest. 4. Set the air fryer to 300°F (149°C). In a medium bowl, toss the shallots with the oil. Place the shallots in the basket and air fry for 5 minutes, then give them a toss and cook for 3 to 5 minutes more, until crispy and golden brown. 5. Place the steaks on serving plates and arrange the shallots on top.

Pork and Tricolor Vegetables Kebabs

Prep time: 1 hour 20 minutes | Cook time: 8 minutes per batch | Serves 4

For the Pork:
1 pound (454 g) pork steak, cut in cubes
1 tablespoon white wine vinegar
3 tablespoons steak sauce
¼ cup soy sauce
1 teaspoon powdered chili
1 teaspoon red chili flakes
2 teaspoons smoked paprika
1 teaspoon garlic salt

For the Vegetable:
1 green squash, deseeded and cut in cubes
1 yellow squash, deseeded and cut in cubes
1 red pepper, cut in cubes
1 green pepper, cut in cubes
Salt and ground black pepper, to taste
Cooking spray
Special Equipment:
4 bamboo skewers, soaked in water for at least 30 minutes

1. Combine the ingredients for the pork in a large bowl. Press the pork to dunk in the marinade. Wrap the bowl in plastic and refrigerate for at least an hour. 2. Preheat the air fryer to 370°F (188°C) and spritz with cooking spray. 3. Remove the pork from the marinade and run the skewers through the pork and vegetables alternatively. Sprinkle with salt and pepper to taste. 4. Arrange the skewers in the preheated air fryer and spritz with cooking spray. Air fry for 8 minutes or until the pork is browned and the vegetables are lightly charred and tender. Flip the skewers halfway through. You may need to work in batches to avoid overcrowding. 5. Serve immediately.

Beef Whirls

Prep time: 30 minutes | Cook time: 18 minutes | Serves 6

3 cube steaks (6 ounces / 170 g each)
1 (16-ounce / 454-g) bottle Italian dressing
1 cup Italian-style bread crumbs
½ cup grated Parmesan cheese
1 teaspoon dried basil

1 teaspoon dried oregano
1 teaspoon dried parsley
¼ cup beef broth
1 to 2 tablespoons oil

1. In a large resealable bag, combine the steaks and Italian dressing. Seal the bag and refrigerate to marinate for 2 hours. 2. In a medium bowl, whisk the bread crumbs, cheese, basil, oregano, and parsley until blended. Stir in the beef broth. 3. Place the steaks on a cutting board and cut each in half so you have 6 equal pieces. Sprinkle with the bread crumb mixture. Roll up the steaks, jelly roll-style, and secure with toothpicks. 4. Preheat the air fryer to 400°F (204°C). 5. Place 3 roll-ups in the air fryer basket. 6. Cook for 5 minutes. Flip the roll-ups and spritz with oil. Cook for 4 minutes more until the internal temperature reaches 145°F (63°C). Repeat with the remaining roll-ups. Let rest for 5 to 10 minutes before serving.

Chapter 6   Fish and Seafood

Cajun Catfish Cakes with Cheese

Prep time: 5 minutes | Cook time: 35 minutes | Serves 4

2 catfish fillets	½ cup buttermilk
3 ounces (85 g) butter	1 teaspoon baking powder
1 cup shredded Parmesan cheese	1 teaspoon baking soda
1 cup shredded Swiss cheese	1 teaspoon Cajun seasoning

1. Bring a pot of salted water to a boil. Add the catfish fillets to the boiling water and let them boil for 5 minutes until they become opaque. 2. Remove the fillets from the pot to a mixing bowl and flake them into small pieces with a fork. 3. Add the remaining ingredients to the bowl of fish and stir until well incorporated. 4. Divide the fish mixture into 12 equal portions and shape each portion into a patty. 5. Preheat the air fryer to 380°F (193°C). 6. Arrange the patties in the air fryer basket and air fry in batches for 15 minutes until golden brown and cooked through. Flip the patties halfway through the cooking time. 7. Let the patties sit for 5 minutes and serve.

Almond Pesto Salmon

Prep time: 5 minutes | Cook time: 12 minutes | Serves 2

¼ cup pesto	(about 4 ounces / 113 g each)
¼ cup sliced almonds, roughly chopped	2 tablespoons unsalted butter, melted
2 (1½-inch-thick) salmon fillets	

1. In a small bowl, mix pesto and almonds. Set aside. 2. Place fillets into a round baking dish. 3. Brush each fillet with butter and place half of the pesto mixture on the top of each fillet. Place dish into the air fryer basket. 4. Adjust the temperature to 390°F (199°C) and set the timer for 12 minutes. 5. Salmon will easily flake when fully cooked and reach an internal temperature of at least 145°F (63°C). Serve warm.

Cod Tacos with Mango Salsa

Prep time: 15 minutes | Cook time: 17 minutes | Serves 4

1 mango, peeled and diced	1 egg
1 small jalapeño pepper, diced	¾ cup cornstarch
½ red bell pepper, diced	¾ cup all-purpose flour
½ red onion, minced	½ teaspoon ground cumin
Pinch chopped fresh cilantro	¼ teaspoon chili powder
Juice of ½ lime	1 pound (454 g) cod, cut into
¼ teaspoon salt	4 pieces
¼ teaspoon ground black pepper	Olive oil spray
½ cup Mexican beer	4 corn tortillas, or flour tortillas, at room temperature

1. In a small bowl, stir together the mango, jalapeño, red bell pepper, red onion, cilantro, lime juice, salt, and pepper. Set aside. 2. In a medium bowl, whisk the beer and egg. 3. In another medium bowl, stir together the cornstarch, flour, cumin, and chili powder. 4. Insert the crisper plate into the basket and the basket into the unit. Preheat the unit by selecting AIR FRY, setting the temperature to 375°F (191°C), and setting the time to 3 minutes. Select START/STOP to begin. 5. Dip the fish pieces into the egg mixture and in the flour mixture to coat completely. 6. Once the unit is preheated, place a parchment paper liner into the basket. Place the fish on the liner in a single layer. 7. Select AIR FRY, set the temperature to 375°F (191°C), and set the time to 17 minutes. Select START/STOP to begin. 8. After about 9 minutes, spray the fish with olive oil. Reinsert the basket to resume cooking. 9. When the cooking is complete, the fish should be golden and crispy. Place the pieces in the tortillas, top with the mango salsa, and serve.

Orange-Mustard Glazed Salmon

Prep time: 10 minutes | Cook time: 10 minutes | Serves 2

1 tablespoon orange marmalade	2 (8-ounce / 227 -g) skin-on salmon fillets, 1½ inches thick
¼ teaspoon grated orange zest plus 1 tablespoon juice	Salt and pepper, to taste
2 teaspoons whole-grain mustard	Vegetable oil spray

1. Preheat the air fryer to 400°F (204°C). 2. Make foil sling for air fryer basket by folding 1 long sheet of aluminum foil so it is 4 inches wide. Lay sheet of foil widthwise across basket, pressing foil into and up sides of basket. Fold excess foil as needed so that edges of foil are flush with top of basket. Lightly spray foil and basket with vegetable oil spray. 3. Combine marmalade, orange zest and juice, and mustard in bowl. Pat salmon dry with paper towels and season with salt and pepper. Brush tops and sides of fillets evenly with glaze. Arrange fillets skin side down on sling in prepared basket, spaced evenly apart. Air fry salmon until center is still translucent when checked with the tip of a paring knife and registers 125°F (52°C) (for medium-rare), 10 to 14 minutes, using sling to rotate fillets halfway through cooking. 4. Using the sling, carefully remove salmon from air fryer. Slide fish spatula along underside of fillets and transfer to individual serving plates, leaving skin behind. Serve.

Crustless Shrimp Quiche

Prep time: 15 minutes | Cook time: 20 minutes | Serves 2

Vegetable oil	¼ cup chopped scallions
4 large eggs	1 teaspoon sweet smoked paprika
½ cup half-and-half	
4 ounces (113 g) raw shrimp, chopped (about 1 cup)	1 teaspoon herbes de Provence
1 cup shredded Parmesan or Swiss cheese	1 teaspoon black pepper
	½ to 1 teaspoon kosher salt

1. Generously grease a baking pan with vegetable oil. (Be sure to grease the pan well, the proteins in eggs stick something fierce. Alternatively, line the bottom of the pan with parchment paper cut to fit and spray the parchment and sides of the pan generously with vegetable oil spray.) 2. In a large bowl, beat together the eggs and half-and-half. Add the shrimp, ¾ cup of the cheese, the scallions, paprika, herbes de Provence, pepper, and salt. Stir with a fork to thoroughly combine. Pour the egg mixture into the prepared pan. 3. Place the pan in the air fryer basket. Set the air fryer to 300°F (149°C) for 20 minutes. After 17 minutes, sprinkle the remaining ¼ cup cheese on top and cook for the remaining 3 minutes, or until the cheese has melted, the eggs are set, and a toothpick inserted into the center comes out clean. 4. Serve the quiche warm or at room temperature.

Scallops with Asparagus and Peas

Prep time: 10 minutes | Cook time: 7 to 10 minutes | Serves 4

Cooking oil spray	lemon juice
1 pound (454 g) asparagus, ends trimmed, cut into 2-inch pieces	2 teaspoons extra-virgin olive oil
1 cup sugar snap peas	½ teaspoon dried thyme
1 pound (454 g) sea scallops	Salt and freshly ground black pepper, to taste
1 tablespoon freshly squeezed	

1. Insert the crisper plate into the basket and the basket into the unit. Preheat the unit by selecting AIR FRY, setting the temperature to 400°F (204°C), and setting the time to 3 minutes. Select START/STOP to begin. 2. Once the unit is preheated, spray the crisper plate with cooking oil. Place the asparagus and sugar snap peas into the basket. 3. Select AIR FRY, set the temperature to 400°F (204°C), and set the time to 10 minutes. Select START/STOP to begin. 4. Meanwhile, check the scallops for a small muscle attached to the side. Pull it off and discard. In a medium bowl, toss together the scallops, lemon juice, olive oil, and thyme. Season with salt and pepper. 5. After 3 minutes, the vegetables should be just starting to get tender. Place the scallops on top of the vegetables. Reinsert the basket to resume cooking. After 3 minutes more, remove the basket and shake it. Again reinsert the basket to resume cooking. 6. When the cooking is complete, the scallops should be firm when tested with your finger and opaque in the center, and the vegetables tender. Serve immediately.

Baked Salmon with Tomatoes and Olives

Prep time: 5 minutes | Cook time: 8 minutes | Serves 4

2 tablespoons olive oil	1 teaspoon chopped fresh dill
4 (1½-inch-thick) salmon fillets	2 Roma tomatoes, diced
½ teaspoon salt	¼ cup sliced Kalamata olives
¼ teaspoon cayenne	4 lemon slices

1. Preheat the air fryer to 380°F(193°C). 2. Brush the olive oil on both sides of the salmon fillets, and then season them lightly with salt, cayenne, and dill. 3. Place the fillets in a single layer in the basket of the air fryer, then layer the tomatoes and olives over the top. Top each fillet with a lemon slice. 4. Bake for 8 minutes, or until the salmon has reached an internal temperature of 145°F(63°C).

Chili Prawns

Prep time: 10 minutes | Cook time: 8 minutes | Serves 2

8 prawns, cleaned	½ teaspoon garlic powder
Salt and black pepper, to taste	½ teaspoon ground cumin
½ teaspoon ground cayenne pepper	½ teaspoon red chili flakes
	Cooking spray

1. Preheat the air fryer to 340°F (171°C). Spritz the air fryer basket with cooking spray. 2. Toss the remaining ingredients in a large bowl until the prawns are well coated. 3. Spread the coated prawns evenly in the basket and spray them with cooking spray. 4. Air fry for 8 minutes, flipping the prawns halfway through, or until the prawns are pink. 5. Remove the prawns from the basket to a plate.

Cornmeal-Crusted Trout Fingers

Prep time: 15 minutes | Cook time: 6 minutes | Serves 2

½ cup yellow cornmeal, medium or finely ground (not coarse)	¾ pound (340 g) skinless trout fillets, cut into strips 1 inch wide and 3 inches long
⅓ cup all-purpose flour	3 large eggs, lightly beaten
1½ teaspoons baking powder	Cooking spray
1 teaspoon kosher salt, plus more as needed	½ cup mayonnaise
½ teaspoon freshly ground black pepper, plus more as needed	2 tablespoons capers, rinsed and finely chopped
	1 tablespoon fresh tarragon
⅛ teaspoon cayenne pepper	1 teaspoon fresh lemon juice, plus lemon wedges, for serving

1. Preheat the air fryer to 400°F (204°C). 2. In a large bowl, whisk together the cornmeal, flour, baking powder, salt, black pepper, and cayenne. Dip the trout strips in the egg, then toss them in the cornmeal mixture until fully coated. Transfer the trout to a rack set over a baking sheet and liberally spray all over with cooking spray. 3. Transfer half the fish to the air fryer and air fry until the fish is cooked through and golden brown, about 6 minutes. Transfer the fish sticks to a plate and repeat with the remaining fish. 4. Meanwhile, in a bowl, whisk together the mayonnaise, capers, tarragon, and lemon juice. Season the tartar sauce with salt and black pepper. 5. Serve the trout fingers hot along with the tartar sauce and lemon wedges.

Coconut Shrimp

Prep time: 5 minutes | Cook time: 6 minutes | Serves 2

8 ounces (227 g) medium shelled and deveined shrimp	½ teaspoon Old Bay seasoning
2 tablespoons salted butter, melted	¼ cup unsweetened shredded coconut

1. In a large bowl, toss the shrimp in butter and Old Bay seasoning. 2. Place shredded coconut in bowl. Coat each piece of shrimp in the coconut and place into the air fryer basket. 3. Adjust the temperature to 400°F (204°C) and air fry for 6 minutes. 4. Gently turn the shrimp halfway through the cooking time. Serve immediately.

Calamari with Hot Sauce

Prep time: 10 minutes | Cook time: 6 minutes | Serves 2

10 ounces (283 g) calamari, trimmed	2 tablespoons keto hot sauce
	1 tablespoon avocado oil

1. Slice the calamari and sprinkle with avocado oil. 2. Put the calamari in the air fryer and cook at 400°F (204°C) for 3 minutes per side. 3. Then transfer the calamari in the serving plate and sprinkle with hot sauce.

Roasted Fish with Almond-Lemon Crumbs

Prep time: 10 minutes | Cook time: 7 to 8 minutes | Serves 4

½ cup raw whole almonds	Freshly ground black pepper,
1 scallion, finely chopped	to taste
Grated zest and juice of 1	4 (6 ounces / 170 g each)
lemon	skinless fish fillets
½ tablespoon extra-virgin olive	Cooking spray
oil	1 teaspoon Dijon mustard
¾ teaspoon kosher salt, divided	

1. In a food processor, pulse the almonds to coarsely chop. Transfer to a small bowl and add the scallion, lemon zest, and olive oil. Season with ¼ teaspoon of the salt and pepper to taste and mix to combine. 2. Spray the top of the fish with oil and squeeze the lemon juice over the fish. Season with the remaining ½ teaspoon salt and pepper to taste. Spread the mustard on top of the fish. Dividing evenly, press the almond mixture onto the top of the fillets to adhere. 3. Preheat the air fryer to 375°F (191°C). 4. Working in batches, place the fillets in the air fryer basket in a single layer. Air fry for 7 to 8 minutes, until the crumbs start to brown and the fish is cooked through. 5. Serve immediately.

Shrimp Kebabs

Prep time: 15 minutes | Cook time: 6 minutes | Serves 4

Oil, for spraying	1 tablespoon packed light
1 pound (454 g) medium raw	brown sugar
shrimp, peeled and deveined	1 teaspoon granulated garlic
4 tablespoons unsalted butter,	1 teaspoon onion powder
melted	½ teaspoon freshly ground
1 tablespoon Old Bay	black pepper
seasoning	

1. Line the air fryer basket with parchment and spray lightly with oil. 2. Thread the shrimp onto the skewers and place them in the prepared basket. 3. In a small bowl, mix together the butter, Old Bay, brown sugar, garlic, onion powder, and black pepper. Brush the sauce on the shrimp. 4. Air fry at 400°F (204°C) for 5 to 6 minutes, or until pink and firm. Serve immediately.

Scallops and Spinach with Cream Sauce

Prep time: 5 minutes | Cook time: 10 minutes | Serves 2

Vegetable oil spray	to taste
1 (10-ounce / 283-g) package	¾ cup heavy cream
frozen spinach, thawed and	1 tablespoon tomato paste
drained	1 tablespoon chopped fresh
8 jumbo sea scallops	basil
Kosher salt and black pepper,	1 teaspoon minced garlic

1. Spray a baking pan with vegetable oil spray. Spread the thawed spinach in an even layer in the bottom of the pan. 2. Spray both sides of the scallops with vegetable oil spray. Season lightly with salt and pepper. Arrange the scallops on top of the spinach. 3. In a small bowl, whisk together the cream, tomato paste, basil, garlic, ½ teaspoon salt, and ½ teaspoon pepper. Pour the sauce over the scallops and spinach. 4. Place the pan in the air fryer basket. Set the air fryer to 350°F (177°C) for 10 minutes. Use a meat thermometer to ensure the scallops have an internal temperature of 135°F (57°C).

Classic Shrimp Empanadas

Prep time: 10 minutes | Cook time: 8 minutes | Serves 5

½ pound (227g) raw shrimp,	½ tablespoon fresh lime juice
peeled, deveined and chopped	¼ teaspoon sweet paprika
¼ cup chopped red onion	⅛ teaspoon kosher salt
1 scallion, chopped	⅛ teaspoon crushed red pepper
2 garlic cloves, minced	flakes (optional)
2 tablespoons minced red bell	1 large egg, beaten
pepper	10 frozen Goya Empanada
2 tablespoons chopped fresh	Discos, thawed
cilantro	Cooking spray

1. In a medium bowl, combine the shrimp, red onion, scallion, garlic, bell pepper, cilantro, lime juice, paprika, salt, and pepper flakes (if using). 2. In a small bowl, beat the egg with 1 teaspoon water until smooth. 3. Place an empanada disc on a work surface and put 2 tablespoons of the shrimp mixture in the center. Brush the outer edges of the disc with the egg wash. Fold the disc over and gently press the edges to seal. Use a fork and press around the edges to crimp and seal completely. Brush the tops of the empanadas with the egg wash. 4. Preheat the air fryer to 380°F (193°C). 5. Spray the bottom of the air fryer basket with cooking spray to prevent sticking. Working in batches, arrange a single layer of the empanadas in the air fryer basket and air fry for about 8 minutes, flipping halfway, until golden brown and crispy. 6. Serve hot.

Trout Amandine with Lemon Butter Sauce

Prep time: 20 minutes | Cook time:8 minutes | Serves 4

Trout Amandine:	8 tablespoons (1 stick) butter,
⅔ cup toasted almonds	melted
⅓ cup grated Parmesan cheese	2 tablespoons freshly squeezed
1 teaspoon salt	lemon juice
½ teaspoon freshly ground	½ teaspoon Worcestershire
black pepper	sauce
2 tablespoons butter, melted	½ teaspoon salt
4 (4-ounce / 113-g) trout fillets,	½ teaspoon freshly ground
or salmon fillets	black pepper
Cooking spray	¼ teaspoon hot sauce
Lemon Butter Sauce:	

1. In a blender or food processor, pulse the almonds for 5 to 10 seconds until finely processed. Transfer to a shallow bowl and whisk in the Parmesan cheese, salt, and pepper. Place the melted butter in another shallow bowl. 2. One at a time, dip the fish in the melted butter, then the almond mixture, coating thoroughly. 3. Preheat the air fryer to 300°F (149°C). Line the air fryer basket with parchment paper. 4. Place the coated fish on the parchment and spritz with oil. 5. Bake for 4 minutes. Flip the fish, spritz it with oil, and bake for 4 minutes more until the fish flakes easily with a fork. 6. In a small bowl, whisk the butter, lemon juice, Worcestershire sauce, salt, pepper, and hot sauce until blended. 7. Serve with the fish.

Parmesan Lobster Tails

Prep time: 5 minutes | Cook time: 7 minutes | Serves 4

4 (4-ounce / 113-g) lobster tails	¼ teaspoon ground black pepper
2 tablespoons salted butter, melted	¼ cup grated Parmesan cheese
1½ teaspoons Cajun seasoning, divided	½ ounce (14 g) plain pork rinds, finely crushed
¼ teaspoon salt	

1. Cut lobster tails open carefully with a pair of scissors and gently pull meat away from shells, resting meat on top of shells. 2. Brush lobster meat with butter and sprinkle with 1 teaspoon Cajun seasoning, ¼ teaspoon per tail. 3. In a small bowl, mix remaining Cajun seasoning, salt, pepper, Parmesan, and pork rinds. Gently press ¼ mixture onto meat on each lobster tail. 4. Carefully place tails into ungreased air fryer basket. Adjust the temperature to 400°F (204°C) and air fry for 7 minutes. Lobster tails will be crispy and golden on top and have an internal temperature of at least 145°F (63°C) when done. Serve warm.

Chili Lime Shrimp

Prep time: 5 minutes | Cook time: 5 minutes | Serves 4

1 pound (454 g) medium shrimp, peeled and deveined	¼ teaspoon salt
1 tablespoon salted butter, melted	¼ teaspoon ground black pepper
2 teaspoons chili powder	½ small lime, zested and juiced, divided
¼ teaspoon garlic powder	

1. In a medium bowl, toss shrimp with butter, then sprinkle with chili powder, garlic powder, salt, pepper, and lime zest. 2. Place shrimp into ungreased air fryer basket. Adjust the temperature to 400°F (204°C) and air fry for 5 minutes. Shrimp will be firm and form a "C" shape when done. 3. Transfer shrimp to a large serving dish and drizzle with lime juice. Serve warm.

Snapper with Shallot and Tomato

Prep time: 20 minutes | Cook time: 15 minutes | Serves 2

2 snapper fillets	1 tablespoon olive oil
1 shallot, peeled and sliced	¼ teaspoon freshly ground black pepper
2 garlic cloves, halved	
1 bell pepper, sliced	½ teaspoon paprika
1 small-sized serrano pepper, sliced	Sea salt, to taste
1 tomato, sliced	2 bay leaves

1. Place two parchment sheets on a working surface. Place the fish in the center of one side of the parchment paper. 2. Top with the shallot, garlic, peppers, and tomato. Drizzle olive oil over the fish and vegetables. Season with black pepper, paprika, and salt. Add the bay leaves. 3. Fold over the other half of the parchment. Now, fold the paper around the edges tightly and create a half moon shape, sealing the fish inside. 4. Cook in the preheated air fryer at 390°F (199°C) for 15 minutes. Serve warm.

Crab-Stuffed Avocado Boats

Prep time: 5 minutes | Cook time: 7 minutes | Serves 4

2 medium avocados, halved and pitted	¼ teaspoon Old Bay seasoning
8 ounces (227 g) cooked crab meat	2 tablespoons peeled and diced yellow onion
	2 tablespoons mayonnaise

1. Scoop out avocado flesh in each avocado half, leaving ½ inch around edges to form a shell. Chop scooped-out avocado. 2. In a medium bowl, combine crab meat, Old Bay seasoning, onion, mayonnaise, and chopped avocado. Place ¼ mixture into each avocado shell. 3. Place avocado boats into ungreased air fryer basket. Adjust the temperature to 350°F (177°C) and air fry for 7 minutes. Avocado will be browned on the top and mixture will be bubbling when done. Serve warm.

Dukkah-Crusted Halibut

Prep time: 15 minutes | Cook time: 17 minutes | Serves 2

Dukkah:	¼ teaspoon black pepper
1 tablespoon coriander seeds	Fish:
1 tablespoon sesame seeds	2 (5-ounce / 142-g) halibut fillets
1½ teaspoons cumin seeds	2 tablespoons mayonnaise
⅓ cup roasted mixed nuts	Vegetable oil spray
¼ teaspoon kosher salt	Lemon wedges, for serving

1. For the dukkah: Combine the coriander, sesame seeds, and cumin in a small baking pan. Place the pan in the air fryer basket. Set the air fryer to 400°F (204°C) for 5 minutes. Toward the end of the cooking time, you will hear the seeds popping. Transfer to a plate and let cool for 5 minutes. 2. Transfer the toasted seeds to a food processor or spice grinder and add the mixed nuts. Pulse until coarsely chopped. Add the salt and pepper and stir well. 3. For the fish: Spread each fillet with 1 tablespoon of the mayonnaise. Press a heaping tablespoon of the dukkah into the mayonnaise on each fillet, pressing lightly to adhere. 4. Spray the air fryer basket with vegetable oil spray. Place the fish in the basket. Set the air fryer to 400°F (204°C) for 12 minutes, or until the fish flakes easily with a fork. 5. Serve the fish with lemon wedges.

Tex-Mex Salmon Bowl

Prep time: 15 minutes | Cook time: 9 to 14 minutes | Serves 4

12 ounces (340 g) salmon fillets, cut into 1½-inch cubes	2 teaspoons peanut oil or safflower oil
1 red onion, chopped	2 tablespoons low-sodium tomato juice
1 jalapeño pepper, minced	1 teaspoon chili powder
1 red bell pepper, chopped	
¼ cup low-sodium salsa	

1. Preheat the air fryer to 370°F (188°C). 2. Mix together the salmon cubes, red onion, jalapeño, red bell pepper, salsa, peanut oil, tomato juice, chili powder in a medium metal bowl and stir until well incorporated. 3. Transfer the bowl to the air fryer basket and bake for 9 to 14 minutes, stirring once, or until the salmon is cooked through and the veggies are fork-tender. 4. Serve warm.

Sea Bass with Potato Scales

Prep time: 10 minutes | Cook time: 10 minutes | Serves 2

2 (6- to 8-ounce / 170- to 227-g) fillets of sea bass	2 Fingerling potatoes, very thinly sliced into rounds
Salt and freshly ground black pepper, to taste	Olive oil
¼ cup mayonnaise	½ clove garlic, crushed into a paste
2 teaspoons finely chopped lemon zest	1 tablespoon capers, drained and rinsed
1 teaspoon chopped fresh thyme	1 tablespoon olive oil
	1 teaspoon lemon juice, to taste

1. Preheat the air fryer to 400ºF (204ºC). 2. Season the fish well with salt and freshly ground black pepper. Mix the mayonnaise, lemon zest and thyme together in a small bowl. Spread a thin layer of the mayonnaise mixture on both fillets. Start layering rows of potato slices onto the fish fillets to simulate the fish scales. The second row should overlap the first row slightly. Dabbing a little more mayonnaise along the upper edge of the row of potatoes where the next row overlaps will help the potato slices stick. Press the potatoes onto the fish to secure them well and season again with salt. Brush or spray the potato layer with olive oil. 3. Transfer the fish to the air fryer and air fry for 8 to 10 minutes, depending on the thickness of your fillets. 1-inch of fish should take 10 minutes at 400ºF (204ºC). 4. While the fish is cooking, add the garlic, capers, olive oil and lemon juice to the remaining mayonnaise mixture to make the caper aïoli. 5. Serve the fish warm with a dollop of the aïoli on top or on the side.

Salmon with Provolone Cheese

Prep time: 5 minutes | Cook time: 15 minutes | Serves 4

1 pound (454 g) salmon fillet, chopped	grated
2 ounces (57 g) Provolone,	1 teaspoon avocado oil
	¼ teaspoon ground paprika

1. Sprinkle the salmon fillets with avocado oil and put in the air fryer. 2. Then sprinkle the fish with ground paprika and top with Provolone cheese. 3. Cook the fish at 360ºF (182ºC) for 15 minutes.

Parmesan Fish Fillets

Prep time: 8 minutes | Cook time: 17 minutes | Serves 4

⅓ cup grated Parmesan cheese	4 (4-ounce / 113-g) fish fillets, halved
½ teaspoon fennel seed	
½ teaspoon tarragon	2 tablespoons dry white wine
⅓ teaspoon mixed peppercorns	1 teaspoon seasoned salt
2 eggs, beaten	

1. Preheat the air fryer to 345ºF (174ºC). 2. Place the grated Parmesan cheese, fennel seed, tarragon, and mixed peppercorns in a food processor and pulse for about 20 seconds until well combined. Transfer the cheese mixture to a shallow dish. 3. Place the beaten eggs in another shallow dish. 4. Drizzle the dry white wine over the top of fish fillets. Dredge each fillet in the beaten eggs on both sides, shaking off any excess, then roll them in the cheese mixture until fully coated. Season with the salt. 5. Arrange the fillets in the air fryer basket and air fry for about 17 minutes, or until the fish is cooked through and no longer translucent. Flip the fillets once halfway through the cooking time. 6. Cool for 5 minutes before serving.

White Fish with Cauliflower

Prep time: 30 minutes | Cook time: 13 minutes | Serves 4

½ pound (227 g) cauliflower florets	½ tablespoon cilantro, minced
	2 tablespoons sour cream
½ teaspoon English mustard	2 ½ cups cooked white fish
2 tablespoons butter, room temperature	Salt and freshly cracked black pepper, to taste

1. Boil the cauliflower until tender. Then, purée the cauliflower in your blender. Transfer to a mixing dish. 2. Now, stir in the fish, cilantro, salt, and black pepper. 3. Add the sour cream, English mustard, and butter; mix until everything's well incorporated. Using your hands, shape into patties. 4. Place in the refrigerator for about 2 hours. Cook for 13 minutes at 395ºF (202ºC). Serve with some extra English mustard.

Crab Cakes with Sriracha Mayonnaise

Prep time: 15 minutes | Cook time: 10 minutes | Serves 4

Sriracha Mayonnaise:	¼ cup diced celery
1 cup mayonnaise	1 pound (454 g) lump crab meat
1 tablespoon sriracha	
1½ teaspoons freshly squeezed lemon juice	1 teaspoon Old Bay seasoning
	1 egg
Crab Cakes:	1½ teaspoons freshly squeezed lemon juice
1 teaspoon extra-virgin olive oil	
	1¾ cups panko bread crumbs, divided
¼ cup finely diced red bell pepper	
	Vegetable oil, for spraying
¼ cup diced onion	

1. Mix the mayonnaise, sriracha, and lemon juice in a small bowl. Place ⅔ cup of the mixture in a separate bowl to form the base of the crab cakes. Cover the remaining sriracha mayonnaise and refrigerate. (This will become dipping sauce for the crab cakes once they are cooked.) 2. Heat the olive oil in a heavy-bottomed, medium skillet over medium-high heat. Add the bell pepper, onion, and celery and sauté for 3 minutes. Transfer the vegetables to the bowl with the reserved ⅔ cup of sriracha mayonnaise. Mix in the crab, Old Bay seasoning, egg, and lemon juice. Add 1 cup of the panko. Form the crab mixture into 8 cakes. Dredge the cakes in the remaining ¾ cup of panko, turning to coat. Place on a baking sheet. Cover and refrigerate for at least 1 hour and up to 8 hours. 3. Preheat the air fryer to 375ºF (191ºC). Spray the air fryer basket with oil. Working in batches as needed so as not to overcrowd the basket, place the chilled crab cakes in a single layer in the basket. Spray the crab cakes with oil. Bake until golden brown, 8 to 10 minutes, carefully turning halfway through cooking. Remove to a platter and keep warm. Repeat with the remaining crab cakes as needed. Serve the crab cakes immediately with sriracha mayonnaise dipping sauce.

Teriyaki Salmon

Prep time: 30 minutes | Cook time: 12 minutes | Serves 4

4 (6-ounce / 170-g) salmon fillets	¼ teaspoon ground ginger
½ cup soy sauce	2 teaspoons olive oil
¼ cup packed light brown sugar	½ teaspoon salt
2 teaspoons rice vinegar	¼ teaspoon freshly ground black pepper
1 teaspoon minced garlic	Oil, for spraying

1. Place the salmon in a small pan, skin-side up. 2. In a small bowl, whisk together the soy sauce, brown sugar, rice vinegar, garlic, ginger, olive oil, salt, and black pepper. 3. Pour the mixture over the salmon and marinate for about 30 minutes. 4. Line the air fryer basket with parchment and spray lightly with oil. Place the salmon in the prepared basket, skin-side down. You may need to work in batches, depending on the size of your air fryer. 5. Air fry at 400°F (204°C) for 6 minutes, brush the salmon with more marinade, and cook for another 6 minutes, or until the internal temperature reaches 145°F (63°C). Serve immediately.

Baked Tilapia with Garlic Aioli

Prep time: 5 minutes | Cook time: 15 minutes | Serves 4

Tilapia:	seasoning
4 tilapia fillets	Garlic Aioli:
1 tablespoon extra-virgin olive oil	2 garlic cloves, minced
1 teaspoon garlic powder	1 tablespoon mayonnaise
1 teaspoon paprika	Juice of ½ lemon
1 teaspoon dried basil	1 teaspoon extra-virgin olive oil
A pinch of lemon-pepper	Salt and pepper, to taste

1. Preheat the air fryer to 400°F (204°C). 2. On a clean work surface, brush both sides of each fillet with the olive oil. Sprinkle with the garlic powder, paprika, basil, and lemon-pepper seasoning. 3. Place the fillets in the air fryer basket and bake for 15 minutes, flipping the fillets halfway through, or until the fish flakes easily and is no longer translucent in the center. 4. Meanwhile, make the garlic aioli: Whisk together the garlic, mayo, lemon juice, olive oil, salt, and pepper in a small bowl until smooth. 5. Remove the fish from the basket and serve with the garlic aioli on the side.

Lemon Mahi-Mahi

Prep time: 5 minutes | Cook time: 14 minutes | Serves 2

Oil, for spraying	¼ teaspoon salt
2 (6-ounce / 170-g) mahi-mahi fillets	¼ teaspoon freshly ground black pepper
1 tablespoon lemon juice	1 tablespoon chopped fresh dill
1 tablespoon olive oil	2 lemon slices

1. Line the air fryer basket with parchment and spray lightly with oil. 2. Place the mahi-mahi in the prepared basket. 3. In a small bowl, whisk together the lemon juice and olive oil. Brush the mixture evenly over the mahi-mahi. 4. Sprinkle the mahi-mahi with the salt and black pepper and top with the dill. 5. Air fry at 400°F (204°C) for 12 to 14 minutes, depending on the thickness of the fillets, until they flake easily. 6. Transfer to plates, top each with a lemon slice, and serve.

Fish Croquettes with Lemon-Dill Aioli

Prep time: 15 minutes | Cook time: 10 minutes | Serves 4

Croquettes:	¾ cup plus 2 tablespoons bread crumbs, divided
3 large eggs, divided	1 teaspoon fresh lemon juice
12 ounces (340 g) raw cod fillet, flaked apart with two forks	1 teaspoon kosher salt
¼ cup 1% milk	½ teaspoon dried thyme
½ cup boxed instant mashed potatoes	¼ teaspoon freshly ground black pepper
2 teaspoons olive oil	Cooking spray
⅓ cup chopped fresh dill	Lemon-Dill Aioli:
1 shallot, minced	5 tablespoons mayonnaise
1 large garlic clove, minced	Juice of ½ lemon
	1 tablespoon chopped fresh dill

1. For the croquettes: In a medium bowl, lightly beat 2 of the eggs. Add the fish, milk, instant mashed potatoes, olive oil, dill, shallot, garlic, 2 tablespoons of the bread crumbs, lemon juice, salt, thyme, and pepper. Mix to thoroughly combine. Place in the refrigerator for 30 minutes. 2. For the lemon-dill aioli: In a small bowl, combine the mayonnaise, lemon juice, and dill. Set aside. 3. Measure out about 3½ tablespoons of the fish mixture and gently roll in your hands to form a log about 3 inches long. Repeat to make a total of 12 logs. 4. Beat the remaining egg in a small bowl. Place the remaining ¾ cup bread crumbs in a separate bowl. Dip the croquettes in the egg, then coat in the bread crumbs, gently pressing to adhere. Place on a work surface and spray both sides with cooking spray. 5. Preheat the air fryer to 350°F (177°C). 6. Working in batches, arrange a single layer of the croquettes in the air fryer basket. Air fry for about 10 minutes, flipping halfway, until golden. 7. Serve with the aioli for dipping.

Lemony Shrimp and Zucchini

Prep time: 15 minutes | Cook time: 7 to 8 minutes | Serves 4

1¼ pounds (567 g) extra-large raw shrimp, peeled and deveined	½ teaspoon garlic salt
	1½ teaspoons dried oregano
2 medium zucchini (about 8 ounces / 227 g each), halved lengthwise and cut into ½-inch-thick slices	⅛ teaspoon crushed red pepper flakes (optional)
	Juice of ½ lemon
	1 tablespoon chopped fresh mint
1½ tablespoons olive oil	1 tablespoon chopped fresh dill

1. Preheat the air fryer to 350°F (177°C). 2. In a large bowl, combine the shrimp, zucchini, oil, garlic salt, oregano, and pepper flakes (if using) and toss to coat. 3. Working in batches, arrange a single layer of the shrimp and zucchini in the air fryer basket. Air fry for 7 to 8 minutes, shaking the basket halfway, until the zucchini is golden and the shrimp are cooked through. 4. Transfer to a serving dish and tent with foil while you air fry the remaining shrimp and zucchini. 5. Top with the lemon juice, mint, and dill and serve.

Sole and Asparagus Bundles

Prep time: 10 minutes | Cook time: 14 minutes | Serves 2

8 ounces (227 g) asparagus, trimmed	4 tablespoons unsalted butter, softened
1 teaspoon extra-virgin olive oil, divided	1 small shallot, minced
Salt and pepper, to taste	1 tablespoon chopped fresh tarragon
4 (3-ounce / 85-g) skinless sole or flounder fillets, ⅛ to ¼ inch thick	¼ teaspoon lemon zest plus ½ teaspoon juice
	Vegetable oil spray

1. Preheat the air fryer to 300°F (149°C). 2. Toss asparagus with ½ teaspoon oil, pinch salt, and pinch pepper in a bowl. Cover and microwave until bright green and just tender, about 3 minutes, tossing halfway through microwaving. Uncover and set aside to cool slightly. 3. Make foil sling for air fryer basket by folding 1 long sheet of aluminum foil so it is 4 inches wide. Lay sheet of foil widthwise across basket, pressing foil into and up sides of basket. Fold excess foil as needed so that edges of foil are flush with top of basket. Lightly spray foil and basket with vegetable oil spray. 4. Pat sole dry with paper towels and season with salt and pepper. Arrange fillets skinned side up on cutting board, with thicker ends closest to you. Arrange asparagus evenly across base of each fillet, then tightly roll fillets away from you around asparagus to form tidy bundles. 5. Rub bundles evenly with remaining ½ teaspoon oil and arrange seam side down on sling in prepared basket. Bake until asparagus is tender and sole flakes apart when gently prodded with a paring knife, 14 to 18 minutes, using a sling to rotate bundles halfway through cooking. 6. Combine butter, shallot, tarragon, and lemon zest and juice in a bowl. Using sling, carefully remove sole bundles from air fryer and transfer to individual plates. Top evenly with butter mixture and serve.

Salmon Burgers

Prep time: 15 minutes | Cook time: 12 minutes | Serves 5

Lemon-Caper Rémoulade:	¼ cup minced red onion plus ¼ cup slivered for serving
½ cup mayonnaise	1 garlic clove, minced
2 tablespoons minced drained capers	1 large egg, lightly beaten
2 tablespoons chopped fresh parsley	1 tablespoon Dijon mustard
2 teaspoons fresh lemon juice	1 teaspoon fresh lemon juice
Salmon Patties:	1 tablespoon chopped fresh parsley
1 pound (454 g) wild salmon fillet, skinned and pin bones removed	½ teaspoon kosher salt
	For Serving:
6 tablespoons panko bread crumbs	5 whole wheat potato buns or gluten-free buns
	10 butter lettuce leaves

1. For the lemon-caper rémoulade: In a small bowl, combine the mayonnaise, capers, parsley, and lemon juice and mix well. 2. For the salmon patties: Cut off a 4-ounce / 113-g piece of the salmon and transfer to a food processor. Pulse until it becomes pasty. With a sharp knife, chop the remaining salmon into small cubes. 3. In a medium bowl, combine the chopped and processed salmon with the panko, minced red onion, garlic, egg, mustard, lemon juice, parsley, and salt. Toss gently to combine. Form the mixture into 5 patties about ¾ inch thick. Refrigerate for at least 30 minutes. 4. Preheat the air fryer to 400°F (204°C). 5. Working in batches, place the patties in the air fryer basket. Air fry for about 12 minutes, gently flipping halfway, until golden and cooked through. 6. To serve, transfer each patty to a bun. Top each with 2 lettuce leaves, 2 tablespoons of the rémoulade, and the slivered red onions.

Chili Tilapia

Prep time: 5 minutes | Cook time: 20 minutes | Serves 4

4 tilapia fillets, boneless	1 tablespoon avocado oil
1 teaspoon chili flakes	1 teaspoon mustard
1 teaspoon dried oregano	

1. Rub the tilapia fillets with chili flakes, dried oregano, avocado oil, and mustard and put in the air fryer. 2. Cook it for 10 minutes per side at 360°F (182°C).

BBQ Shrimp with Creole Butter Sauce

Prep time: 10 minutes | Cook time: 12 to 15 minutes | Serves 4

6 tablespoons unsalted butter	1 teaspoon Creole seasoning
⅓ cup Worcestershire sauce	1½ pounds (680 g) large uncooked shrimp, peeled and deveined
3 cloves garlic, minced	
Juice of 1 lemon	
1 teaspoon paprika	2 tablespoons fresh parsley

1. Preheat the air fryer to 370°F (188°C). 2. In a large microwave-safe bowl, combine the butter, Worcestershire, and garlic. Microwave on high for 1 to 2 minutes until the butter is melted. Stir in the lemon juice, paprika, and Creole seasoning. Add the shrimp and toss until thoroughly coated. 3. Transfer the mixture to a casserole dish or pan that fits in your air fryer. Pausing halfway through the cooking time to turn the shrimp, air fry for 12 to 15 minutes, until the shrimp are cooked through. Top with the parsley just before serving.

New Orleans-Style Crab Cakes

Prep time: 10 minutes | Cook time: 8 to 10 minutes | Serves 4

1¼ cups bread crumbs	1½ cups crab meat
2 teaspoons Creole Seasoning	2 large eggs, beaten
1 teaspoon dry mustard	1 teaspoon butter, melted
1 teaspoon salt	⅓ cup minced onion
1 teaspoon freshly ground black pepper	Cooking spray
	Pecan Tartar Sauce, for serving

1. Preheat the air fryer to 350°F (177°C). Line the air fryer basket with parchment paper. 2. In a medium bowl, whisk the bread crumbs, Creole Seasoning, dry mustard, salt, and pepper until blended. Add the crab meat, eggs, butter, and onion. Stir until blended. Shape the crab mixture into 8 patties. 3. Place the crab cakes on the parchment and spritz with oil. 4. Air fry for 4 minutes. Flip the cakes, spritz them with oil, and air fry for 4 to 6 minutes more until the outsides are firm and a fork inserted into the center comes out clean. Serve with the Pecan Tartar Sauce.

Tuna-Stuffed Tomatoes

Prep time: 5 minutes | Cook time: 5 minutes | Serves 2

2 medium beefsteak tomatoes, tops removed, seeded, membranes removed	2 tablespoons mayonnaise
	¼ teaspoon salt
2 (2.6-ounce / 74-g) pouches tuna packed in water, drained	¼ teaspoon ground black pepper
1 medium stalk celery, trimmed and chopped	2 teaspoons coconut oil
	¼ cup shredded mild Cheddar cheese

1. Scoop pulp out of each tomato, leaving ½-inch shell. 2. In a medium bowl, mix tuna, celery, mayonnaise, salt, and pepper. Drizzle with coconut oil. Spoon ½ mixture into each tomato and top each with 2 tablespoons Cheddar. 3. Place tomatoes into ungreased air fryer basket. Adjust the temperature to 320ºF (160ºC) and air fry for 5 minutes. Cheese will be melted when done. Serve warm.

Cripsy Shrimp with Cilantro

Prep time: 40 minutes | Cook time: 10 minutes | Serves 4

1 pound (454 g) raw large shrimp, peeled and deveined with tails on or off	1 egg
	¾ cup bread crumbs
½ cup chopped fresh cilantro	Salt and freshly ground black pepper, to taste
Juice of 1 lime	Cooking oil spray
½ cup all-purpose flour	1 cup cocktail sauce

1. Place the shrimp in a resealable plastic bag and add the cilantro and lime juice. Seal the bag. Shake it to combine. Marinate the shrimp in the refrigerator for 30 minutes. 2. Place the flour in a small bowl. 3. In another small bowl, beat the egg. 4. Place the bread crumbs in a third small bowl, season with salt and pepper, and stir to combine. 5. Insert the crisper plate into the basket and the basket into the unit. Preheat the unit by selecting AIR FRY, setting the temperature to 400ºF (204ºC), and setting the time to 3 minutes. Select START/STOP to begin. 6. Remove the shrimp from the plastic bag. Dip each in the flour, the egg, and the bread crumbs to coat. Gently press the crumbs onto the shrimp. 7. Once the unit is preheated, spray the crisper plate and the basket with cooking oil. Place the shrimp in the basket. It is okay to stack them. Spray the shrimp with the cooking oil. 8. Select AIR FRY, set the temperature to 400ºF (204ºC), and set the time to 8 minutes. Select START/STOP to begin. 9. After 4 minutes, remove the basket and flip the shrimp one at a time. Reinsert the basket to resume cooking. 10. When the cooking is complete, the shrimp should be crisp. Let cool for 5 minutes. Serve with cocktail sauce.

Mackerel with Spinach

Prep time: 15 minutes | Cook time: 20 minutes | Serves 5

1 pound (454 g) mackerel, trimmed	1 tablespoon avocado oil
	1 teaspoon ground black pepper
1 bell pepper, chopped	1 teaspoon keto tomato paste
½ cup spinach, chopped	

1. In the mixing bowl, mix bell pepper with spinach, ground black pepper, and tomato paste. 2. Fill the mackerel with spinach mixture. 3. Then brush the fish with avocado oil and put it in the air fryer. 4. Cook the fish at 365ºF (185ºC) for 20 minutes.

Seasoned Breaded Shrimp

Prep time: 15 minutes | Cook time: 10 to 15 minutes | Serves 4

2 teaspoons Old Bay seasoning, divided	deveined, with tails on
	2 large eggs
½ teaspoon garlic powder	½ cup whole-wheat panko bread crumbs
½ teaspoon onion powder	
1 pound (454 g) large shrimp,	Cooking spray

1. Preheat the air fryer to 380ºF (193ºC). 2. Spray the air fryer basket lightly with cooking spray. 3. In a medium bowl, mix together 1 teaspoon of Old Bay seasoning, garlic powder, and onion powder. Add the shrimp and toss with the seasoning mix to lightly coat. 4. In a separate small bowl, whisk the eggs with 1 teaspoon water. 5. In a shallow bowl, mix together the remaining 1 teaspoon Old Bay seasoning and the panko bread crumbs. 6. Dip each shrimp in the egg mixture and dredge in the bread crumb mixture to evenly coat. 7. Place the shrimp in the air fryer basket, in a single layer. Lightly spray the shrimp with cooking spray. You many need to cook the shrimp in batches. 8. Air fry for 10 to 15 minutes, or until the shrimp is cooked through and crispy, shaking the basket at 5-minute intervals to redistribute and evenly cook. 9. Serve immediately.

Stuffed Shrimp

Prep time: 20 minutes | Cook time: 12 minutes per batch | Serves 4

16 tail-on shrimp, peeled and deveined (last tail section intact)	2 tablespoons chopped celery
	2 tablespoons chopped green bell pepper
¾ cup crushed panko bread crumbs	½ cup crushed saltine crackers
	1 teaspoon Old Bay Seasoning
Oil for misting or cooking spray	1 teaspoon garlic powder
Stuffing:	¼ teaspoon ground thyme
2 (6-ounce / 170-g) cans lump crab meat	2 teaspoons dried parsley flakes
	2 teaspoons fresh lemon juice
2 tablespoons chopped shallots	2 teaspoons Worcestershire sauce
2 tablespoons chopped green onions	1 egg, beaten

1. Rinse shrimp. Remove tail section (shell) from 4 shrimp, discard, and chop the meat finely. 2. To prepare the remaining 12 shrimp, cut a deep slit down the back side so that the meat lies open flat. Do not cut all the way through. 3. Preheat the air fryer to 360ºF (182ºC). 4. Place chopped shrimp in a large bowl with all of the stuffing ingredients and stir to combine. 5. Divide stuffing into 12 portions, about 2 tablespoons each. 6. Place one stuffing portion onto the back of each shrimp and form into a ball or oblong shape. Press firmly so that stuffing sticks together and adheres to shrimp. 7. Gently roll each stuffed shrimp in panko crumbs and mist with oil or cooking spray. 8. Place 6 shrimp in air fryer basket and air fry at 360ºF (182ºC) for 10 minutes. Mist with oil or spray and cook 2 minutes longer or until stuffing cooks through inside and is crispy outside. 9. Repeat step 8 to cook remaining shrimp.

Crispy Fish Sticks

Prep time: 15 minutes | Cook time: 10 minutes | Serves 4

1 ounce (28 g) pork rinds, finely ground	1 tablespoon coconut oil
¼ cup blanched finely ground almond flour	1 large egg
½ teaspoon Old Bay seasoning	1 pound (454 g) cod fillet, cut into ¾-inch strips

1. Place ground pork rinds, almond flour, Old Bay seasoning, and coconut oil into a large bowl and mix together. In a medium bowl, whisk egg. 2. Dip each fish stick into the egg and then gently press into the flour mixture, coating as fully and evenly as possible. Place fish sticks into the air fryer basket. 3. Adjust the temperature to 400°F (204°C) and air fry for 10 minutes or until golden. 4. Serve immediately.

Italian Tuna Roast

Prep time: 15 minutes | Cook time: 21 to 24 minutes | Serves 8

Cooking spray	oil
1 tablespoon Italian seasoning	1 teaspoon lemon juice
⅛ teaspoon ground black pepper	1 tuna loin (approximately 2 pounds / 907 g, 3 to 4 inches thick)
1 tablespoon extra-light olive	

1. Spray baking dish with cooking spray and place in air fryer basket. Preheat the air fryer to 390°F (199°C). 2. Mix together the Italian seasoning, pepper, oil, and lemon juice. 3. Using a dull table knife or butter knife, pierce top of tuna about every half inch: Insert knife into top of tuna roast and pierce almost all the way to the bottom. 4. Spoon oil mixture into each of the holes and use the knife to push seasonings into the tuna as deeply as possible. 5. Spread any remaining oil mixture on all outer surfaces of tuna. 6. Place tuna roast in baking dish and roast at 390°F (199°C) for 20 minutes. Check temperature with a meat thermometer. Cook for an additional 1 to 4 minutes or until temperature reaches 145°F (63°C). 7. Remove basket from the air fryer and let tuna sit in the basket for 10 minutes.

Snapper Scampi

Prep time: 5 minutes | Cook time: 8 to 10 minutes | Serves 4

4 (6-ounce / 170-g) skinless snapper or arctic char fillets	Pinch salt
1 tablespoon olive oil	Freshly ground black pepper, to taste
3 tablespoons lemon juice, divided	2 tablespoons butter
½ teaspoon dried basil	2 cloves garlic, minced

1. Rub the fish fillets with olive oil and 1 tablespoon of the lemon juice. Sprinkle with the basil, salt, and pepper, and place in the air fryer basket. 2. Air fry the fish at 380°F (193°C) for 7 to 8 minutes or until the fish just flakes when tested with a fork. Remove the fish from the basket and put on a serving plate. Cover to keep warm. 3. In a baking pan, combine the butter, remaining 2 tablespoons lemon juice, and garlic. Bake in the air fryer for 1 to 2 minutes or until the

garlic is sizzling. Pour this mixture over the fish and serve

Greek Fish Pitas

Prep time: 10 minutes | Cook time: 15 minutes | Serves 4

1 pound (454 g) pollock, cut into 1-inch pieces	¼ teaspoon cayenne
¼ cup olive oil	4 whole wheat pitas
1 teaspoon salt	1 cup shredded lettuce
½ teaspoon dried oregano	2 Roma tomatoes, diced
½ teaspoon dried thyme	Nonfat plain Greek yogurt
½ teaspoon garlic powder	Lemon, quartered

1. Preheat the air fryer to 380°F(193°C). 2. In a medium bowl, combine the pollock with olive oil, salt, oregano, thyme, garlic powder, and cayenne. 3. Put the pollock into the air fryer basket and roast for 15 minutes. 4. Serve inside pitas with lettuce, tomato, and Greek yogurt with a lemon wedge on the side.

Snapper with Fruit

Prep time: 15 minutes | Cook time: 9 to 13 minutes | Serves 4

4 (4-ounce / 113-g) red snapper fillets	1 cup red grapes
2 teaspoons olive oil	1 tablespoon freshly squeezed lemon juice
3 nectarines, halved and pitted	1 tablespoon honey
3 plums, halved and pitted	½ teaspoon dried thyme

1. Put the red snapper in the air fryer basket and drizzle with the olive oil. Air fry at 390°F (199°C) for 4 minutes. 2. Remove the basket and add the nectarines and plums. Scatter the grapes over all. 3. Drizzle with the lemon juice and honey and sprinkle with the thyme. 4. Return the basket to the air fryer and air fry for 5 to 9 minutes more, or until the fish flakes when tested with a fork and the fruit is tender. Serve immediately.

Cucumber and Salmon Salad

Prep time: 10 minutes | Cook time: 8 to 10 minutes | Serves 2

1 pound (454 g) salmon fillet	sliced
1½ tablespoons olive oil, divided	¼ Vidalia onion, thinly sliced
1 tablespoon sherry vinegar	2 tablespoons chopped fresh parsley
1 tablespoon capers, rinsed and drained	Salt and freshly ground black pepper, to taste
1 seedless cucumber, thinly	

1. Preheat the air fryer to 400°F (204°C). 2. Lightly coat the salmon with ½ tablespoon of the olive oil. Place skin-side down in the air fryer basket and air fry for 8 to 10 minutes until the fish is opaque and flakes easily with a fork. Transfer the salmon to a plate and let cool to room temperature. Remove the skin and carefully flake the fish into bite-size chunks. 3. In a small bowl, whisk the remaining 1 tablespoon olive oil and the vinegar until thoroughly combined. Add the flaked fish, capers, cucumber, onion, and parsley. Season to taste with salt and freshly ground black pepper. Toss gently to coat. Serve immediately or cover and refrigerate for up to 4 hours.

Shrimp Scampi

Prep time: 8 minutes | Cook time: 8 minutes | Serves 4

4 tablespoons (½ stick) salted butter or ghee	2 tablespoons chicken broth or dry white wine
1 tablespoon fresh lemon juice	2 tablespoons chopped fresh basil, plus more for sprinkling, or 1 teaspoon dried
1 tablespoon minced garlic	
2 teaspoons red pepper flakes	
1 pound (454 g) shrimp (21 to 25 count), peeled and deveined	1 tablespoon chopped fresh chives, or 1 teaspoon dried

1. Place a baking pan in the air fryer basket. Set the air fryer to 325ºF (163ºC) for 8 minutes (this will preheat the pan so the butter will melt faster). 2. Carefully remove the pan from the fryer and add the butter, lemon juice, garlic, and red pepper flakes. Place the pan back in the fryer. 3. Cook for 2 minutes, stirring once, until the butter has melted. (Do not skip this step; this is what infuses the butter with garlic flavor, which is what makes it all taste so good.) 4. Carefully remove the pan from the fryer and add the shrimp, broth, basil, and chives. Stir gently until the ingredients are well combined. 5. Return the pan to the air fryer and cook for 5 minutes, stirring once. 6. Thoroughly stir the shrimp mixture and let it rest for 1 minute on a wire rack. (This is so the shrimp cooks in the residual heat rather than getting overcooked and rubbery.) 7. Stir once more, sprinkle with additional chopped fresh basil, and serve.

Tuna Avocado Bites

Prep time: 10 minutes | Cook time: 7 minutes | Makes 12 bites

1 (10-ounce / 283-g) can tuna, drained	pitted, and mashed
¼ cup full-fat mayonnaise	½ cup blanched finely ground almond flour, divided
1 stalk celery, chopped	2 teaspoons coconut oil
1 medium avocado, peeled,	

1. In a large bowl, mix tuna, mayonnaise, celery, and mashed avocado. Form the mixture into balls. 2. Roll balls in almond flour and spritz with coconut oil. Place balls into the air fryer basket. 3. Adjust the temperature to 400ºF (204ºC) and set the timer for 7 minutes. 4. Gently turn tuna bites after 5 minutes. Serve warm.

Cod with Creamy Mustard Sauce

Prep time: 10 minutes | Cook time: 10 minutes | Serves 4

Fish:	black pepper
Oil, for spraying	Mustard Sauce:
1 pound (454 g) cod fillets	½ cup heavy cream
2 tablespoons olive oil	3 tablespoons Dijon mustard
1 tablespoon lemon juice	1 tablespoon unsalted butter
1 teaspoon salt	1 teaspoon salt
½ teaspoon freshly ground	

Make the Fish 1. Line the air fryer basket with parchment and spray lightly with oil. 2. Rub the cod with the olive oil and lemon juice. Season with the salt and black pepper. 3. Place the cod in the prepared basket. You may need to work in batches, depending on the size of your air fryer. 4. Roast at 350ºF (177ºC) for 5 minutes. Increase the temperature to 400ºF (204ºC) and cook for another 5 minutes, until flaky and the internal temperature reaches 145ºF (63ºC). Make the Mustard Sauce 5. In a small saucepan, mix together the heavy cream, mustard, butter, and salt and bring to a simmer over low heat. Cook for 3 to 4 minutes, or until the sauce starts to thicken. 6. Transfer the cod to a serving plate and drizzle with the mustard sauce. Serve immediately.

Panko Catfish Nuggets

Prep time: 10 minutes | Cook time: 7 to 8 minutes | Serves 4

2 medium catfish fillets, cut into chunks (approximately 1 × 2 inch)	2 tablespoons skim milk
	½ cup cornstarch
Salt and pepper, to taste	1 cup panko bread crumbs
2 eggs	Cooking spray

1. Preheat the air fryer to 390ºF (199ºC). 2. In a medium bowl, season the fish chunks with salt and pepper to taste. 3. In a small bowl, beat together the eggs with milk until well combined. 4. Place the cornstarch and bread crumbs into separate shallow dishes. 5. Dredge the fish chunks one at a time in the cornstarch, coating well on both sides, then dip in the egg mixture, shaking off any excess, finally press well into the bread crumbs. Spritz the fish chunks with cooking spray. 6. Arrange the fish chunks in the air fryer basket in a single layer. You may need to cook in batches depending on the size of your air fryer basket. 7. Fry the fish chunks for 7 to 8 minutes until they are no longer translucent in the center and golden brown. Shake the basket once during cooking. 8. Remove the fish chunks from the basket to a plate. Repeat with the remaining fish chunks. 9. Serve warm.

Fish Sandwich with Tartar Sauce

Prep time: 10 minutes | Cook time: 17 minutes | Serves 2

Tartar Sauce:	pepper
½ cup mayonnaise	Fish:
2 tablespoons dried minced onion	2 tablespoons all-purpose flour
	1 egg, lightly beaten
1 dill pickle spear, finely chopped	1 cup panko
	2 teaspoons lemon pepper
2 teaspoons pickle juice	2 tilapia fillets
¼ teaspoon salt	Cooking spray
⅛ teaspoon ground black	2 hoagie rolls

1. Preheat the air fryer to 400ºF (204ºC). 2. In a small bowl, combine the mayonnaise, dried minced onion, pickle, pickle juice, salt, and pepper. 3. Whisk to combine and chill in the refrigerator while you make the fish. 4. Place a parchment liner in the air fryer basket. 5. Scoop the flour out onto a plate; set aside. 6. Put the beaten egg in a medium shallow bowl. 7. On another plate, mix to combine the panko and lemon pepper. 8. Dredge the tilapia fillets in the flour, then dip in the egg, and then press into the panko mixture. 9. Place the prepared fillets on the liner in the air fryer in a single layer. 10. Spray lightly with cooking spray and air fry for 8 minutes. Carefully flip the fillets, spray with more cooking spray, and air fry for an additional 9 minutes, until golden and crispy. 11. Place each cooked fillet in a hoagie roll, top with a little bit of tartar sauce, and serve.

Air Fried Spring Rolls

Prep time: 10 minutes | Cook time: 17 to 22 minutes | Serves 4

2 teaspoons minced garlic	4 teaspoons soy sauce
2 cups finely sliced cabbage	Salt and freshly ground black
1 cup matchstick cut carrots	pepper, to taste
2 (4-ounce / 113-g) cans tiny shrimp, drained	16 square spring roll wrappers Cooking spray

1. Preheat the air fryer to 370°F (188°C). 2. Spray the air fryer basket lightly with cooking spray. Spray a medium sauté pan with cooking spray. 3. Add the garlic to the sauté pan and cook over medium heat until fragrant, 30 to 45 seconds. Add the cabbage and carrots and sauté until the vegetables are slightly tender, about 5 minutes. 4. Add the shrimp and soy sauce and season with salt and pepper, then stir to combine. Sauté until the moisture has evaporated, 2 more minutes. Set aside to cool. 5. Place a spring roll wrapper on a work surface so it looks like a diamond. Place 1 tablespoon of the shrimp mixture on the lower end of the wrapper. 6. Roll the wrapper away from you halfway, then fold in the right and left sides, like an envelope. Continue to roll to the very end, using a little water to seal the edge. Repeat with the remaining wrappers and filling. 7. Place the spring rolls in the air fryer basket in a single layer, leaving room between each roll. Lightly spray with cooking spray. You may need to cook them in batches. 8. Air fry for 5 minutes. Turn the rolls over, lightly spray with cooking spray, and air fry until heated through and the rolls start to brown, 5 to 10 more minutes. Cool for 5 minutes before serving.

Herbed Shrimp Pita

Prep time: 5 minutes | Cook time: 8 minutes | Serves 4

1 pound (454 g) medium shrimp, peeled and deveined	¼ teaspoon black pepper
2 tablespoons olive oil	4 whole wheat pitas
1 teaspoon dried oregano	4 ounces (113 g) feta cheese, crumbled
½ teaspoon dried thyme	1 cup shredded lettuce
½ teaspoon garlic powder	1 tomato, diced
¼ teaspoon onion powder	¼ cup black olives, sliced
½ teaspoon salt	1 lemon

1. Preheat the oven to 380°F(193°C). 2. In a medium bowl, combine the shrimp with the olive oil, oregano, thyme, garlic powder, onion powder, salt, and black pepper. 3. Pour shrimp in a single layer in the air fryer basket and roast for 6 to 8 minutes, or until cooked through. 4. Remove from the air fryer and divide into warmed pitas with feta, lettuce, tomato, olives, and a squeeze of lemon.

Popcorn Crawfish

Prep time: 15 minutes | Cook time: 18 to 20 minutes | Serves 4

½ cup flour, plus 2 tablespoons	1 (12-ounce / 340-g) package
½ teaspoon garlic powder	frozen crawfish tail meat,
1½ teaspoons Old Bay Seasoning	thawed and drained Oil for misting or cooking
½ teaspoon onion powder	spray
½ cup beer, plus 2 tablespoons	Coating:

1½ cups panko crumbs	½ teaspoon ground black
1 teaspoon Old Bay Seasoning	pepper

1. In a large bowl, mix together the flour, garlic powder, Old Bay Seasoning, and onion powder. Stir in beer to blend. 2. Add crawfish meat to batter and stir to coat. 3. Combine the coating ingredients in food processor and pulse to finely crush the crumbs. Transfer crumbs to shallow dish. 4. Preheat the air fryer to 390°F (199°C). 5. Pour the crawfish and batter into a colander to drain. Stir with a spoon to drain excess batter. 6. Working with a handful of crawfish at a time, roll in crumbs and place on a cookie sheet. It's okay if some of the smaller pieces of crawfish meat stick together. 7. Spray breaded crawfish with oil or cooking spray and place all at once into air fryer basket. 8. Air fry at 390°F (199°C) for 5 minutes. Shake basket or stir and mist again with olive oil or spray. Cook 5 more minutes, shake basket again, and mist lightly again. Continue cooking 3 to 5 more minutes, until browned and crispy.

Garlic Lemon Scallops

Prep time: 5 minutes | Cook time: 10 minutes | Serves 4

4 tablespoons salted butter, melted	8 (1-ounce / 28-g) sea scallops, cleaned and patted dry
4 teaspoons peeled and finely minced garlic	¼ teaspoon salt
½ small lemon, zested and juiced	¼ teaspoon ground black pepper

1. In a small bowl, mix butter, garlic, lemon zest, and lemon juice. Place scallops in an ungreased round nonstick baking dish. Pour butter mixture over scallops, then sprinkle with salt and pepper. 2. Place dish into air fryer basket. Adjust the temperature to 360°F (182°C) and bake for 10 minutes. Scallops will be opaque and firm, and have an internal temperature of 135°F (57°C) when done. Serve warm.

Seasoned Tuna Steaks

Prep time: 5 minutes | Cook time: 9 minutes | Serves 4

1 teaspoon garlic powder	4 tuna steaks
½ teaspoon salt	2 tablespoons olive oil
¼ teaspoon dried thyme	1 lemon, quartered
¼ teaspoon dried oregano	

1. Preheat the air fryer to 380°F(193°C). 2. In a small bowl, whisk together the garlic powder, salt, thyme, and oregano. 3. Coat the tuna steaks with olive oil. Season both sides of each steak with the seasoning blend. Place the steaks in a single layer in the air fryer basket. 4. Roast for 5 minutes, then flip and roast for an additional 3 to 4 minutes.

Lime Lobster Tails

Prep time: 10 minutes | Cook time: 6 minutes | Serves 4

4 lobster tails, peeled	½ teaspoon dried basil
2 tablespoons lime juice	½ teaspoon coconut oil, melted

1. Mix lobster tails with lime juice, dried basil, and coconut oil. 2. Put the lobster tails in the air fryer and cook at 380°F (193°C) for 6 minutes.

Cheesy Tuna Patties

Prep time: 5 minutes | Cook time: 17 to 18 minutes | Serves 4

Tuna Patties:
1 pound (454 g) canned tuna, drained
1 egg, whisked
2 tablespoons shallots, minced
1 garlic clove, minced
1 cup grated Romano cheese

Sea salt and ground black pepper, to taste
1 tablespoon sesame oil
Cheese Sauce:
1 tablespoon butter
1 cup beer
2 tablespoons grated Colby cheese

1. Mix together the canned tuna, whisked egg, shallots, garlic, cheese, salt, and pepper in a large bowl and stir to incorporate. 2. Divide the tuna mixture into four equal portions and form each portion into a patty with your hands. Refrigerate the patties for 2 hours. 3. When ready, brush both sides of each patty with sesame oil. 4. Preheat the air fryer to 360°F (182°C). 5. Place the patties in the air fryer basket and bake for 14 minutes, flipping the patties halfway through, or until lightly browned and cooked through. 6. Meanwhile, melt the butter in a pan over medium heat. 7. Pour in the beer and whisk constantly, or until it begins to bubble. 8. Add the grated Colby cheese and mix well. Continue cooking for 3 to 4 minutes, or until the cheese melts. Remove the patties from the basket to a plate. Drizzle them with the cheese sauce and serve immediately.

Chapter 7   Snacks and Appetizers

Crispy Green Tomatoes with Horseradish

Prep time: 18 minutes | Cook time: 10 to 15 minutes | Serves 4

2 eggs
¼ cup buttermilk
½ cup bread crumbs
½ cup cornmeal
¼ teaspoon salt
1½ pounds (680 g) firm green tomatoes, cut into ¼-inch slices
Cooking spray
Horseradish Sauce:
¼ cup sour cream
¼ cup mayonnaise
2 teaspoons prepared horseradish
½ teaspoon lemon juice
½ teaspoon Worcestershire sauce
⅛ teaspoon black pepper

1. Preheat air fryer to 390°F (199°C). Spritz the air fryer basket with cooking spray. 2. In a small bowl, whisk together all the ingredients for the horseradish sauce until smooth. Set aside. 3. In a shallow dish, beat the eggs and buttermilk. 4. In a separate shallow dish, thoroughly combine the bread crumbs, cornmeal, and salt. 5. Dredge the tomato slices, one at a time, in the egg mixture, then roll in the bread crumb mixture until evenly coated. 6. Working in batches, place the tomato slices in the air fryer basket in a single layer. Spray them with cooking spray. 7. Air fry for 10 to 15 minutes, flipping the slices halfway through, or until the tomato slices are nicely browned and crisp. 8. Remove from the basket to a platter and repeat with the remaining tomato slices. 9. Serve drizzled with the prepared horseradish sauce.

Classic Spring Rolls

Prep time: 10 minutes | Cook time: 9 minutes | Makes 16 spring rolls

4 teaspoons toasted sesame oil
6 medium garlic cloves, minced or pressed
1 tablespoon grated peeled fresh ginger
2 cups thinly sliced shiitake mushrooms
4 cups chopped green cabbage
1 cup grated carrot
½ teaspoon sea salt
16 rice paper wrappers
Cooking oil spray (sunflower, safflower, or refined coconut)
Gluten-free sweet and sour sauce or Thai sweet chili sauce, for serving (optional)

1. Place a wok or sauté pan over medium heat until hot. 2. Add the sesame oil, garlic, ginger, mushrooms, cabbage, carrot, and salt. Cook for 3 to 4 minutes, stirring often, until the cabbage is lightly wilted. Remove the pan from the heat. 3. Gently run a rice paper under water. Lay it on a flat nonabsorbent surface. Place about ¼ cup of the cabbage filling in the middle. Once the wrapper is soft enough to roll, fold the bottom up over the filling, fold in the sides, and roll the wrapper all the way up. (Basically, make a tiny burrito.) 4. Repeat step 3 to make the remaining spring rolls until you have the number of spring rolls you want to cook right now (and the amount that will fit in the air fryer basket in a single layer without them touching each other). Refrigerate any leftover filling in an airtight container for about 1 week. 5. Insert the crisper plate into the basket and the basket into the unit. Preheat the unit by selecting AIR FRY, setting the temperature to 390°F (199°C), and setting the time to 3 minutes. Select START/STOP to begin. 6. Once the unit is preheated, spray the crisper plate and the basket with cooking oil. Place the spring rolls into the basket, leaving a little room between them so they don't stick to each other. Spray the top of each spring roll with cooking oil. 7. Select AIR FRY, set the temperature to 390°F (199°C), and set the time to 9 minutes. Select START/STOP to begin. 8. When the cooking is complete, the egg rolls should be crisp-ish and lightly browned. Serve immediately, plain or with a sauce of choice.

Homemade Sweet Potato Chips

Prep time: 5 minutes | Cook time: 15 minutes | Serves 2

1 large sweet potato, sliced thin
⅛ teaspoon salt
2 tablespoons olive oil

1. Preheat the air fryer to 380°F(193°C). 2. In a small bowl, toss the sweet potatoes, salt, and olive oil together until the potatoes are well coated. 3. Put the sweet potato slices into the air fryer and spread them out in a single layer. 4. Fry for 10 minutes. Stir, then air fry for 3 to 5 minutes more, or until the chips reach the preferred level of crispiness.

Parmesan French Fries

Prep time: 10 minutes | Cook time: 25 minutes | Serves 2 to 3

2 to 3 large russet potatoes, peeled and cut into ½-inch sticks
2 teaspoons vegetable or canola oil
¾ cup grated Parmesan cheese
½ teaspoon salt
Freshly ground black pepper, to taste
1 teaspoon fresh chopped parsley

1. Bring a large saucepan of salted water to a boil on the stovetop while you peel and cut the potatoes. Blanch the potatoes in the boiling salted water for 4 minutes while you preheat the air fryer to 400°F (204°C). Strain the potatoes and rinse them with cold water. Dry them well with a clean kitchen towel. 2. Toss the dried potato sticks gently with the oil and place them in the air fryer basket. Air fry for 25 minutes, shaking the basket a few times while the fries cook to help them brown evenly. 3. Combine the Parmesan cheese, salt and pepper. With 2 minutes left on the air fryer cooking time, sprinkle the fries with the Parmesan cheese mixture. Toss the fries to coat them evenly with the cheese mixture and continue to air fry for the final 2 minutes, until the cheese has melted and just starts to brown. Sprinkle the finished fries with chopped parsley, a little more grated Parmesan cheese if you like, and serve.

Ranch Oyster Snack Crackers

Prep time: 3 minutes | Cook time: 12 minutes | Serves 6

Oil, for spraying
¼ cup olive oil
2 teaspoons dry ranch seasoning
1 teaspoon chili powder
½ teaspoon dried dill
½ teaspoon granulated garlic
½ teaspoon salt
1 (9-ounce / 255-g) bag oyster crackers

1. Preheat the air fryer to 325°F (163°C). Line the air fryer basket with parchment and spray lightly with oil. 2. In a large bowl, mix together the olive oil, ranch seasoning, chili powder, dill, garlic, and salt. Add the crackers and toss until evenly coated. 3. Place the mixture in the prepared basket. 4. Cook for 10 to 12 minutes, shaking or stirring every 3 to 4 minutes, or until crisp and golden brown.

Garlicky and Cheesy French Fries

Prep time: 5 minutes | Cook time: 20 to 25 minutes | Serves 4

3 medium russet potatoes, rinsed, dried, and cut into thin wedges or classic fry shapes	½ teaspoon salt
	¼ teaspoon freshly ground black pepper
2 tablespoons extra-virgin olive oil	Cooking oil spray
1 tablespoon granulated garlic	2 tablespoons finely chopped fresh parsley (optional)
⅓ cup grated Parmesan cheese	

1. In a large bowl combine the potato wedges or fries and the olive oil. Toss to coat. 2. Sprinkle the potatoes with the granulated garlic, Parmesan cheese, salt, and pepper, and toss again. 3. Insert the crisper plate into the basket and the basket into the unit. Preheat the unit by selecting AIR FRY, setting the temperature to 400°F (204°C), and setting the time to 3 minutes. Select START/STOP to begin. 4. Once the unit is preheated, spray the crisper plate with cooking oil. Place the potatoes into the basket. 5. Select AIR FRY, set the temperature to 400°F (204°C), and set the time to 20 to 25 minutes. Select START/STOP to begin. 6. After about 10 minutes, remove the basket and shake it so the fries at the bottom come up to the top. Reinsert the basket to resume cooking. 7. When the cooking is complete, top the fries with the parsley (if using) and serve hot.

Crispy Phyllo Artichoke Triangles

Prep time: 15 minutes | Cook time: 9 to 12 minutes | Makes 18 triangles

¼ cup Ricotta cheese	Mozzarella cheese
1 egg white	½ teaspoon dried thyme
⅓ cup minced and drained artichoke hearts	6 sheets frozen phyllo dough, thawed
3 tablespoons grated	2 tablespoons melted butter

1. Preheat the air fryer to 400°F (204°C). 2. In a small bowl, combine the Ricotta cheese, egg white, artichoke hearts, Mozzarella cheese, and thyme, and mix well. 3. Cover the phyllo dough with a damp kitchen towel while you work so it doesn't dry out. Using one sheet at a time, place on the work surface and cut into thirds lengthwise. 4. Put about 1½ teaspoons of the filling on each strip at the base. Fold the bottom right-hand tip of phyllo over the filling to meet the other side in a triangle, then continue folding in a triangle. Brush each triangle with butter to seal the edges. Repeat with the remaining phyllo dough and filling. 5. Place the triangles in the air fryer basket. Bake, 6 at a time, for about 3 to 4 minutes, or until the phyllo is golden brown and crisp. 6. Serve hot.

Spiced Roasted Cashews

Prep time: 5 minutes | Cook time: 10 minutes | Serves 4

2 cups raw cashews	¼ teaspoon chili powder
2 tablespoons olive oil	⅛ teaspoon garlic powder
¼ teaspoon salt	⅛ teaspoon smoked paprika

1. Preheat the air fryer to 360°F (182°C). 2. In a large bowl, toss all of the ingredients together. 3. Pour the cashews into the air fryer basket and roast them for 5 minutes. Shake the basket, then cook for

5 minutes more. 4. Serve immediately.

Eggplant Fries

Prep time: 10 minutes | Cook time: 7 to 8 minutes per batch | Serves 4

1 medium eggplant	crumbs
1 teaspoon ground coriander	1 large egg
1 teaspoon cumin	2 tablespoons water
1 teaspoon garlic powder	Oil for misting or cooking spray
½ teaspoon salt	
1 cup crushed panko bread	

1. Peel and cut the eggplant into fat fries, ⅜- to ½-inch thick. 2. Preheat the air fryer to 390°F (199°C). 3. In a small cup, mix together the coriander, cumin, garlic, and salt. 4. Combine 1 teaspoon of the seasoning mix and panko crumbs in a shallow dish. 5. Place eggplant fries in a large bowl, sprinkle with remaining seasoning, and stir well to combine. 6. Beat eggs and water together and pour over eggplant fries. Stir to coat. 7. Remove eggplant from egg wash, shaking off excess, and roll in panko crumbs. 8. Spray with oil. 9. Place half of the fries in air fryer basket. You should have only a single layer, but it's fine if they overlap a little. 10. Cook for 5 minutes. Shake basket, mist lightly with oil, and cook 2 to 3 minutes longer, until browned and crispy. 11. Repeat step 10 to cook remaining eggplant.

Bacon-Wrapped Shrimp and Jalapeño

Prep time: 20 minutes | Cook time: 26 minutes | Serves 8

24 large shrimp, peeled and deveined, about ¾ pound (340 g)	divided
	12 strips bacon, cut in half
5 tablespoons barbecue sauce,	24 small pickled jalapeño slices

1. Toss together the shrimp and 3 tablespoons of the barbecue sauce. Let stand for 15 minutes. Soak 24 wooden toothpicks in water for 10 minutes. Wrap 1 piece bacon around the shrimp and jalapeño slice, then secure with a toothpick. 2. Preheat the air fryer to 350°F (177°C). 3. Working in batches, place half of the shrimp in the air fryer basket, spacing them ½ inch apart. Air fry for 10 minutes. Turn shrimp over with tongs and air fry for 3 minutes more, or until bacon is golden brown and shrimp are cooked through. 4. Brush with the remaining barbecue sauce and serve.

Garlic-Parmesan Croutons

Prep time: 3 minutes | Cook time: 12 minutes | Serves 4

Oil, for spraying	3 tablespoons olive oil
4 cups cubed French bread	1 tablespoon granulated garlic
1 tablespoon grated Parmesan cheese	½ teaspoon unsalted salt

1. Line the air fryer basket with parchment and spray lightly with oil. 2. In a large bowl, mix together the bread, Parmesan cheese, olive oil, garlic, and salt, tossing with your hands to evenly distribute the seasonings. Transfer the coated bread cubes to the prepared basket. 3. Air fry at 350°F (177°C) for 10 to 12 minutes, stirring once after 5 minutes, or until crisp and golden brown.

Vegetable Pot Stickers

Prep time: 12 minutes | Cook time: 11 to 18 minutes | Makes 12 pot stickers

cup shredded red cabbage	2 garlic cloves, minced
¼ cup chopped button mushrooms	2 teaspoons grated fresh ginger
¼ cup grated carrot	12 gyoza/pot sticker wrappers
2 tablespoons minced onion	2½ teaspoons olive oil, divided

1. In a baking pan, combine the red cabbage, mushrooms, carrot, onion, garlic, and ginger. Add 1 tablespoon of water. Place in the air fryer and air fry at 370°F (188°C) for 3 to 6 minutes, until the vegetables are crisp-tender. Drain and set aside. 2. Working one at a time, place the pot sticker wrappers on a work surface. Top each wrapper with a scant 1 tablespoon of the filling. Fold half of the wrapper over the other half to form a half circle. Dab one edge with water and press both edges together. 3. To another pan, add 1¼ teaspoons of olive oil. Put half of the pot stickers, seam-side up, in the pan. Air fry for 5 minutes, or until the bottoms are light golden brown. Add 1 tablespoon of water and return the pan to the air fryer. 4. Air fry for 4 to 6 minutes more, or until hot. Repeat with the remaining pot stickers, remaining 1¼ teaspoons of oil, and another tablespoon of water. Serve immediately.

Roasted Pearl Onion Dip

Prep time: 5 minutes | Cook time: 12 minutes | Serves 4

2 cups peeled pearl onions	1 tablespoon lemon juice
3 garlic cloves	¼ teaspoon black pepper
3 tablespoons olive oil, divided	⅛ teaspoon red pepper flakes
½ teaspoon salt	Pita chips, vegetables, or
1 cup nonfat plain Greek yogurt	toasted bread for serving (optional)

1. Preheat the air fryer to 360°F(182°C). 2. In a large bowl, combine the pearl onions and garlic with 2 tablespoons of the olive oil until the onions are well coated. 3. Pour the garlic-and-onion mixture into the air fryer basket and roast for 12 minutes. 4. Transfer the garlic and onions to a food processor. Pulse the vegetables several times, until the onions are minced but still have some chunks. 5. In a large bowl, combine the garlic and onions and the remaining 1 tablespoon of olive oil, along with the salt, yogurt, lemon juice, black pepper, and red pepper flakes. 6. Cover and chill for 1 hour before serving with pita chips, vegetables, or toasted bread.

Spinach and Crab Meat Cups

Prep time: 10 minutes | Cook time: 10 minutes | Makes 30 cups

1 (6-ounce / 170-g) can crab meat, drained to yield ⅓ cup meat	3 tablespoons plain yogurt
	¼ teaspoon lemon juice
¼ cup frozen spinach, thawed, drained, and chopped	½ teaspoon Worcestershire sauce
1 clove garlic, minced	30 mini frozen phyllo shells, thawed
½ cup grated Parmesan cheese	Cooking spray

1. Preheat the air fryer to 390°F (199°C). 2. Remove any bits of shell that might remain in the crab meat. 3. Mix the crab meat, spinach, garlic, and cheese together. 4. Stir in the yogurt, lemon juice, and Worcestershire sauce and mix well. 5. Spoon a teaspoon of filling into each phyllo shell. 6. Spray the air fryer basket with cooking spray and arrange half the shells in the basket. Air fry for 5 minutes. Repeat with the remaining shells. 7. Serve immediately.

Baked Ricotta

Prep time: 10 minutes | Cook time: 15 minutes | Makes 2 cups

1 (15-ounce / 425-g) container whole milk Ricotta cheese	1 teaspoon grated lemon zest
3 tablespoons grated Parmesan cheese, divided	1 clove garlic, crushed with press
2 tablespoons extra-virgin olive oil	¼ teaspoon salt
	¼ teaspoon pepper
1 teaspoon chopped fresh thyme leaves	Toasted baguette slices or crackers, for serving

1. Preheat the air fryer to 380°F (193°C). 2. To get the baking dish in and out of the air fryer, create a sling using a 24-inch length of foil, folded lengthwise into thirds. 3. Whisk together the Ricotta, 2 tablespoons of the Parmesan, oil, thyme, lemon zest, garlic, salt, and pepper. Pour into a baking dish. Cover the dish tightly with foil. 4. Place the sling under dish and lift by the ends into the air fryer, tucking the ends of the sling around the dish. Bake for 10 minutes. Remove the foil cover and sprinkle with the remaining 1 tablespoon of the Parmesan. Air fry for 5 more minutes, or until bubbly at edges and the top is browned. 5. Serve warm with toasted baguette slices or crackers.

Asian Rice Logs

Prep time: 30 minutes | Cook time: 5 minutes | Makes 8 rice logs

1½ cups cooked jasmine or sushi rice	⅓ cup plain bread crumbs
	¾ cup panko bread crumbs
¼ teaspoon salt	2 tablespoons sesame seeds
2 teaspoons five-spice powder	Orange Marmalade Dipping Sauce:
2 teaspoons diced shallots	
1 tablespoon tamari sauce	½ cup all-natural orange marmalade
1 egg, beaten	
1 teaspoon sesame oil	1 tablespoon soy sauce
2 teaspoons water	

1. Make the rice according to package instructions. While the rice is cooking, make the dipping sauce by combining the marmalade and soy sauce and set aside. 2. Stir together the cooked rice, salt, five-spice powder, shallots, and tamari sauce. 3. Divide rice into 8 equal pieces. With slightly damp hands, mold each piece into a log shape. Chill in freezer for 10 to 15 minutes. 4. Mix the egg, sesame oil, and water together in a shallow bowl. 5. Place the plain bread crumbs on a sheet of wax paper. 6. Mix the panko bread crumbs with the sesame seeds and place on another sheet of wax paper. 7. Roll the rice logs in plain bread crumbs, then dip in egg wash, and then dip in the panko and sesame seeds. 8. Cook the logs at 390°F (199°C) for approximately 5 minutes, until golden brown. 9. Cool slightly before serving with Orange Marmalade Dipping Sauce.

Cheese Wafers

Prep time: 30 minutes | Cook time: 5 to 6 minutes per batch | Makes 4 dozen

4 ounces (113 g) sharp Cheddar cheese, grated	¼ teaspoon salt
¼ cup butter	½ cup crisp rice cereal
½ cup flour	Oil for misting or cooking spray

1. Cream the butter and grated cheese together. You can do it by hand, but using a stand mixer is faster and easier. 2. Sift flour and salt together. Add it to the cheese mixture and mix until well blended. 3. Stir in cereal. 4. Place dough on wax paper and shape into a long roll about 1 inch in diameter. Wrap well with the wax paper and chill for at least 4 hours. 5. When ready to cook, preheat the air fryer to 360°F (182°C). 6. Cut cheese roll into ¼-inch slices. 7. Spray the air fryer basket with oil or cooking spray and place slices in a single layer, close but not touching. 8. Cook for 5 to 6 minutes or until golden brown. When done, place them on paper towels to cool. 9. Repeat previous step to cook remaining cheese bites.

Carrot Chips

Prep time: 15 minutes | Cook time: 8 to 10 minutes | Serves 4

1 tablespoon olive oil, plus more for greasing the basket	and thinly sliced
4 to 5 medium carrots, trimmed	1 teaspoon seasoned salt

1. Preheat the air fryer to 390°F (199°C). Grease the air fryer basket with the olive oil. 2. Toss the carrot slices with 1 tablespoon of olive oil and salt in a medium bowl until thoroughly coated. 3. Arrange the carrot slices in the greased basket. You may need to work in batches to avoid overcrowding. 4. Air fry for 8 to 10 minutes until the carrot slices are crisp-tender. Shake the basket once during cooking. 5. Transfer the carrot slices to a bowl and repeat with the remaining carrots. 6. Allow to cool for 5 minutes and serve.

Shishito Peppers with Herb Dressing

Prep time: 10 minutes | Cook time: 6 minutes | Serves 2 to 4

6 ounces (170 g) shishito peppers	fresh flat-leaf parsley
1 tablespoon vegetable oil	1 tablespoon finely chopped fresh tarragon
Kosher salt and freshly ground black pepper, to taste	1 tablespoon finely chopped fresh chives
½ cup mayonnaise	Finely grated zest of ½ lemon
2 tablespoons finely chopped fresh basil leaves	1 tablespoon fresh lemon juice
2 tablespoons finely chopped	Flaky sea salt, for serving

1. Preheat the air fryer to 400°F (204°C). 2. In a bowl, toss together the shishitos and oil to evenly coat and season with kosher salt and black pepper. Transfer to the air fryer and air fry for 6 minutes, shaking the basket halfway through, or until the shishitos are blistered and lightly charred. 3. Meanwhile, in a small bowl, whisk together the mayonnaise, basil, parsley, tarragon, chives, lemon zest, and lemon juice. 4. Pile the peppers on a plate, sprinkle with flaky sea salt, and serve hot with the dressing.

Tangy Fried Pickle Spears

Prep time: 5 minutes | Cook time: 15 minutes | Serves 6

2 jars sweet and sour pickle spears, patted dry	1 teaspoon sea salt
2 medium-sized eggs	½ teaspoon shallot powder
⅓ cup milk	⅓ teaspoon chili powder
1 teaspoon garlic powder	⅓ cup all-purpose flour
	Cooking spray

1. Preheat the air fryer to 385°F (196°C). Spritz the air fryer basket with cooking spray. 2. In a bowl, beat together the eggs with milk. In another bowl, combine garlic powder, sea salt, shallot powder, chili powder and all-purpose flour until well blended. 3. One by one, roll the pickle spears in the powder mixture, then dredge them in the egg mixture. Dip them in the powder mixture a second time for additional coating. 4. Arrange the coated pickles in the prepared basket. Air fry for 15 minutes until golden and crispy, shaking the basket halfway through to ensure even cooking. 5. Transfer to a plate and let cool for 5 minutes before serving.

Rumaki

Prep time: 30 minutes | Cook time: 10 to 12 minutes per batch | Makes about 24 rumaki

10 ounces (283 g) raw chicken livers	¼ cup low-sodium teriyaki sauce
1 can sliced water chestnuts, drained	12 slices turkey bacon

1. Cut livers into 1½-inch pieces, trimming out tough veins as you slice. 2. Place livers, water chestnuts, and teriyaki sauce in small container with lid. If needed, add another tablespoon of teriyaki sauce to make sure livers are covered. Refrigerate for 1 hour. 3. When ready to cook, cut bacon slices in half crosswise. 4. Wrap 1 piece of liver and 1 slice of water chestnut in each bacon strip. Secure with toothpick. 5. When you have wrapped half of the livers, place them in the air fryer basket in a single layer. 6. Air fry at 390°F (199°C) for 10 to 12 minutes, until liver is done and bacon is crispy. 7. While first batch cooks, wrap the remaining livers. Repeat step 6 to cook your second batch.

Veggie Salmon Nachos

Prep time: 10 minutes | Cook time: 9 to 12 minutes | Serves 6

2 ounces (57 g) baked no-salt corn tortilla chips	1 red bell pepper, chopped
1 (5-ounce / 142-g) baked salmon fillet, flaked	½ cup grated carrot
½ cup canned low-sodium black beans, rinsed and drained	1 jalapeño pepper, minced
	⅓ cup shredded low-sodium low-fat Swiss cheese
	1 tomato, chopped

1. Preheat the air fryer to 360°F (182°C). 2. In a baking pan, layer the tortilla chips. Top with the salmon, black beans, red bell pepper, carrot, jalapeño, and Swiss cheese. 3. Bake in the air fryer for 9 to 12 minutes, or until the cheese is melted and starts to brown. 4. Top with the tomato and serve.

Polenta Fries with Chili-Lime Mayo

Prep time: 10 minutes | Cook time: 28 minutes | Serves 4

Polenta Fries:	½ cup mayonnaise
2 teaspoons vegetable or olive oil	1 teaspoon chili powder
¼ teaspoon paprika	1 teaspoon chopped fresh cilantro
1 pound (454 g) prepared polenta, cut into 3-inch × ½-inch strips	¼ teaspoon ground cumin
	Juice of ½ lime
Chili-Lime Mayo:	Salt and freshly ground black pepper, to taste

1. Preheat the air fryer to 400°F (204°C). 2. Mix the oil and paprika in a bowl. Add the polenta strips and toss until evenly coated. 3. Transfer the polenta strips to the air fry basket and air fry for 28 minutes until the fries are golden brown, shaking the basket once during cooking. Season as desired with salt and pepper. 4. Meanwhile, whisk together all the ingredients for the chili-lime mayo in a small bowl. 5. Remove the polenta fries from the air fryer to a plate and serve alongside the chili-lime mayo as a dipping sauce.

Cheesy Steak Fries

Prep time: 5 minutes | Cook time: 20 minutes | Serves 5

1 (28-ounce / 794-g) bag frozen steak fries	1 cup shredded Mozzarella cheese
Cooking spray	2 scallions, green parts only, chopped
Salt and pepper, to taste	
½ cup beef gravy	

1. Preheat the air fryer to 400°F (204°C). 2. Place the frozen steak fries in the air fryer. Air fry for 10 minutes. Shake the basket and spritz the fries with cooking spray. Sprinkle with salt and pepper. Air fry for an additional 8 minutes. 3. Pour the beef gravy into a medium, microwave-safe bowl. Microwave for 30 seconds, or until the gravy is warm. 4. Sprinkle the fries with the cheese. Air fry for an additional 2 minutes, until the cheese is melted. 5. Transfer the fries to a serving dish. Drizzle the fries with gravy and sprinkle the scallions on top for a green garnish. Serve.

Tortellini with Spicy Dipping Sauce

Prep time: 5 minutes | Cook time: 20 minutes | Serves 4

¾ cup mayonnaise	½ teaspoon dried oregano
2 tablespoons mustard	1½ cups bread crumbs
1 egg	2 tablespoons olive oil
½ cup flour	2 cups frozen cheese tortellini

1. Preheat the air fryer to 380°F (193°C). 2. In a small bowl, combine the mayonnaise and mustard and mix well. Set aside. 3. In a shallow bowl, beat the egg. In a separate bowl, combine the flour and oregano. In another bowl, combine the bread crumbs and olive oil, and mix well. 4. Drop the tortellini, a few at a time, into the egg, then into the flour, then into the egg again, and then into the bread crumbs to coat. Put into the air fryer basket, cooking in batches. 5. Air fry for about 10 minutes, shaking halfway through the cooking time, or until the tortellini are crisp and golden brown on the outside. Serve

with the mayonnaise mixture.

Greek Yogurt Deviled Eggs

Prep time: 15 minutes | Cook time: 15 minutes | Serves 4

4 eggs	⅛ teaspoon paprika
¼ cup nonfat plain Greek yogurt	⅛ teaspoon garlic powder
1 teaspoon chopped fresh dill	Chopped fresh parsley, for garnish
⅛ teaspoon salt	

1. Preheat the air fryer to 260°F(127°C). 2. Place the eggs in a single layer in the air fryer basket and cook for 15 minutes. 3. Quickly remove the eggs from the air fryer and place them into a cold water bath. Let the eggs cool in the water for 10 minutes before removing and peeling them. 4. After peeling the eggs, cut them in half. 5. Spoon the yolk into a small bowl. Add the yogurt, dill, salt, paprika, and garlic powder and mix until smooth. 6. Spoon or pipe the yolk mixture into the halved egg whites. Serve with a sprinkle of fresh parsley on top.

Cream Cheese Wontons

Prep time: 15 minutes | Cook time: 6 minutes | Makes 20 wontons

Oil, for spraying	4 ounces (113 g) cream cheese
20 wonton wrappers	

1. Line the air fryer basket with parchment and spray lightly with oil. 2. Pour some water in a small bowl. 3. Lay out a wonton wrapper and place 1 teaspoon of cream cheese in the center. 4. Dip your finger in the water and moisten the edge of the wonton wrapper. Fold over the opposite corners to make a triangle and press the edges together. 5. Pinch the corners of the triangle together to form a classic wonton shape. Place the wonton in the prepared basket. Repeat with the remaining wrappers and cream cheese. You may need to work in batches, depending on the size of your air fryer. 6. Air fry at 400°F (204°C) for 6 minutes, or until golden brown around the edges.

Peppery Chicken Meatballs

Prep time: 5 minutes | Cook time: 13 to 20 minutes | Makes 16 meatballs

2 teaspoons olive oil	1 egg white
¼ cup minced onion	½ teaspoon dried thyme
¼ cup minced red bell pepper	½ pound (227 g) ground chicken breast
2 vanilla wafers, crushed	

1. Preheat the air fryer to 370°F (188°C). 2. In a baking pan, mix the olive oil, onion, and red bell pepper. Put the pan in the air fryer. Air fry for 3 to 5 minutes, or until the vegetables are tender. 3. In a medium bowl, mix the cooked vegetables, crushed wafers, egg white, and thyme until well combined 4. Mix in the chicken, gently but thoroughly, until everything is combined. 5. Form the mixture into 16 meatballs and place them in the air fryer basket. Air fry for 10 to 15 minutes, or until the meatballs reach an internal temperature of 165°F (74°C) on a meat thermometer. 6. Serve immediately.

Zucchini Feta Roulades

Prep time: 10 minutes | Cook time: 10 minutes | Serves 6

½ cup feta
1 garlic clove, minced
2 tablespoons fresh basil, minced
1 tablespoon capers, minced
⅛ teaspoon salt
⅛ teaspoon red pepper flakes
1 tablespoon lemon juice
2 medium zucchini
12 toothpicks

1. Preheat the air fryer to 360°F (182°C).(If using a grill attachment, make sure it is inside the air fryer during preheating.) 2. In a small bowl, combine the feta, garlic, basil, capers, salt, red pepper flakes, and lemon juice. 3. Slice the zucchini into ⅛-inch strips lengthwise. (Each zucchini should yield around 6 strips.) 4. Spread 1 tablespoon of the cheese filling onto each slice of zucchini, then roll it up and secure it with a toothpick through the middle. 5. Place the zucchini roulades into the air fryer basket in a single layer, making sure that they don't touch each other. 6. Bake or grill in the air fryer for 10 minutes. 7. Remove the zucchini roulades from the air fryer and gently remove the toothpicks before serving.

Jalapeño Poppers

Prep time: 10 minutes | Cook time: 20 minutes | Serves 4

Oil, for spraying
8 ounces (227 g) cream cheese
¾ cup gluten-free bread crumbs, divided
2 tablespoons chopped fresh
parsley
½ teaspoon granulated garlic
½ teaspoon salt
10 jalapeño peppers, halved and seeded

1. Line the air fryer basket with parchment and spray lightly with oil. 2. In a medium bowl, mix together the cream cheese, half of the bread crumbs, the parsley, garlic, and salt. 3. Spoon the mixture into the jalapeño halves. Gently press the stuffed jalapeños in the remaining bread crumbs. 4. Place the stuffed jalapeños in the prepared basket. 5. Air fry at 370°F (188°C) for 20 minutes, or until the cheese is melted and the bread crumbs are crisp and golden brown.

Crispy Mozzarella Sticks

Prep time: 8 minutes | Cook time: 5 minutes | Serves 4

½ cup all-purpose flour
1 egg, beaten
½ cup panko bread crumbs
½ cup grated Parmesan cheese
1 teaspoon Italian seasoning
½ teaspoon garlic salt
6 Mozzarella sticks, halved crosswise
Olive oil spray

1. Put the flour in a small bowl. 2. Put the beaten egg in another small bowl. 3. In a medium bowl, stir together the panko, Parmesan cheese, Italian seasoning, and garlic salt. 4. Roll a Mozzarella-stick half in the flour, dip it into the egg, and then roll it in the panko mixture to coat. Press the coating lightly to make sure the bread crumbs stick to the cheese. Repeat with the remaining 11 Mozzarella sticks. 5. Insert the crisper plate into the basket and the basket into the unit. Preheat the unit by selecting AIR FRY, setting the temperature to 400°F (204°C), and setting the time to 3 minutes. Select START/ STOP to begin. 6. Once the unit is preheated, spray the crisper plate with olive oil and place a parchment paper liner in the basket. Place the Mozzarella sticks into the basket and lightly spray them with olive oil. 7. Select AIR FRY, set the temperature to 400°F (204°C), and set the time to 5 minutes. Select START/STOP to begin. 8. When the cooking is complete, the Mozzarella sticks should be golden and crispy. Let the sticks stand for 1 minute before transferring them to a serving plate. Serve warm.

Roasted Grape Dip

Prep time: 10 minutes | Cook time: 8 to 12 minutes | Serves 6

2 cups seedless red grapes, rinsed and patted dry
1 tablespoon apple cider vinegar
1 tablespoon honey
1 cup low-fat Greek yogurt
2 tablespoons 2% milk
2 tablespoons minced fresh basil

1. In the air fryer basket, sprinkle the grapes with the cider vinegar and drizzle with the honey. Toss to coat. Roast the grapes at 380°F (193°C) for 8 to 12 minutes, or until shriveled but still soft. Remove from the air fryer. 2. In a medium bowl, stir together the yogurt and milk. 3. Gently blend in the grapes and basil. Serve immediately, or cover and chill for 1 to 2 hours.

Black Bean Corn Dip

Prep time: 10 minutes | Cook time: 10 minutes | Serves 4

½ (15-ounce / 425-g) can black beans, drained and rinsed
½ (15-ounce / 425-g) can corn, drained and rinsed
¼ cup chunky salsa
2 ounces (57 g) reduced-fat cream cheese, softened
¼ cup shredded reduced-fat Cheddar cheese
½ teaspoon ground cumin
½ teaspoon paprika
Salt and freshly ground black pepper, to taste

1. Preheat the air fryer to 325°F (163°C). 2. In a medium bowl, mix together the black beans, corn, salsa, cream cheese, Cheddar cheese, cumin, and paprika. Season with salt and pepper and stir until well combined. 3. Spoon the mixture into a baking dish. 4. Place baking dish in the air fryer basket and bake until heated through, about 10 minutes. 5. Serve hot.

Crispy Chili Chickpeas

Prep time: 5 minutes | Cook time: 15 minutes | Serves 4

1 (15-ounce / 425-g) can cooked chickpeas, drained and rinsed
1 tablespoon olive oil
¼ teaspoon salt
⅛ teaspoon chili powder
⅛ teaspoon garlic powder
⅛ teaspoon paprika

1. Preheat the air fryer to 380°F(193°C). 2. In a medium bowl, toss all of the ingredients together until the chickpeas are well coated. 3. Pour the chickpeas into the air fryer and spread them out in a single layer. 4. Roast for 15 minutes, stirring once halfway through the cook time.

Crispy Breaded Beef Cubes

Prep time: 10 minutes | Cook time: 12 to 16 minutes | Serves 4

1 pound (454 g) sirloin tip, cut into 1-inch cubes	1½ cups soft bread crumbs
1 cup cheese pasta sauce	2 tablespoons olive oil
	½ teaspoon dried marjoram

1. Preheat the air fryer to 360°F (182°C). 2. In a medium bowl, toss the beef with the pasta sauce to coat. 3. In a shallow bowl, combine the bread crumbs, oil, and marjoram, and mix well. Drop the beef cubes, one at a time, into the bread crumb mixture to coat thoroughly. 4. Air fry the beef in two batches for 6 to 8 minutes, shaking the basket once during cooking time, until the beef is at least 145°F (63°C) and the outside is crisp and brown. 5. Serve hot.

Chile-Brined Fried Calamari

Prep time: 20 minutes | Cook time: 8 minutes | Serves 2

1 (8-ounce / 227-g) jar sweet or hot pickled cherry peppers	black pepper, to taste
½ pound (227 g) calamari bodies and tentacles, bodies cut into ½-inch-wide rings	3 large eggs, lightly beaten
	Cooking spray
	½ cup mayonnaise
1 lemon	1 teaspoon finely chopped rosemary
2 cups all-purpose flour	
Kosher salt and freshly ground	1 garlic clove, minced

1. Drain the pickled pepper brine into a large bowl and tear the peppers into bite-size strips. Add the pepper strips and calamari to the brine and let stand in the refrigerator for 20 minutes or up to 2 hours. 2. Grate the lemon zest into a large bowl then whisk in the flour and season with salt and pepper. Dip the calamari and pepper strips in the egg, then toss them in the flour mixture until fully coated. Spray the calamari and peppers liberally with cooking spray, then transfer half to the air fryer. Air fry at 400°F (204°C), shaking the basket halfway into cooking, until the calamari is cooked through and golden brown, about 8 minutes. Transfer to a plate and repeat with the remaining pieces. 3. In a small bowl, whisk together the mayonnaise, rosemary, and garlic. Squeeze half the zested lemon to get 1 tablespoon of juice and stir it into the sauce. Season with salt and pepper. Cut the remaining zested lemon half into 4 small wedges and serve alongside the calamari, peppers, and sauce.

Skinny Fries

Prep time: 10 minutes | Cook time: 15 minutes per batch | Serves 2

2 to 3 russet potatoes, peeled and cut into ¼-inch sticks	vegetable oil
2 to 3 teaspoons olive or	Salt, to taste

1. Cut the potatoes into ¼-inch strips. (A mandolin with a julienne blade is really helpful here.) Rinse the potatoes with cold water several times and let them soak in cold water for at least 10 minutes or as long as overnight. 2. Preheat the air fryer to 380°F (193°C). 3. Drain and dry the potato sticks really well, using a clean kitchen towel. Toss the fries with the oil in a bowl and then air fry the fries in two batches at 380°F (193°C) for 15 minutes, shaking the basket a couple of times while they cook. 4. Add the first batch of French fries back into the air fryer basket with the finishing batch and let everything warm through for a few minutes. As soon as the fries are done, season them with salt and transfer to a plate or basket. Serve them warm with ketchup or your favorite dip.

Italian Rice Balls

Prep time: 20 minutes | Cook time: 10 minutes | Makes 8 rice balls

1½ cups cooked sticky rice	(small enough to stuff into olives)
½ teaspoon Italian seasoning blend	2 eggs
¾ teaspoon salt, divided	⅓ cup Italian bread crumbs
8 black olives, pitted	¾ cup panko bread crumbs
1 ounce (28 g) Mozzarella cheese, cut into tiny pieces	Cooking spray

1. Preheat air fryer to 390°F (199°C). 2. Stuff each black olive with a piece of Mozzarella cheese. Set aside. 3. In a bowl, combine the cooked sticky rice, Italian seasoning blend, and ½ teaspoon of salt and stir to mix well. Form the rice mixture into a log with your hands and divide it into 8 equal portions. Mold each portion around a black olive and roll into a ball. 4. Transfer to the freezer to chill for 10 to 15 minutes until firm. 5. In a shallow dish, place the Italian bread crumbs. In a separate shallow dish, whisk the eggs. In a third shallow dish, combine the panko bread crumbs and remaining salt. 6. One by one, roll the rice balls in the Italian bread crumbs, then dip in the whisked eggs, finally coat them with the panko bread crumbs. 7. Arrange the rice balls in the air fryer basket and spritz both sides with cooking spray. 8. Air fry for 10 minutes until the rice balls are golden brown. Flip the balls halfway through the cooking time. 9. Serve warm.

Greek Potato Skins with Olives and Feta

Prep time: 5 minutes | Cook time: 45 minutes | Serves 4

2 russet potatoes	2 tablespoons fresh cilantro, chopped, plus more for serving
3 tablespoons olive oil, divided, plus more for drizzling (optional)	¼ cup Kalamata olives, diced
	¼ cup crumbled feta
1 teaspoon kosher salt, divided	Chopped fresh parsley, for garnish (optional)
¼ teaspoon black pepper	

1. Preheat the air fryer to 380°F (193°C). 2. Using a fork, poke 2 to 3 holes in the potatoes, then coat each with about ½ tablespoon olive oil and ½ teaspoon salt. 3. Place the potatoes into the air fryer basket and bake for 30 minutes. 4. Remove the potatoes from the air fryer, and slice in half. Using a spoon, scoop out the flesh of the potatoes, leaving a ½-inch layer of potato inside the skins, and set the skins aside. 5. In a medium bowl, combine the scooped potato middles with the remaining 2 tablespoons of olive oil, ½ teaspoon of salt, black pepper, and cilantro. Mix until well combined. 6. Divide the potato filling into the now-empty potato skins, spreading it evenly over them. Top each potato with a tablespoon each of the olives and feta. 7. Place the loaded potato skins back into the air fryer and bake for 15 minutes. 8. Serve with additional chopped cilantro or parsley and a drizzle of olive oil, if desired.

Cinnamon-Apple Chips

Prep time: 10 minutes | Cook time: 32 minutes | Serves 4

Oil, for spraying
2 Red Delicious or Honeycrisp apples

¼ teaspoon ground cinnamon, divided

1. Line the air fryer basket with parchment and spray lightly with oil. 2. Trim the uneven ends off the apples. Using a mandoline on the thinnest setting or a sharp knife, cut the apples into very thin slices. Discard the cores. 3. Place half of the apple slices in a single layer in the prepared basket and sprinkle with half of the cinnamon. 4. Place a metal air fryer trivet on top of the apples to keep them from flying around while they are cooking. 5. Air fry at 300°F (149°C) for 16 minutes, flipping every 5 minutes to ensure even cooking. Repeat with the remaining apple slices and cinnamon. 6. Let cool to room temperature before serving. The chips will firm up as they cool.

Corn Dog Muffins

Prep time: 10 minutes | Cook time: 8 to 10 minutes per batch | Makes 8 muffins

1¼ cups sliced kosher hotdogs (3 or 4, depending on size)
½ cup flour
½ cup yellow cornmeal
2 teaspoons baking powder
½ cup skim milk
1 egg

2 tablespoons canola oil
8 foil muffin cups, paper liners removed
Cooking spray
Mustard or your favorite dipping sauce

1. Slice each hotdog in half lengthwise, then cut in ¼-inch half-moon slices. Set aside. 2. Preheat the air fryer to 390°F (199°C). 3. In a large bowl, stir together flour, cornmeal, and baking powder. 4. In a small bowl, beat together the milk, egg, and oil until just blended. 5. Pour egg mixture into dry ingredients and stir with a spoon to mix well. 6. Stir in sliced hot dogs. 7. Spray the foil cups lightly with cooking spray. 8. Divide mixture evenly into muffin cups. 9. Place 4 muffin cups in the air fryer basket and cook for 5 minutes. 10. Reduce temperature to 360°F (182°C) and cook 3 to 5 minutes or until toothpick inserted in center of muffin comes out clean. 11. Repeat steps 9 and 10 to bake remaining corn dog muffins. 12. Serve with mustard or other sauces for dipping.

Mozzarella Arancini

Prep time: 5 minutes | Cook time: 8 to 11 minutes | Makes 16 arancini

2 cups cooked rice, cooled
2 eggs, beaten
1½ cups panko bread crumbs, divided
½ cup grated Parmesan cheese

2 tablespoons minced fresh basil
16 ¾-inch cubes Mozzarella cheese
2 tablespoons olive oil

1. Preheat the air fryer to 400°F (204°C). 2. In a medium bowl, combine the rice, eggs, ½ cup of the bread crumbs, Parmesan cheese, and basil. Form this mixture into 16 1½-inch balls. 3. Poke a hole in each of the balls with your finger and insert a Mozzarella cube. Form the rice mixture firmly around the cheese. 4. On a shallow plate, combine the remaining 1 cup of the bread crumbs with the olive oil and mix well. Roll the rice balls in the bread crumbs to coat. 5. Air fry the arancini in batches for 8 to 11 minutes or until golden brown. 6. Serve hot.

Cheese-Stuffed Blooming Onion

Prep time: 10 minutes | Cook time: 15 minutes | Serves 2

1 large yellow onion (14 ounces / 397 g)
1 tablespoon olive oil
Kosher salt and freshly ground black pepper, to taste
¼ cup plus 2 tablespoons panko bread crumbs
¼ cup grated Parmesan cheese

3 tablespoons mayonnaise
1 tablespoon fresh lemon juice
1 tablespoon chopped fresh flat-leaf parsley
2 teaspoons whole-grain Dijon mustard
1 garlic clove, minced

1. Place the onion on a cutting board and trim the top off and peel off the outer skin. Turn the onion upside down and use a paring knife, cut vertical slits halfway through the onion at ½-inch intervals around the onion, keeping the root intact. When you turn the onion right side up, it should open up like the petals of a flower. Drizzle the cut sides of the onion with the olive oil and season with salt and pepper. Place petal-side up in the air fryer and air fry at 350°F (177°C) for 10 minutes. 2. Meanwhile, in a bowl, stir together the panko, Parmesan, mayonnaise, lemon juice, parsley, mustard, and garlic until incorporated into a smooth paste. 3. Remove the onion from the fryer and stuff the paste all over and in between the onion "petals." Return the onion to the air fryer and air fry at 375°F (191°C) until the onion is tender in the center and the bread crumb mixture is golden brown, about 5 minutes. Remove the onion from the air fryer, transfer to a plate, and serve hot.

Cream Cheese Stuffed Jalapeño Poppers

Prep time: 12 minutes | Cook time: 6 to 8 minutes | Serves 10

8 ounces (227 g) cream cheese, at room temperature
1 cup panko bread crumbs, divided
2 tablespoons fresh parsley,

minced
1 teaspoon chili powder
10 jalapeño peppers, halved and seeded
Cooking oil spray

1. In a small bowl, whisk the cream cheese, ½ cup of panko, the parsley, and chili powder until combined. Stuff the cheese mixture into the jalapeño halves. 2. Sprinkle the tops of the stuffed jalapeños with the remaining ½ cup of panko and press it lightly into the filling. 3. Insert the crisper plate into the basket and the basket into the unit. Preheat the unit by selecting AIR FRY, setting the temperature to 375°F (191°C), and setting the time to 3 minutes. Select START/STOP to begin. 4. Once the unit is preheated, spray the crisper plate with cooking oil. Place the poppers into the basket. 5. Select AIR FRY, set the temperature to 375°F (191°C), and set the time to 8 minutes. Select START/STOP to begin. 6. After 6 minutes, check the poppers. If they are softened and the cheese is melted, they are done. If not, resume cooking. 7. When the cooking is complete, serve warm.

Cheesy Zucchini Tots

Prep time: 15 minutes | Cook time: 6 minutes | Serves 8

2 medium zucchini (about 12 ounces / 340 g), shredded	½ cup panko bread crumbs
1 large egg, whisked	¼ teaspoon black pepper
½ cup grated pecorino romano cheese	1 clove garlic, minced
	Cooking spray

1. Using your hands, squeeze out as much liquid from the zucchini as possible. In a large bowl, mix the zucchini with the remaining ingredients except the oil until well incorporated. 2. Make the zucchini tots: Use a spoon or cookie scoop to place tablespoonfuls of the zucchini mixture onto a lightly floured cutting board and form into 1-inch logs. 3. Preheat air fryer to 375°F (191°C). Spritz the air fryer basket with cooking spray. 4. Place the tots in the basket. You may need to cook in batches to avoid overcrowding. 5. Air fry for 6 minutes until golden brown. 6. Remove from the basket to a serving plate and repeat with the remaining zucchini tots. 7. Serve immediately.

Lemon-Pepper Chicken Drumsticks

Prep time: 30 minutes | Cook time: 30 minutes | Serves 2

2 teaspoons freshly ground coarse black pepper	4 chicken drumsticks (4 ounces / 113 g each)
1 teaspoon baking powder	Kosher salt, to taste
½ teaspoon garlic powder	1 lemon

1. In a small bowl, stir together the pepper, baking powder, and garlic powder. Place the drumsticks on a plate and sprinkle evenly with the baking powder mixture, turning the drumsticks so they're well coated. Let the drumsticks stand in the refrigerator for at least 1 hour or up to overnight. 2. Sprinkle the drumsticks with salt, then transfer them to the air fryer, standing them bone-end up and leaning against the wall of the air fryer basket. Air fry at 375°F (191°C) until cooked through and crisp on the outside, about 30 minutes. 3. Transfer the drumsticks to a serving platter and finely grate the zest of the lemon over them while they're hot. Cut the lemon into wedges and serve with the warm drumsticks.

Old Bay Chicken Wings

Prep time: 10 minutes | Cook time: 12 to 15 minutes | Serves 4

2 tablespoons Old Bay seasoning	2 pounds (907 g) chicken wings, patted dry
2 teaspoons baking powder	Cooking spray
2 teaspoons salt	

1. Preheat the air fryer to 400°F (204°C). Lightly spray the air fryer basket with cooking spray. 2. Combine the Old Bay seasoning, baking powder, and salt in a large zip-top plastic bag. Add the chicken wings, seal, and shake until the wings are thoroughly coated in the seasoning mixture. 3. Lay the chicken wings in the air fryer basket in a single layer and lightly mist with cooking spray. You may need to work in batches to avoid overcrowding. 4. Air fry for 12 to 15 minutes, flipping the wings halfway through, or until the wings are lightly browned and the internal temperature reaches at least 165°F (74°C) on a meat thermometer. 5. Remove from the basket to a plate and repeat with the remaining chicken wings. 6. Serve hot.

Spicy Tortilla Chips

Prep time: 5 minutes | Cook time: 8 to 12 minutes | Serves 4

½ teaspoon ground cumin	Pinch cayenne pepper
½ teaspoon paprika	8 (6-inch) corn tortillas, each cut into 6 wedges
½ teaspoon chili powder	Cooking spray
½ teaspoon salt	

1. Preheat the air fryer to 375°F (191°C). Lightly spritz the air fryer basket with cooking spray. 2. Stir together the cumin, paprika, chili powder, salt, and pepper in a small bowl. 3. Working in batches, arrange the tortilla wedges in the air fryer basket in a single layer. Lightly mist them with cooking spray. Sprinkle some seasoning mixture on top of the tortilla wedges. 4. Air fry for 4 to 6 minutes, shaking the basket halfway through, or until the chips are lightly browned and crunchy. 5. Repeat with the remaining tortilla wedges and seasoning mixture. 6. Let the tortilla chips cool for 5 minutes and serve.

Air Fryer Popcorn with Garlic Salt

Prep time: 3 minutes | Cook time: 10 minutes | Serves 2

2 tablespoons olive oil	1 teaspoon garlic salt
¼ cup popcorn kernels	

1. Preheat the air fryer to 380°F(193°C). 2. Tear a square of aluminum foil the size of the bottom of the air fryer and place into the air fryer. 3. Drizzle olive oil over the top of the foil, and then pour in the popcorn kernels. 4. Roast for 8 to 10 minutes, or until the popcorn stops popping. 5. Transfer the popcorn to a large bowl and sprinkle with garlic salt before serving.

Caramelized Onion Dip

Prep time: 5 minutes | Cook time: 30 minutes | Serves 8 to 10

1 tablespoon butter	½ cup sour cream
1 medium yellow onion, halved and thinly sliced	¼ teaspoon onion powder
¼ teaspoon kosher salt, plus additional for seasoning	1 tablespoon chopped fresh chives
4 ounces (113 g) cream cheese, softened	Black pepper, to taste
	Thick-cut potato chips or vegetable chips

1. Place the butter in a baking pan. Place the pan in the air fryer basket. Set the air fryer to 200°F (93°C) for 1 minute, or until the butter is melted. Add the onions and salt to the pan. 2. Set the air fryer to 200°F (93°C) for 15 minutes, or until onions are softened. Set the air fryer to 375°F (191°C) for 15 minutes, until onions are a deep golden brown, stirring two or three times during the cooking time. Let cool completely. 3. In a medium bowl, stir together the cooked onions, cream cheese, sour cream, onion powder, and chives. Season with salt and pepper. Cover and refrigerate for 2 hours to allow the flavors to blend. 4. Serve the dip with potato chips or vegetable chips.

Grilled Ham and Cheese on Raisin Bread

Prep time: 5 minutes | Cook time: 10 minutes | Serves 1

2 slices raisin bread	ham (about 3 ounces / 85 g)
2 tablespoons butter, softened	4 slices Muenster cheese (about
2 teaspoons honey mustard	3 ounces / 85 g)
3 slices thinly sliced honey	2 toothpicks

1. Preheat the air fryer to 370°F (188°C). 2. Spread the softened butter on one side of both slices of raisin bread and place the bread, buttered side down on the counter. Spread the honey mustard on the other side of each slice of bread. Layer 2 slices of cheese, the ham and the remaining 2 slices of cheese on one slice of bread and top with the other slice of bread. Remember to leave the buttered side of the bread on the outside. 3. Transfer the sandwich to the air fryer basket and secure the sandwich with toothpicks. 4. Air fry for 5 minutes. Flip the sandwich over, remove the toothpicks and air fry for another 5 minutes. Cut the sandwich in half and enjoy!

Cheese Drops

Prep time: 15 minutes | Cook time: 10 minutes per batch | Serves 8

¾ cup all-purpose flour	Dash garlic powder (optional)
½ teaspoon kosher salt	¼ cup butter, softened
¼ teaspoon cayenne pepper	1 cup shredded sharp Cheddar
¼ teaspoon smoked paprika	cheese, at room temperature
¼ teaspoon black pepper	Olive oil spray

1. In a small bowl, combine the flour, salt, cayenne, paprika, pepper, and garlic powder, if using. 2. Using a food processor, cream the butter and cheese until smooth. Gently add the seasoned flour and process until the dough is well combined, smooth, and no longer sticky. (Or make the dough in a stand mixer fitted with the paddle attachment: Cream the butter and cheese on medium speed until smooth, then add the seasoned flour and beat at low speed until smooth.) 3. Divide the dough into 32 equal-size pieces. On a lightly floured surface, roll each piece into a small ball. 4. Spray the air fryer basket with oil spray. Arrange 16 cheese drops in the basket. Set the air fryer to 325°F (163°C) for 10 minutes, or until drops are just starting to brown. Transfer to a wire rack. Repeat with remaining dough, checking for doneness at 8 minutes. 5. Cool the cheese drops completely on the wire rack. Store in an airtight container until ready to serve, or up to 1 or 2 days.

Five-Ingredient Falafel with Garlic-Yogurt Sauce

Prep time: 5 minutes | Cook time: 15 minutes | Serves 4

Falafel:	Salt
1 (15-ounce / 425-g) can	Garlic-Yogurt Sauce:
chickpeas, drained and rinsed	1 cup nonfat plain Greek
½ cup fresh parsley	yogurt
2 garlic cloves, minced	1 garlic clove, minced
½ tablespoon ground cumin	1 tablespoon chopped fresh dill
1 tablespoon whole wheat flour	2 tablespoons lemon juice

Make the Falafel: 1. Preheat the air fryer to 360°F(182°C). 2. Put the chickpeas into a food processor. Pulse until mostly chopped, then add the parsley, garlic, and cumin and pulse for another 1 to 2 minutes, or until the ingredients are combined and turning into a dough. 3. Add the flour. Pulse a few more times until combined. The dough will have texture, but the chickpeas should be pulsed into small bits. 4. Using clean hands, roll the dough into 8 balls of equal size, then pat the balls down a bit so they are about ½-thick disks. 5. Spray the basket of the air fryer with olive oil cooking spray, then place the falafel patties in the basket in a single layer, making sure they don't touch each other. 6. Fry in the air fryer for 15 minutes. Make the garlic-yogurt sauce 7. In a small bowl, combine the yogurt, garlic, dill, and lemon juice. 8. Once the falafel are done cooking and nicely browned on all sides, remove them from the air fryer and season with salt. 9. Serve hot with a side of dipping sauce.

Onion Pakoras

Prep time: 30 minutes | Cook time: 10 minutes per batch | Serves 2

2 medium yellow or white	tablespoons chickpea flour
onions, sliced (2 cups)	1 teaspoon ground turmeric
½ cup chopped fresh cilantro	1 teaspoon cumin seeds
2 tablespoons vegetable oil	1 teaspoon kosher salt
1 tablespoon chickpea flour	½ teaspoon cayenne pepper
1 tablespoon rice flour, or 2	Vegetable oil spray

1. In a large bowl, combine the onions, cilantro, oil, chickpea flour, rice flour, turmeric, cumin seeds, salt, and cayenne. Stir to combine. Cover and let stand for 30 minutes or up to overnight. (This allows the onions to release moisture, creating a batter.) Mix well before using. 2. Spray the air fryer basket generously with vegetable oil spray. Drop half of the batter in 6 heaping tablespoons into the basket. Set the air fryer to 350°F (177°C) for 8 minutes. Carefully turn the pakoras over and spray with oil spray. Set the air fryer for 2 minutes, or until the batter is cooked through and crisp. 3. Repeat with remaining batter to make 6 more pakoras, checking at 6 minutes for doneness. Serve hot.

Onion Pakoras

Prep time: 30 minutes | Cook time: 10 minutes per batch | Serves 2

2 medium yellow or white	tablespoons chickpea flour
onions, sliced (2 cups)	1 teaspoon ground turmeric
½ cup chopped fresh cilantro	1 teaspoon cumin seeds
2 tablespoons vegetable oil	1 teaspoon kosher salt
1 tablespoon chickpea flour	½ teaspoon cayenne pepper
1 tablespoon rice flour, or 2	Vegetable oil spray

1. In a large bowl, combine the onions, cilantro, oil, chickpea flour, rice flour, turmeric, cumin seeds, salt, and cayenne. Stir to combine. Cover and let stand for 30 minutes or up to overnight. (This allows the onions to release moisture, creating a batter.) Mix well before using. 2. Spray the air fryer basket generously with vegetable oil spray. Drop half of the batter in 6 heaping tablespoons into the basket. Set the air fryer to 350°F (177°C) for 8 minutes. Carefully turn the pakoras over and spray with oil spray. Set the air fryer for 2 minutes, or until the batter is cooked through and crisp. 3. Repeat with remaining batter to make 6 more pakoras, checking at 6 minutes for doneness. Serve hot.

Golden Onion Rings

Prep time: 15 minutes | Cook time: 14 minutes per batch | Serves 4

1 large white onion, peeled and cut into ½ to ¾-inch-thick slices (about 2 cups)	black pepper, divided
½ cup 2% milk	¾ teaspoon granulated garlic, divided
1 cup whole-wheat pastry flour, or all-purpose flour	1½ cups whole-grain bread crumbs, or gluten-free bread crumbs
2 tablespoons cornstarch	Cooking oil spray (coconut, sunflower, or safflower)
¾ teaspoon sea salt, divided	Ketchup, for serving (optional)
½ teaspoon freshly ground	

1. Carefully separate the onion slices into rings—a gentle touch is important here. 2. Place the milk in a shallow bowl and set aside. 3. Make the first breading: In a medium bowl, stir together the flour, cornstarch, ¼ teaspoon of salt, ¼ teaspoon of pepper, and ¼ teaspoon of granulated garlic. Set aside. 4. Make the second breading: In a separate medium bowl, stir together the bread crumbs with the remaining ½ teaspoon of salt, the remaining ½ teaspoon of garlic, and the remaining ½ teaspoon of pepper. Set aside. 5. Insert the crisper plate into the basket and the basket into the unit. Preheat the unit by selecting AIR FRY, setting the temperature to 390°F (199°C), and setting the time to 3 minutes. Select START/STOP to begin. 6. Once the unit is preheated, spray the crisper plate and the basket with cooking oil. 7. To make the onion rings, dip one ring into the milk and into the first breading mixture. Dip the ring into the milk again and back into the first breading mixture, coating thoroughly. Dip the ring into the milk one last time and then into the second breading mixture, coating thoroughly. Gently lay the onion ring in the basket. Repeat with additional rings and, as you place them into the basket, do not overlap them too much. Once all the onion rings are in the basket, generously spray the tops with cooking oil. 8. Select AIR FRY, set the temperature to 390°F (199°C), and set the time to 14 minutes. Insert the basket into the unit. Select START/STOP to begin. 9. After 4 minutes, open the unit and spray the rings generously with cooking oil. Close the unit to resume cooking. After 3 minutes, remove the basket and spray the onion rings again. Remove the rings, turn them over, and place them back into the basket. Generously spray them again with oil. Reinsert the basket to resume cooking. After 4 minutes, generously spray the rings with oil one last time. Resume cooking for the remaining 3 minutes, or until the onion rings are very crunchy and brown. 10. When the cooking is complete, serve the hot rings with ketchup, or other sauce of choice.

Mexican Potato Skins

Prep time: 10 minutes | Cook time: 55 minutes | Serves 6

Olive oil	beans
6 medium russet potatoes, scrubbed	1 tablespoon taco seasoning
Salt and freshly ground black pepper, to taste	½ cup salsa
	¾ cup reduced-fat shredded Cheddar cheese
1 cup fat-free refried black	

1. Spray the air fryer basket lightly with olive oil. 2. Spray the potatoes lightly with oil and season with salt and pepper. Pierce each potato a few times with a fork. 3. Place the potatoes in the air fryer basket. Air fry at 400°F (204°C) until fork-tender, 30 to 40 minutes. The cooking time will depend on the size of the potatoes. You can cook the potatoes in the microwave or a standard oven, but they won't get the same lovely crispy skin they will get in the air fryer. 4. While the potatoes are cooking, in a small bowl, mix together the beans and taco seasoning. Set aside until the potatoes are cool enough to handle. 5. Cut each potato in half lengthwise. Scoop out most of the insides, leaving about ¼ inch in the skins so the potato skins hold their shape. 6. Season the insides of the potato skins with salt and black pepper. Lightly spray the insides of the potato skins with oil. You may need to cook them in batches. 7. Place them into the air fryer basket, skin-side down, and air fry until crisp and golden, 8 to 10 minutes. 8. Transfer the skins to a work surface and spoon ½ tablespoon of seasoned refried black beans into each one. Top each with 2 teaspoons salsa and 1 tablespoon shredded Cheddar cheese. 9. Place filled potato skins in the air fryer basket in a single layer. Lightly spray with oil. 10. Air fry until the cheese is melted and bubbly, 2 to 3 minutes.

Pork and Cabbage Egg Rolls

Prep time: 15 minutes | Cook time: 12 minutes | Makes 12 egg rolls

Cooking oil spray	ginger
2 garlic cloves, minced	2 cups shredded green cabbage
12 ounces (340 g) ground pork	4 scallions, green parts (white parts optional), chopped
1 teaspoon sesame oil	24 egg roll wrappers
¼ cup soy sauce	
2 teaspoons grated peeled fresh	

1. Spray a skillet with the cooking oil and place it over medium-high heat. Add the garlic and cook for 1 minute until fragrant. 2. Add the ground pork to the skillet. Using a spoon, break the pork into smaller chunks. 3. In a small bowl, whisk the sesame oil, soy sauce, and ginger until combined. Add the sauce to the skillet. Stir to combine and continue cooking for about 5 minutes until the pork is browned and thoroughly cooked. 4. Stir in the cabbage and scallions. Transfer the pork mixture to a large bowl. 5. Lay the egg roll wrappers on a flat surface. Dip a basting brush in water and glaze each egg roll wrapper along the edges with the wet brush. This will soften the dough and make it easier to roll. 6. Stack 2 egg roll wrappers (it works best if you double-wrap the egg rolls). Scoop 1 to 2 tablespoons of the pork mixture into the center of each wrapper stack. 7. Roll one long side of the wrappers up over the filling. Press firmly on the area with the filling, tucking it in lightly to secure it in place. Fold in the left and right sides. Continue rolling to close. Use the basting brush to wet the seam and seal the egg roll. Repeat with the remaining ingredients. 8. Insert the crisper plate into the basket and the basket into the unit. Preheat the unit by selecting AIR FRY, setting the temperature to 400°F (204°C), and setting the time to 3 minutes. Select START/STOP to begin. 9. Once the unit is preheated, spray the crisper plate with cooking oil. Place the egg rolls into the basket. It is okay to stack them. Spray them with cooking oil. 10. Select AIR FRY, set the temperature to 400°F (204°C), and set the time to 12 minutes. Insert the basket into the unit. Select START/STOP to begin. 11. After 8 minutes, use tongs to flip the egg rolls. Reinsert the basket to resume cooking. 12. When the cooking is complete, serve the egg rolls hot.

Shrimp Pirogues

Prep time: 15 minutes | Cook time: 4 to 5 minutes | Serves 8

12 ounces (340 g) small, peeled, and deveined raw shrimp
3 ounces (85 g) cream cheese, room temperature
2 tablespoons plain yogurt
1 teaspoon lemon juice

1 teaspoon dried dill weed, crushed
Salt, to taste
4 small hothouse cucumbers, each approximately 6 inches long

1. Pour 4 tablespoons water in bottom of air fryer drawer. 2. Place shrimp in air fryer basket in single layer and air fry at 390°F (199°C) for 4 to 5 minutes, just until done. Watch carefully because shrimp cooks quickly, and overcooking makes it tough. 3. Chop shrimp into small pieces, no larger than ½ inch. Refrigerate while mixing the remaining ingredients. 4. With a fork, mash and whip the cream cheese until smooth. 5. Stir in the yogurt and beat until smooth. Stir in lemon juice, dill weed, and chopped shrimp. 6. Taste for seasoning. If needed, add ¼ to ½ teaspoon salt to suit your taste. 7. Store in refrigerator until serving time. 8. When ready to serve, wash and dry cucumbers and split them lengthwise. Scoop out the seeds and turn cucumbers upside down on paper towels to drain for 10 minutes. 9. Just before filling, wipe centers of cucumbers dry. Spoon the shrimp mixture into the pirogues and cut in half crosswise. Serve immediately.

Sausage Balls with Cheese

Prep time: 10 minutes | Cook time: 10 to 11 minutes | Serves 8

12 ounces (340 g) mild ground sausage
1½ cups baking mix
1 cup shredded mild Cheddar cheese

3 ounces (85 g) cream cheese, at room temperature
1 to 2 tablespoons olive oil

1. Preheat the air fryer to 325°F (163°C). Line the air fryer basket with parchment paper. 2. Mix together the ground sausage, baking mix, Cheddar cheese, and cream cheese in a large bowl and stir to incorporate. 3. Divide the sausage mixture into 16 equal portions and roll them into 1-inch balls with your hands. 4. Arrange the sausage balls on the parchment, leaving space between each ball. You may need to work in batches to avoid overcrowding. 5. Brush the sausage balls with the olive oil. Bake for 10 to 11 minutes, shaking the basket halfway through, or until the balls are firm and lightly browned on both sides. 6. Remove from the basket to a plate and repeat with the remaining balls. 7. Serve warm.

Sweet Potato Fries with Mayonnaise

Prep time: 5 minutes | Cook time: 20 minutes | Serves 2 to 3

1 large sweet potato (about 1 pound / 454 g), scrubbed
1 teaspoon vegetable or canola oil
Salt, to taste
Dipping Sauce:

¼ cup light mayonnaise
½ teaspoon sriracha sauce
1 tablespoon spicy brown mustard
1 tablespoon sweet Thai chili sauce

1. Preheat the air fryer to 200°F (93°C). 2. On a flat work surface, cut the sweet potato into fry-shaped strips about ¼ inch wide and ¼ inch thick. You can use a mandoline to slice the sweet potato quickly and uniformly. 3. In a medium bowl, drizzle the sweet potato strips with the oil and toss well. 4. Transfer to the air fryer basket and air fry for 10 minutes, shaking the basket twice during cooking. 5. Remove the air fryer basket and sprinkle with the salt and toss to coat. 6. Increase the air fryer temperature to 400°F (204°C) and air fry for an additional 10 minutes, or until the fries are crispy and tender. Shake the basket a few times during cooking. 7. Meanwhile, whisk together all the ingredients for the sauce in a small bowl. 8. Remove the sweet potato fries from the basket to a plate and serve warm alongside the dipping sauce.

Chapter 8   Vegetables and Sides

Corn and Cilantro Salad

Prep time: 10 minutes | Cook time: 10 minutes | Serves 2

2 ears of corn, shucked (halved crosswise if too large to fit in your air fryer)	cilantro leaves
	1 tablespoon sour cream
1 tablespoon unsalted butter, at room temperature	1 tablespoon mayonnaise
	1 teaspoon adobo sauce (from a can of chipotle peppers in adobo sauce)
1 teaspoon chili powder	
¼ teaspoon garlic powder	
Kosher salt and freshly ground black pepper, to taste	2 tablespoons crumbled queso fresco
1 cup lightly packed fresh	Lime wedges, for serving

1. Brush the corn all over with the butter, then sprinkle with the chili powder and garlic powder, and season with salt and pepper. Place the corn in the air fryer and air fry at 400°F (204°C), turning over halfway through, until the kernels are lightly charred and tender, about 10 minutes. 2. Transfer the ears to a cutting board, let stand 1 minute, then carefully cut the kernels off the cobs and move them to a bowl. Add the cilantro leaves and toss to combine (the cilantro leaves will wilt slightly). 3. In a small bowl, stir together the sour cream, mayonnaise, and adobo sauce. Divide the corn and cilantro among plates and spoon the adobo dressing over the top. Sprinkle with the queso fresco and serve with lime wedges on the side.

Garlic Zucchini and Red Peppers

Prep time: 5 minutes | Cook time: 15 minutes | Serves 6

2 medium zucchini, cubed	2 tablespoons olive oil
1 red bell pepper, diced	½ teaspoon salt
2 garlic cloves, sliced	

1. Preheat the air fryer to 380°F(193°C). 2. In a large bowl, mix together the zucchini, bell pepper, and garlic with the olive oil and salt. 3. Pour the mixture into the air fryer basket, and roast for 7 minutes. Shake or stir, then roast for 7 to 8 minutes more.

Tofu Bites

Prep time: 15 minutes | Cook time: 30 minutes | Serves 4

1 packaged firm tofu, cubed and pressed to remove excess water	1 teaspoon liquid smoke
	1 teaspoon hot sauce
	2 tablespoons sesame seeds
1 tablespoon soy sauce	1 teaspoon garlic powder
1 tablespoon ketchup	Salt and ground black pepper, to taste
1 tablespoon maple syrup	
½ teaspoon vinegar	Cooking spray

1. Preheat the air fryer to 375°F (191°C). 2. Spritz a baking dish with cooking spray. 3. Combine all the ingredients to coat the tofu completely and allow the marinade to absorb for half an hour. 4. Transfer the tofu to the baking dish, then air fry for 15 minutes. Flip the tofu over and air fry for another 15 minutes on the other side. 5. Serve immediately.

Air Fried Potatoes with Olives

Prep time: 15 minutes | Cook time: 40 minutes | Serves 1

1 medium russet potatoes, scrubbed and peeled	Dollop of butter
	Dollop of cream cheese
1 teaspoon olive oil	1 tablespoon Kalamata olives
¼ teaspoon onion powder	1 tablespoon chopped chives
⅛ teaspoon salt	

1. Preheat the air fryer to 400°F (204°C). 2. In a bowl, coat the potatoes with the onion powder, salt, olive oil, and butter. 3. Transfer to the air fryer and air fry for 40 minutes, turning the potatoes over at the halfway point. 4. Take care when removing the potatoes from the air fryer and serve with the cream cheese, Kalamata olives and chives on top.

Radish Chips

Prep time: 10 minutes | Cook time: 5 minutes | Serves 4

2 cups water	½ teaspoon garlic powder
1 pound (454 g) radishes	2 tablespoons coconut oil, melted
¼ teaspoon onion powder	
¼ teaspoon paprika	

1. Place water in a medium saucepan and bring to a boil on stovetop. 2. Remove the top and bottom from each radish, then use a mandoline to slice each radish thin and uniformly. You may also use the slicing blade in the food processor for this step. 3. Place the radish slices into the boiling water for 5 minutes or until translucent. Remove them from the water and place them into a clean kitchen towel to absorb excess moisture. 4. Toss the radish chips in a large bowl with remaining ingredients until fully coated in oil and seasoning. Place radish chips into the air fryer basket. 5. Adjust the temperature to 320°F (160°C) and air fry for 5 minutes. 6. Shake the basket two or three times during the cooking time. Serve warm.

Broccoli with Sesame Dressing

Prep time: 5 minutes | Cook time: 10 minutes | Serves 4

6 cups broccoli florets, cut into bite-size pieces	2 tablespoons coconut aminos
	2 tablespoons sesame oil
1 tablespoon olive oil	½ teaspoon Swerve
¼ teaspoon salt	¼ teaspoon red pepper flakes (optional)
2 tablespoons sesame seeds	
2 tablespoons rice vinegar	

1. Preheat the air fryer to 400°F (204°C). 2. In a large bowl, toss the broccoli with the olive oil and salt until thoroughly coated. 3. Transfer the broccoli to the air fryer basket. Pausing halfway through the cooking time to shake the basket, air fry for 10 minutes until the stems are tender and the edges are beginning to crisp. 4. Meanwhile, in the same large bowl, whisk together the sesame seeds, vinegar, coconut aminos, sesame oil, Swerve, and red pepper flakes (if using). 5. Transfer the broccoli to the bowl and toss until thoroughly coated with the seasonings. Serve warm or at room temperature.

Rosemary New Potatoes

Prep time: 10 minutes | Cook time: 5 to 6 minutes | Serves 4

3 large red potatoes (enough to make 3 cups sliced)	⅛ teaspoon salt
¼ teaspoon ground rosemary	⅛ teaspoon ground black pepper
¼ teaspoon ground thyme	2 teaspoons extra-light olive oil

1. Preheat the air fryer to 330°F (166°C). 2. Place potatoes in large bowl and sprinkle with rosemary, thyme, salt, and pepper. 3. Stir with a spoon to distribute seasonings evenly. 4. Add oil to potatoes and stir again to coat well. 5. Air fry at 330°F (166°C) for 4 minutes. Stir and break apart any that have stuck together. 6. Cook an additional 1 to 2 minutes or until fork-tender.

Buttery Green Beans

Prep time: 5 minutes | Cook time: 8 to 10 minutes | Serves 6

1 pound (454 g) green beans, trimmed	black pepper, to taste
1 tablespoon avocado oil	¼ cup (4 tablespoons) unsalted butter, melted
1 teaspoon garlic powder	¼ cup freshly grated Parmesan cheese
Sea salt and freshly ground	

1. In a large bowl, toss together the green beans, avocado oil, and garlic powder and season with salt and pepper. 2. Set the air fryer to 400°F (204°C). Arrange the green beans in a single layer in the air fryer basket. Air fry for 8 to 10 minutes, tossing halfway through. 3. Transfer the beans to a large bowl and toss with the melted butter. Top with the Parmesan cheese and serve warm.

Buffalo Cauliflower with Blue Cheese

Prep time: 15 minutes | Cook time: 5 to 7 minutes per batch | Serves 6

1 large head cauliflower, rinsed and separated into small florets	
1 tablespoon extra-virgin olive oil	¼ cup buttermilk
½ teaspoon garlic powder	½ teaspoon hot sauce
Cooking oil spray	1 celery stalk, chopped
⅓ cup hot wing sauce	2 tablespoons crumbled blue cheese
⅔ cup nonfat Greek yogurt	

1. Insert the crisper plate into the basket and the basket into the unit. Preheat the unit by selecting AIR FRY, setting the temperature to 375°F (191°C), and setting the time to 3 minutes. Select START/STOP to begin. 2. In a large bowl, toss together the cauliflower florets and olive oil. Sprinkle with the garlic powder and toss again to coat. 3. Once the unit is preheated, spray the crisper plate with cooking oil. Put half the cauliflower into the basket. 4. Select AIR FRY, set the temperature to 375°F (191°C), and set the time to 7 minutes. Select START/STOP to begin. 5. After 3 minutes, remove the basket and shake the cauliflower. Reinsert the basket to resume cooking. After 2 minutes, check the cauliflower. It is done when it is browned. If not, resume cooking. 6. When the cooking is complete, transfer the cauliflower to a serving bowl and toss with half the hot wing sauce.

7. Repeat steps 4, 5, and 6 with the remaining cauliflower and hot wing sauce. 8. In a small bowl, stir together the yogurt, buttermilk, hot sauce, celery, and blue cheese. Drizzle the sauce over the finished cauliflower and serve.

Green Tomato Salad

Prep time: 10 minutes | Cook time: 8 to 10 minutes | Serves 4

4 green tomatoes	2 teaspoons fresh lemon juice
½ teaspoon salt	2 tablespoons finely chopped fresh parsley
1 large egg, lightly beaten	
½ cup peanut flour	1 teaspoon dried dill
1 tablespoon Creole seasoning	1 teaspoon dried chives
1 (5-ounce / 142-g) bag arugula	½ teaspoon salt
Buttermilk Dressing:	½ teaspoon garlic powder
1 cup mayonnaise	½ teaspoon onion powder
½ cup sour cream	

1. Preheat the air fryer to 400°F (204°C). 2. Slice the tomatoes into ½-inch slices and sprinkle with the salt. Let sit for 5 to 10 minutes. 3. Place the egg in a small shallow bowl. In another small shallow bowl, combine the peanut flour and Creole seasoning. Dip each tomato slice into the egg wash, then dip into the peanut flour mixture, turning to coat evenly. 4. Working in batches if necessary, arrange the tomato slices in a single layer in the air fryer basket and spray both sides lightly with olive oil. Air fry until browned and crisp, 8 to 10 minutes. 5. To make the buttermilk dressing: In a small bowl, whisk together the mayonnaise, sour cream, lemon juice, parsley, dill, chives, salt, garlic powder, and onion powder. 6. Serve the tomato slices on top of a bed of the arugula with the dressing on the side.

Broccoli-Cheddar Twice-Baked Potatoes

Prep time: 10 minutes | Cook time: 46 minutes | Serves 4

Oil, for spraying	1 teaspoon granulated garlic
2 medium russet potatoes	1 teaspoon onion powder
1 tablespoon olive oil	½ cup shredded Cheddar cheese
¼ cup broccoli florets	
1 tablespoon sour cream	

1. Line the air fryer basket with parchment and spray lightly with oil. 2. Rinse the potatoes and pat dry with paper towels. Rub the outside of the potatoes with the olive oil and place them in the prepared basket. 3. Air fry at 400°F (204°C) for 40 minutes, or until easily pierced with a fork. Let cool just enough to handle, then cut the potatoes in half lengthwise. 4. Meanwhile, place the broccoli in a microwave-safe bowl, cover with water, and microwave on high for 5 to 8 minutes. Drain and set aside. 5. Scoop out most of the potato flesh and transfer to a medium bowl. 6. Add the sour cream, garlic, and onion powder and stir until the potatoes are mashed. 7. Spoon the potato mixture back into the hollowed potato skins, mounding it to fit, if necessary. Top with the broccoli and cheese. Return the potatoes to the basket. You may need to work in batches, depending on the size of your air fryer. 8. Air fry at 400°F (204°C) for 3 to 6 minutes, or until the cheese has melted. Serve immediately.

Dinner Rolls

Prep time: 10 minutes | Cook time: 12 minutes | Serves 6

1 cup shredded Mozzarella cheese	almond flour
1 ounce (28 g) full-fat cream cheese	¼ cup ground flaxseed
	½ teaspoon baking powder
1 cup blanched finely ground	1 large egg

1. Place Mozzarella, cream cheese, and almond flour in a large microwave-safe bowl. Microwave for 1 minute. Mix until smooth. 2. Add flaxseed, baking powder, and egg until fully combined and smooth. Microwave an additional 15 seconds if it becomes too firm. 3. Separate the dough into six pieces and roll into balls. Place the balls into the air fryer basket. 4. Adjust the temperature to 320°F (160°C) and air fry for 12 minutes. 5. Allow rolls to cool completely before serving.

Roasted Sweet Potatoes

Prep time: 10 minutes | Cook time: 25 minutes | Serves 4

Cooking oil spray	Freshly ground black pepper, to taste
2 sweet potatoes, peeled and cut into 1-inch cubes	½ teaspoon dried thyme
1 tablespoon extra-virgin olive oil	½ teaspoon dried marjoram
Pinch salt	¼ cup grated Parmesan cheese

1. Insert the crisper plate into the basket and the basket into the unit. Preheat the unit by selecting AIR ROAST, setting the temperature to 330°F (166°C), and setting the time to 3 minutes. Select START/STOP to begin. 2. Once the unit is preheated, spray the crisper plate with cooking oil. Put the sweet potato cubes into the basket and drizzle with olive oil. Toss gently to coat. Sprinkle with the salt, pepper, thyme, and marjoram and toss again. 3. Select AIR ROAST, set the temperature to 330°F (166°C), and set the time to 25 minutes. Select START/STOP to begin. 4. After 10 minutes, remove the basket and shake the potatoes. Reinsert the basket to resume cooking. After another 10 minutes, remove the basket and shake the potatoes one more time. Sprinkle evenly with the Parmesan cheese. Reinsert the basket to resume cooking. 5. When the cooking is complete, the potatoes should be tender. Serve immediately.

Zucchini Balls

Prep time: 5 minutes | Cook time: 10 minutes | Serves 4

4 zucchinis	1 tablespoon Italian herbs
1 egg	1 cup grated coconut
½ cup grated Parmesan cheese	

1. Thinly grate the zucchinis and dry with a cheesecloth, ensuring to remove all the moisture. 2. In a bowl, combine the zucchinis with the egg, Parmesan, Italian herbs, and grated coconut, mixing well to incorporate everything. Using the hands, mold the mixture into balls. 3. Preheat the air fryer to 400°F (204°C). 4. Lay the zucchini balls in the air fryer basket and air fry for 10 minutes. 5. Serve hot.

Chili Fingerling Potatoes

Prep time: 10 minutes | Cook time: 16 minutes | Serves 4

1 pound (454 g) fingerling potatoes, rinsed and cut into wedges	1 teaspoon black pepper
	1 teaspoon cayenne pepper
1 teaspoon olive oil	1 teaspoon nutritional yeast
1 teaspoon salt	½ teaspoon garlic powder

1. Preheat the air fryer to 400°F (204°C). 2. Coat the potatoes with the rest of the ingredients. 3. Transfer to the air fryer basket and air fry for 16 minutes, shaking the basket at the halfway point. 4. Serve immediately.

Easy Potato Croquettes

Prep time: 15 minutes | Cook time: 15 minutes | Serves 10

¼ cup nutritional yeast	Salt and ground black pepper, to taste
2 cups boiled potatoes, mashed	
1 flax egg	2 tablespoons vegetable oil
1 tablespoon flour	¼ cup bread crumbs
2 tablespoons chopped chives	

1. Preheat the air fryer to 400°F (204°C). 2. In a bowl, combine the nutritional yeast, potatoes, flax egg, flour, and chives. Sprinkle with salt and pepper as desired. 3. In a separate bowl, mix the vegetable oil and bread crumbs to achieve a crumbly consistency. 4. Shape the potato mixture into small balls and dip each one into the bread crumb mixture. 5. Put the croquettes inside the air fryer and air fry for 15 minutes, ensuring the croquettes turn golden brown. 6. Serve immediately.

Blackened Zucchini with Kimchi-Herb Sauce

Prep time: 10 minutes | Cook time: 15 minutes | Serves 2

2 medium zucchini, ends trimmed (about 6 ounces / 170 g each)	flat-leaf parsley, plus more for garnish
	2 tablespoons rice vinegar
2 tablespoons olive oil	2 teaspoons Asian chili-garlic sauce
½ cup kimchi, finely chopped	
¼ cup finely chopped fresh cilantro	1 teaspoon grated fresh ginger
	Kosher salt and freshly ground
¼ cup finely chopped fresh	black pepper, to taste

1. Brush the zucchini with half of the olive oil, place in the air fryer, and air fry at 400°F (204°C), turning halfway through, until lightly charred on the outside and tender, about 15 minutes. 2. Meanwhile, in a small bowl, combine the remaining 1 tablespoon olive oil, the kimchi, cilantro, parsley, vinegar, chili-garlic sauce, and ginger. 3. Once the zucchini is finished cooking, transfer it to a colander and let it cool for 5 minutes. Using your fingers, pinch and break the zucchini into bite-size pieces, letting them fall back into the colander. Season the zucchini with salt and pepper, toss to combine, then let sit a further 5 minutes to allow some of its liquid to drain. Pile the zucchini atop the kimchi sauce on a plate and sprinkle with more parsley to serve.

Maple-Roasted Tomatoes

Prep time: 15 minutes | Cook time: 20 minutes | Serves 2

10 ounces (283 g) cherry tomatoes, halved	2 sprigs fresh thyme, stems removed
Kosher salt, to taste	1 garlic clove, minced
2 tablespoons maple syrup	Freshly ground black pepper
1 tablespoon vegetable oil	

1. Place the tomatoes in a colander and sprinkle liberally with salt. Let stand for 10 minutes to drain. 2. Transfer the tomatoes cut-side up to a cake pan, then drizzle with the maple syrup, followed by the oil. Sprinkle with the thyme leaves and garlic and season with pepper. Place the pan in the air fryer and roast at 325°F (163°C) until the tomatoes are soft, collapsed, and lightly caramelized on top, about 20 minutes. 3. Serve straight from the pan or transfer the tomatoes to a plate and drizzle with the juices from the pan to serve.

Glazed Carrots

Prep time: 10 minutes | Cook time: 8 to 10 minutes | Serves 4

2 teaspoons honey	1 pound (454 g) baby carrots
1 teaspoon orange juice	2 teaspoons olive oil
½ teaspoon grated orange rind	¼ teaspoon salt
⅛ teaspoon ginger	

1. Combine honey, orange juice, grated rind, and ginger in a small bowl and set aside. 2. Toss the carrots, oil, and salt together to coat well and pour them into the air fryer basket. 3. Roast at 390°F (199°C) for 5 minutes. Shake basket to stir a little and cook for 2 to 4 minutes more, until carrots are barely tender. 4. Pour carrots into a baking pan. 5. Stir the honey mixture to combine well, pour glaze over carrots, and stir to coat. 6. Roast at 360°F (182°C) for 1 minute or just until heated through.

Garlic Cauliflower with Tahini

Prep time: 10 minutes | Cook time: 20 minutes | Serves 4

Cauliflower:	½ teaspoon kosher salt
5 cups cauliflower florets (about 1 large head)	Sauce:
6 garlic cloves, smashed and cut into thirds	2 tablespoons tahini (sesame paste)
3 tablespoons vegetable oil	2 tablespoons hot water
½ teaspoon ground cumin	1 tablespoon fresh lemon juice
½ teaspoon ground coriander	1 teaspoon minced garlic
	½ teaspoon kosher salt

1. For the cauliflower: In a large bowl, combine the cauliflower florets and garlic. Drizzle with the vegetable oil. Sprinkle with the cumin, coriander, and salt. Toss until well coated. 2. Place the cauliflower in the air fryer basket. Set the air fryer to 400°F (204°C) for 20 minutes, turning the cauliflower halfway through the cooking time. 3. Meanwhile, for the sauce: In a small bowl, combine the tahini, water, lemon juice, garlic, and salt. (The sauce will appear curdled at first, but keep stirring until you have a thick, creamy, smooth mixture.) 4. Transfer the cauliflower to a large serving bowl.

Pour the sauce over and toss gently to coat. Serve immediately.

Bacon-Wrapped Asparagus

Prep time: 10 minutes | Cook time: 10 minutes | Serves 4

8 slices reduced-sodium bacon, cut in half	g) asparagus spears, trimmed of woody ends
16 thick (about 1 pound / 454	

1. Preheat the air fryer to 350°F (177°C). 2. Wrap a half piece of bacon around the center of each stalk of asparagus. 3. Working in batches, if necessary, arrange seam-side down in a single layer in the air fryer basket. Air fry for 10 minutes until the bacon is crisp and the stalks are tender.

Creamed Spinach

Prep time: 10 minutes | Cook time: 15 minutes | Serves 4

Vegetable oil spray	4 ounces (113 g) cream cheese, diced
1 (10-ounce / 283-g) package frozen spinach, thawed and squeezed dry	½ teaspoon ground nutmeg
½ cup chopped onion	1 teaspoon kosher salt
2 cloves garlic, minced	1 teaspoon black pepper
	½ cup grated Parmesan cheese

1. Spray a baking pan with vegetable oil spray. 2. In a medium bowl, combine the spinach, onion, garlic, cream cheese, nutmeg, salt, and pepper. Transfer to the prepared pan. 3. Place the pan in the air fryer basket. Set the air fryer to 350°F (177°C) for 10 minutes. Open and stir to thoroughly combine the cream cheese and spinach. 4. Sprinkle the Parmesan cheese on top. Set the air fryer to 400°F (204°C) for 5 minutes, or until the cheese has melted and browned.

Sesame Carrots and Sugar Snap Peas

Prep time: 10 minutes | Cook time: 16 minutes | Serves 4

1 pound (454 g) carrots, peeled sliced on the bias (½-inch slices)	1 tablespoon sesame oil
	1 tablespoon soy sauce
1 teaspoon olive oil	½ teaspoon minced fresh ginger
Salt and freshly ground black pepper, to taste	4 ounces (113 g) sugar snap peas (about 1 cup)
⅓ cup honey	1½ teaspoons sesame seeds

1. Preheat the air fryer to 360°F (182°C). 2. Toss the carrots with the olive oil, season with salt and pepper and air fry for 10 minutes, shaking the basket once or twice during the cooking process. 3. Combine the honey, sesame oil, soy sauce and minced ginger in a large bowl. Add the sugar snap peas and the air-fried carrots to the honey mixture, toss to coat and return everything to the air fryer basket. 4. Turn up the temperature to 400°F (204°C) and air fry for an additional 6 minutes, shaking the basket once during the cooking process. 5. Transfer the carrots and sugar snap peas to a serving bowl. Pour the sauce from the bottom of the cooker over the vegetables and sprinkle sesame seeds over top. Serve immediately.

Crispy Zucchini Sticks

Prep time: 5 minutes | Cook time: 14 minutes | Serves 4

2 small zucchini, cut into 2-inch × ½-inch sticks	¼ teaspoon sea salt
3 tablespoons chickpea flour	⅛ teaspoon freshly ground black pepper
2 teaspoons arrowroot (or cornstarch)	1 tablespoon water
½ teaspoon garlic granules	Cooking spray

1. Preheat the air fryer to 392°F (200°C). 2. Combine the zucchini sticks with the chickpea flour, arrowroot, garlic granules, salt, and pepper in a medium bowl and toss to coat. Add the water and stir to mix well. 3. Spritz the air fryer basket with cooking spray and spread out the zucchini sticks in the basket. Mist the zucchini sticks with cooking spray. 4. Air fry for 14 minutes, shaking the basket halfway through, or until the zucchini sticks are crispy and nicely browned. 5. Serve warm.

Cheese-Walnut Stuffed Mushrooms

Prep time: 5 minutes | Cook time: 10 minutes | Serves 4

4 large portobello mushrooms	⅓ cup minced walnuts
1 tablespoon canola oil	2 tablespoons chopped fresh parsley
½ cup shredded Mozzarella cheese	Cooking spray

1. Preheat the air fryer to 350°F (177°C). Spritz the air fryer basket with cooking spray. 2. On a clean work surface, remove the mushroom stems. Scoop out the gills with a spoon and discard. Coat the mushrooms with canola oil. Top each mushroom evenly with the shredded Mozzarella cheese, followed by the minced walnuts. 3. Arrange the mushrooms in the air fryer and roast for 10 minutes until golden brown. 4. Transfer the mushrooms to a plate and sprinkle the parsley on top for garnish before serving.

Garlic-Parmesan Jícama Fries

Prep time: 10 minutes | Cook time: 25 to 35 minutes | Serves 4

1 medium jícama, peeled	¾ teaspoon sea salt
1 tablespoon avocado oil	½ teaspoon freshly ground black pepper
¼ cup (4 tablespoons) unsalted butter	⅓ cup grated Parmesan cheese
1 tablespoon minced garlic	Chopped fresh parsley, for garnish
¾ teaspoon chopped dried rosemary	Maldon sea salt, for garnish

1. Using a spiralizer or julienne peeler, cut the jícama into shoestrings, then cut them into 3-inch-long sticks. 2. Bring a large pot of water to boil. Add the jícama and cook for about 10 minutes. Drain and dry on paper towels. Transfer to a medium bowl and toss with the oil. 3. Set the air fryer to 400°F (204°C). Arrange the jícama in a single layer in the basket, working in batches if necessary. Air fry for 15 to 25 minutes, checking at intervals, until tender and golden brown. 4. While the fries cook, melt the butter over medium-high heat. Add the garlic, rosemary, salt, and pepper. Cook for about 1 minute. 5. Toss the fries with the garlic butter. Top with the Parmesan cheese, and sprinkle with parsley and Maldon sea salt.

Dill-and-Garlic Beets

Prep time: 10 minutes | Cook time: 30 minutes | Serves 4

4 beets, cleaned, peeled, and sliced	dill
1 garlic clove, minced	¼ teaspoon salt
2 tablespoons chopped fresh	¼ teaspoon black pepper
	3 tablespoons olive oil

1. Preheat the air fryer to 380°F (193°C). 2. In a large bowl, mix together all of the ingredients so the beets are well coated with the oil. 3. Pour the beet mixture into the air fryer basket, and roast for 15 minutes before stirring, then continue roasting for 15 minutes more.

Air-Fried Okra

Prep time: 10 minutes | Cook time: 10 minutes | Serves 4

1 egg	¼ teaspoon freshly ground black pepper
½ cup almond milk	½ pound (227 g) fresh okra, stems removed and chopped into 1-inch slices
½ cup crushed pork rinds	
¼ cup grated Parmesan cheese	
¼ cup almond flour	
1 teaspoon garlic powder	

1. Preheat the air fryer to 400°F (204°C). 2. In a shallow bowl, whisk together the egg and milk. 3. In a second shallow bowl, combine the pork rinds, Parmesan, almond flour, garlic powder, and black pepper. 4. Working with a few slices at a time, dip the okra into the egg mixture followed by the crumb mixture. Press lightly to ensure an even coating. 5. Working in batches if necessary, arrange the okra in a single layer in the air fryer basket and spray lightly with olive oil. Pausing halfway through the cooking time to turn the okra, air fry for 10 minutes until tender and golden brown. Serve warm.

Brussels Sprouts with Pecans and Gorgonzola

Prep time: 10 minutes | Cook time: 25 minutes | Serves 4

½ cup pecans	Salt and freshly ground black pepper, to taste
1½ pounds (680 g) fresh Brussels sprouts, trimmed and quartered	¼ cup crumbled Gorgonzola cheese
2 tablespoons olive oil	

1. Spread the pecans in a single layer of the air fryer and set the heat to 350°F (177°C). Air fry for 3 to 5 minutes until the pecans are lightly browned and fragrant. Transfer the pecans to a plate and continue preheating the air fryer, increasing the heat to 400°F (204°C). 2. In a large bowl, toss the Brussels sprouts with the olive oil and season with salt and black pepper to taste. 3. Working in batches if necessary, arrange the Brussels sprouts in a single layer in the air fryer basket. Pausing halfway through the baking time to shake the basket, air fry for 20 to 25 minutes until the sprouts are tender and starting to brown on the edges. 4. Transfer the sprouts to a serving bowl and top with the toasted pecans and Gorgonzola. Serve warm or at room temperature.

Parmesan Mushrooms

Prep time: 5 minutes | Cook time: 15 minutes | Serves 4

Oil, for spraying	mix
1 pound (454 g) cremini	½ teaspoon salt
mushrooms, stems trimmed	¼ teaspoon freshly ground
2 tablespoons olive oil	black pepper
2 teaspoons granulated garlic	⅓ cup grated Parmesan cheese,
1 teaspoon dried onion soup	divided

1. Line the air fryer basket with parchment and spray lightly with oil. 2. In a large bowl, toss the mushrooms with the olive oil, garlic, onion soup mix, salt, and black pepper until evenly coated. 3. Place the mushrooms in the prepared basket. 4. Roast at 370°F (188°C) for 13 minutes. 5. Sprinkle half of the cheese over the mushrooms and cook for another 2 minutes. 6. Transfer the mushrooms to a serving bowl, add the remaining Parmesan cheese, and toss until evenly coated. Serve immediately.

Grits Casserole

Prep time: 5 minutes | Cook time: 28 to 30 minutes | Serves 4

10 fresh asparagus spears, cut into 1-inch pieces	½ teaspoon garlic powder
	¼ teaspoon salt
2 cups cooked grits, cooled to room temperature	2 slices provolone cheese (about 1½ ounces / 43 g)
1 egg, beaten	Oil for misting or cooking
2 teaspoons Worcestershire sauce	spray

1. Mist asparagus spears with oil and air fry at 390°F (199°C) for 5 minutes, until crisp-tender. 2. In a medium bowl, mix together the grits, egg, Worcestershire, garlic powder, and salt. 3. Spoon half of grits mixture into a baking pan and top with asparagus. 4. Tear cheese slices into pieces and layer evenly on top of asparagus. 5. Top with remaining grits. 6. Bake at 360°F (182°C) for 23 to 25 minutes. The casserole will rise a little as it cooks. When done, the top will have browned lightly with just a hint of crispiness.

Lemon-Garlic Mushrooms

Prep time: 10 minutes | Cook time: 10 to 15 minutes | Serves 6

12 ounces (340 g) sliced mushrooms	1 teaspoon minced garlic
	1 teaspoon freshly squeezed
1 tablespoon avocado oil	lemon juice
Sea salt and freshly ground black pepper, to taste	½ teaspoon red pepper flakes
	2 tablespoons chopped fresh
3 tablespoons unsalted butter	parsley

1. Place the mushrooms in a medium bowl and toss with the oil. Season to taste with salt and pepper. 2. Place the mushrooms in a single layer in the air fryer basket. Set your air fryer to 375°F (191°C) and roast for 10 to 15 minutes, until the mushrooms are tender. 3. While the mushrooms cook, melt the butter in a small pot or skillet over medium-low heat. Stir in the garlic and cook for 30 seconds. Remove the pot from the heat and stir in the lemon juice and red

pepper flakes. 4. Toss the mushrooms with the lemon-garlic butter and garnish with the parsley before serving.

Bacon Potatoes and Green Beans

Prep time: 10 minutes | Cook time: 25 minutes | Serves 4

Oil, for spraying	beans
2 pounds (907 g) medium	1 teaspoon salt
russet potatoes, quartered	½ teaspoon freshly ground
¾ cup bacon bits	black pepper
10 ounces (283 g) fresh green	

1. Line the air fryer basket with parchment and spray lightly with oil. 2. Place the potatoes in the prepared basket. Top with the bacon bits and green beans. Sprinkle with the salt and black pepper and spray liberally with oil. 3. Air fry at 355°F (179°C) for 25 minutes, stirring after 12 minutes and spraying with oil, until the potatoes are easily pierced with a fork.

Curry Roasted Cauliflower

Prep time: 10 minutes | Cook time: 20 minutes | Serves 4

¼ cup olive oil	1 head cauliflower, cut into
2 teaspoons curry powder	bite-size florets
½ teaspoon salt	½ red onion, sliced
¼ teaspoon freshly ground black pepper	2 tablespoons freshly chopped parsley, for garnish (optional)

1. Preheat the air fryer to 400°F (204°C). 2. In a large bowl, combine the olive oil, curry powder, salt, and pepper. Add the cauliflower and onion. Toss gently until the vegetables are completely coated with the oil mixture. Transfer the vegetables to the basket of the air fryer. 3. Pausing about halfway through the cooking time to shake the basket, air fry for 20 minutes until the cauliflower is tender and beginning to brown. Top with the parsley, if desired, before serving.

Crispy Garlic Sliced Eggplant

Prep time: 5 minutes | Cook time: 25 minutes | Serves 4

1 egg	½ teaspoon salt
1 tablespoon water	½ teaspoon paprika
½ cup whole wheat bread crumbs	1 medium eggplant, sliced into ¼-inch-thick rounds
1 teaspoon garlic powder	1 tablespoon olive oil
½ teaspoon dried oregano	

1. Preheat the air fryer to 360°F(182°C). 2. In a medium shallow bowl, beat together the egg and water until frothy. 3. In a separate medium shallow bowl, mix together bread crumbs, garlic powder, oregano, salt, and paprika. 4. Dip each eggplant slice into the egg mixture, then into the bread crumb mixture, coating the outside with crumbs. Place the slices in a single layer in the bottom of the air fryer basket. 5. Drizzle the tops of the eggplant slices with the olive oil, then fry for 15 minutes. Turn each slice and cook for an additional 10 minutes.

Parmesan and Herb Sweet Potatoes

Prep time: 10 minutes | Cook time: 18 minutes | Serves 4

2 large sweet potatoes, peeled and cubed	½ teaspoon salt
¼ cup olive oil	2 tablespoons shredded Parmesan
1 teaspoon dried rosemary	

1. Preheat the air fryer to 360°F(182°C). 2. In a large bowl, toss the sweet potatoes with the olive oil, rosemary, and salt. 3. Pour the potatoes into the air fryer basket and roast for 10 minutes, then stir the potatoes and sprinkle the Parmesan over the top. Continue roasting for 8 minutes more. 4. Serve hot and enjoy.

Parmesan Herb Focaccia Bread

Prep time: 10 minutes | Cook time: 10 minutes | Serves 6

1 cup shredded Mozzarella cheese	½ teaspoon baking soda
1 ounce (28 g) full-fat cream cheese	2 large eggs
1 cup blanched finely ground almond flour	½ teaspoon garlic powder
	¼ teaspoon dried basil
¼ cup ground golden flaxseed	¼ teaspoon dried rosemary
¼ cup grated Parmesan cheese	2 tablespoons salted butter, melted and divided

1. Place Mozzarella, cream cheese, and almond flour into a large microwave-safe bowl and microwave for 1 minute. Add the flaxseed, Parmesan, and baking soda and stir until smooth ball forms. If the mixture cools too much, it will be hard to mix. Return to microwave for 10 to 15 seconds to rewarm if necessary. 2. Stir in eggs. You may need to use your hands to get them fully incorporated. Just keep stirring and they will absorb into the dough. 3. Sprinkle dough with garlic powder, basil, and rosemary and knead into dough. Grease a baking pan with 1 tablespoon melted butter. Press the dough evenly into the pan. Place pan into the air fryer basket. 4. Adjust the temperature to 400°F (204°C) and bake for 10 minutes. 5. At 7 minutes, cover with foil if bread begins to get too dark. 6. Remove and let cool at least 30 minutes. Drizzle with remaining butter and serve.

Golden Garlicky Mushrooms

Prep time: 10 minutes | Cook time: 10 minutes | Serves 4

6 small mushrooms	1 teaspoon parsley
1 tablespoon bread crumbs	1 teaspoon garlic purée
1 tablespoon olive oil	Salt and ground black pepper, to taste
1 ounce (28 g) onion, peeled and diced	

1. Preheat the air fryer to 350°F (177°C). 2. Combine the bread crumbs, oil, onion, parsley, salt, pepper and garlic in a bowl. Cut out the mushrooms' stalks and stuff each cap with the crumb mixture. 3. Air fry in the air fryer for 10 minutes. 4. Serve hot.

Blistered Shishito Peppers with Lime Juice

Prep time: 5 minutes | Cook time: 9 minutes | Serves 3

½ pound (227 g) shishito peppers, rinsed	1 tablespoon tamari or shoyu
	2 teaspoons fresh lime juice
Cooking spray	2 large garlic cloves, minced
Sauce:	

1. Preheat the air fryer to 392°F (200°C). Spritz the air fryer basket with cooking spray. 2. Place the shishito peppers in the basket and spritz them with cooking spray. Roast for 3 minutes. 3. Meanwhile, whisk together all the ingredients for the sauce in a large bowl. Set aside. 4. Shake the basket and spritz them with cooking spray again, then roast for an additional 3 minutes. 5. Shake the basket one more time and spray the peppers with cooking spray. Continue roasting for 3 minutes until the peppers are blistered and nicely browned. 6. Remove the peppers from the basket to the bowl of sauce. Toss to coat well and serve immediately.

Gold Artichoke Hearts

Prep time: 15 minutes | Cook time: 8 minutes | Serves 4

12 whole artichoke hearts packed in water, drained	⅓ cup panko bread crumbs
	1 teaspoon Italian seasoning
½ cup all-purpose flour	Cooking oil spray
1 egg	

1. Squeeze any excess water from the artichoke hearts and place them on paper towels to dry. 2. Place the flour in a small bowl. 3. In another small bowl, beat the egg. 4. In a third small bowl, stir together the panko and Italian seasoning. 5. Dip the artichoke hearts in the flour, in the egg, and into the panko mixture until coated. 6. Insert the crisper plate into the basket and the basket into the unit. Preheat the unit by selecting AIR FRY, setting the temperature to 375°F (191°C), and setting the time to 3 minutes. Select START/STOP to begin. 7. Once the unit is preheated, spray the crisper plate and the basket with cooking oil. Place the breaded artichoke hearts into the basket, stacking them if needed. 8. Select AIR FRY, set the temperature to 375°F (191°C), and set the time to 8 minutes. Select START/STOP to begin. 9. After 4 minutes, use tongs to flip the artichoke hearts. I recommend flipping instead of shaking because the hearts are small, and this will help keep the breading intact. Re-insert the basket to resume cooking. 10. When the cooking is complete, the artichoke hearts should be deep golden brown and crisp. Cool for 5 minutes before serving.

Corn on the Cob

Prep time: 5 minutes | Cook time: 12 to 15 minutes | Serves 4

2 large ears fresh corn	Salt, to taste (optional)
Olive oil for misting	

1. Shuck corn, remove silks, and wash. 2. Cut or break each ear in half crosswise. 3. Spray corn with olive oil. 4. Air fry at 390°F (199°C) for 12 to 15 minutes or until browned as much as you like. 5. Serve plain or with coarsely ground salt.

Lush Vegetable Salad

Prep time: 15 minutes | Cook time: 10 minutes | Serves 4

6 plum tomatoes, halved	oil
2 large red onions, sliced	1 teaspoon paprika
4 long red pepper, sliced	½ lemon, juiced
2 yellow pepper, sliced	Salt and ground black pepper,
6 cloves garlic, crushed	to taste
1 tablespoon extra-virgin olive	1 tablespoon baby capers

1. Preheat the air fryer to 420°F (216°C). 2. Put the tomatoes, onions, peppers, and garlic in a large bowl and cover with the extra-virgin olive oil, paprika, and lemon juice. Sprinkle with salt and pepper as desired. 3. Line the inside of the air fryer basket with aluminum foil. Put the vegetables inside and air fry for 10 minutes, ensuring the edges turn brown. 4. Serve in a salad bowl with the baby capers.

Mexican Corn in a Cup

Prep time: 5 minutes | Cook time: 10 minutes | Serves 4

4 cups frozen corn kernels (do not thaw)	2 tablespoons fresh lemon or lime juice
Vegetable oil spray	1 teaspoon chili powder
2 tablespoons butter	Chopped fresh green onion
¼ cup sour cream	(optional)
¼ cup mayonnaise	Chopped fresh cilantro
¼ cup grated Parmesan cheese (or feta, cotija, or queso fresco)	(optional)

1. Place the corn in the bottom of the air fryer basket and spray with vegetable oil spray. Set the air fryer to 350°F (177°C) for 10 minutes. 2. Transfer the corn to a serving bowl. Add the butter and stir until melted. Add the sour cream, mayonnaise, cheese, lemon juice, and chili powder; stir until well combined. Serve immediately with green onion and cilantro (if using).

Parsnip Fries with Romesco Sauce

Prep time: 20 minutes | Cook time: 24 minutes | Serves 4

Romesco Sauce:	2 Roma tomatoes, peeled
1 red bell pepper, halved and seeded	and seeded (or ⅓ cup canned crushed tomatoes)
1 (1-inch) thick slice of Italian bread, torn into pieces (about 1 to 1½ cups)	1 tablespoon red wine vinegar
	¼ teaspoon smoked paprika
1 cup almonds, toasted	½ teaspoon salt
Olive oil	¾ cup olive oil
½ Jalapeño pepper, seeded	3 parsnips, peeled and cut into long strips
1 tablespoon fresh parsley leaves	2 teaspoons olive oil
1 clove garlic	Salt and freshly ground black pepper, to taste

1. Preheat the air fryer to 400°F (204°C). 2. Place the red pepper halves, cut side down, in the air fryer basket and air fry for 8 to 10 minutes, or until the skin turns black all over. Remove the pepper from the air fryer and let it cool. When it is cool enough to handle, peel the pepper. 3. Toss the torn bread and almonds with a little olive oil and air fry for 4 minutes, shaking the basket a couple times throughout the cooking time. When the bread and almonds are nicely toasted, remove them from the air fryer and let them cool for just a minute or two. 4. Combine the toasted bread, almonds, roasted red pepper, Jalapeño pepper, parsley, garlic, tomatoes, vinegar, smoked paprika and salt in a food processor or blender. Process until smooth. With the processor running, add the olive oil through the feed tube until the sauce comes together in a smooth paste that is barely pourable. 5. Toss the parsnip strips with the olive oil, salt and freshly ground black pepper and air fry at 400°F (204°C) for 10 minutes, shaking the basket a couple times during the cooking process so they brown and cook evenly. Serve the parsnip fries warm with the Romesco sauce to dip into.

Garlic-Parmesan Crispy Baby Potatoes

Prep time: 10 minutes | Cook time: 15 minutes | Serves 4

Oil, for spraying	½ teaspoon salt
1 pound (454 g) baby potatoes	¼ teaspoon freshly ground
½ cup grated Parmesan cheese, divided	black pepper
	¼ teaspoon paprika
3 tablespoons olive oil	2 tablespoons chopped fresh
2 teaspoons granulated garlic	parsley, for garnish
½ teaspoon onion powder	

1. Line the air fryer basket with parchment and spray lightly with oil. 2. Rinse the potatoes, pat dry with paper towels, and place in a large bowl. 3. In a small bowl, mix together ¼ cup of Parmesan cheese, the olive oil, garlic, onion powder, salt, black pepper, and paprika. Pour the mixture over the potatoes and toss to coat. 4. Transfer the potatoes to the prepared basket and spread them out in an even layer, taking care to keep them from touching. You may need to work in batches, depending on the size of your air fryer. 5. Air fry at 400°F (204°C) for 15 minutes, stirring after 7 to 8 minutes, or until easily pierced with a fork. Continue to cook for another 1 to 2 minutes, if needed. 6. Sprinkle with the parsley and the remaining Parmesan cheese and serve.

Herbed Shiitake Mushrooms

Prep time: 10 minutes | Cook time: 5 minutes | Serves 4

8 ounces (227 g) shiitake mushrooms, stems removed and caps roughly chopped	1 teaspoon chopped fresh thyme leaves
	1 teaspoon chopped fresh
1 tablespoon olive oil	oregano
½ teaspoon salt	1 tablespoon chopped fresh
Freshly ground black pepper, to taste	parsley

1. Preheat the air fryer to 400°F (204°C). 2. Toss the mushrooms with the olive oil, salt, pepper, thyme and oregano. Air fry for 5 minutes, shaking the basket once or twice during the cooking process. The mushrooms will still be somewhat chewy with a meaty texture. If you'd like them a little more tender, add a couple of minutes to this cooking time. 3. Once cooked, add the parsley to the mushrooms and toss. Season again to taste and serve.

Glazed Sweet Potato Bites

Prep time: 10 minutes | Cook time: 25 minutes | Serves 4

Oil, for spraying	2 tablespoons honey
3 medium sweet potatoes, peeled and cut into 1-inch pieces	1 tablespoon olive oil
	2 teaspoons ground cinnamon

1. Line the air fryer basket with parchment and spray lightly with oil. 2. In a large bowl, toss together the sweet potatoes, honey, olive oil, and cinnamon until evenly coated. 3. Place the potatoes in the prepared basket. 4. Air fry at 400°F (204°C) for 20 to 25 minutes, or until crispy and easily pierced with a fork.

Garlic and Thyme Tomatoes

Prep time: 10 minutes | Cook time: 15 minutes | Serves 2 to 4

4 Roma tomatoes	pepper, to taste
1 tablespoon olive oil	1 clove garlic, minced
Salt and freshly ground black	½ teaspoon dried thyme

1. Preheat the air fryer to 390°F (199°C). 2. Cut the tomatoes in half and scoop out the seeds and any pithy parts with your fingers. Place the tomatoes in a bowl and toss with the olive oil, salt, pepper, garlic and thyme. 3. Transfer the tomatoes to the air fryer, cut side up. Air fry for 15 minutes. The edges should just start to brown. Let the tomatoes cool to an edible temperature for a few minutes and then use in pastas, on top of crostini, or as an accompaniment to any poultry, meat or fish.

Shishito Pepper Roast

Prep time: 4 minutes | Cook time: 9 minutes | Serves 4

Cooking oil spray (sunflower, safflower, or refined coconut)	
1 pound (454 g) shishito, Anaheim, or bell peppers, rinsed	2 teaspoons freshly squeezed lime juice
1 tablespoon soy sauce	2 large garlic cloves, pressed

1. Insert the crisper plate into the basket and the basket into the unit. Preheat the unit by selecting AIR ROAST, setting the temperature to 390°F (199°C), and setting the time to 3 minutes. Select START/STOP to begin. 2. Once the unit is preheated, spray the crisper plate and the basket with cooking oil. Place the peppers into the basket and spray them with oil. 3. Select AIR ROAST, set the temperature to 390°F (199°C), and set the time to 9 minutes. Select START/STOP to begin. 4. After 3 minutes, remove the basket and shake the peppers. Spray the peppers with more oil. Reinsert the basket to resume cooking. Repeat this step again after 3 minutes. 5. While the peppers roast, in a medium bowl, whisk the soy sauce, lime juice, and garlic until combined. Set aside. 6. When the cooking is complete, several of the peppers should have lots of nice browned spots on them. If using Anaheim or bell peppers, cut a slit in the side of each pepper and remove the seeds, which can be bitter. 7. Place the roasted peppers in the bowl with the sauce. Toss to coat the peppers evenly and serve.

Roasted Brussels Sprouts with Bacon

Prep time: 10 minutes | Cook time: 20 minutes | Serves 4

4 slices thick-cut bacon, chopped (about ¼ pound / 113 g)	sprouts, halved (or quartered if large)
1 pound (454 g) Brussels	Freshly ground black pepper, to taste

1. Preheat the air fryer to 380°F (193°C). 2. Air fry the bacon for 5 minutes, shaking the basket once or twice during the cooking time. 3. Add the Brussels sprouts to the basket and drizzle a little bacon fat from the bottom of the air fryer drawer into the basket. Toss the sprouts to coat with the bacon fat. Air fry for an additional 15 minutes, or until the Brussels sprouts are tender to a knifepoint. 4. Season with freshly ground black pepper.

Chiles Rellenos with Red Chile Sauce

Prep time: 20 minutes | Cook time: 20 minutes | Serves 2

Peppers:	½ cup finely chopped yellow onion
2 poblano peppers, rinsed and dried	2 teaspoons minced garlic
⅔ cup thawed frozen or drained canned corn kernels	1 (6-ounce / 170-g) can tomato paste
1 scallion, sliced	2 tablespoons ancho chile powder
2 tablespoons chopped fresh cilantro	1 teaspoon dried oregano
½ teaspoon kosher salt	1 teaspoon ground cumin
¼ teaspoon black pepper	½ teaspoon kosher salt
⅔ cup grated Monterey Jack cheese	2 cups chicken broth
Sauce:	2 tablespoons fresh lemon juice
3 tablespoons extra-virgin olive oil	Mexican crema or sour cream, for serving

1. For the peppers: Place the peppers in the air fryer basket. Set the air fryer to 400°F (204°C) for 10 minutes, turning the peppers halfway through the cooking time, until their skins are charred. Transfer the peppers to a resealable plastic bag, seal, and set aside to steam for 5 minutes. Peel the peppers and discard the skins. Cut a slit down the center of each pepper, starting at the stem and continuing to the tip. Remove the seeds, being careful not to tear the chile. 2. In a medium bowl, combine the corn, scallion, cilantro, salt, black pepper, and cheese; set aside. 3. Meanwhile, for the sauce: In a large skillet, heat the olive oil over medium-high heat. Add the onion and cook, stirring, until tender, about 5 minutes. Add the garlic and cook, stirring, for 30 seconds. Stir in the tomato paste, chile powder, oregano, and cumin, and salt. Cook, stirring, for 1 minute. Whisk in the broth and lemon juice. Bring to a simmer and cook, stirring occasionally, while the stuffed peppers finish cooking. 4. Cut a slit down the center of each poblano pepper, starting at the stem and continuing to the tip. Remove the seeds, being careful not to tear the chile. 5. Carefully stuff each pepper with half the corn mixture. Place the stuffed peppers in a baking pan. Place the pan in the air fryer basket. Set the air fryer to 400°F (204°C) for 10 minutes, or until the cheese has melted. 6. Transfer the stuffed peppers to a serving platter and drizzle with the sauce and some crema.

Broccoli Tots

Prep time: 15 minutes | Cook time: 10 minutes | Makes 24 tots

2 cups broccoli florets (about ½ pound / 227 g broccoli crowns)
1 egg, beaten
⅛ teaspoon onion powder
¼ teaspoon salt

⅛ teaspoon pepper
2 tablespoons grated Parmesan cheese
¼ cup panko bread crumbs
Oil for misting

1. Steam broccoli for 2 minutes. Rinse in cold water, drain well, and chop finely. 2. In a large bowl, mix broccoli with all other ingredients except the oil. 3. Scoop out small portions of mixture and shape into 24 tots. Lay them on a cookie sheet or wax paper as you work. 4. Spray tots with oil and place in air fryer basket in single layer. 5. Air fry at 390°F (199°C) for 5 minutes. Shake basket and spray with oil again. Cook 5 minutes longer or until browned and crispy.

Simple Zucchini Crisps

Prep time: 5 minutes | Cook time: 14 minutes | Serves 4

2 zucchini, sliced into ¼- to ½-inch-thick rounds (about 2 cups)
¼ teaspoon garlic granules
⅛ teaspoon sea salt
Freshly ground black pepper, to taste (optional)
Cooking spray

1. Preheat the air fryer to 392°F (200°C). Spritz the air fryer basket with cooking spray. 2. Put the zucchini rounds in the air fryer basket, spreading them out as much as possible. Top with a sprinkle of garlic granules, sea salt, and black pepper (if desired). Spritz the zucchini rounds with cooking spray. 3. Roast for 14 minutes, flipping the zucchini rounds halfway through, or until the zucchini rounds are crisp-tender. 4. Let them rest for 5 minutes and serve.

Marinara Pepperoni Mushroom Pizza

Prep time: 5 minutes | Cook time: 18 minutes | Serves 4

4 large portobello mushrooms, stems removed
4 teaspoons olive oil
1 cup marinara sauce

1 cup shredded Mozzarella cheese
10 slices sugar-free pepperoni

1. Preheat the air fryer to 375°F (191°C). 2. Brush each mushroom cap with the olive oil, one teaspoon for each cap. 3. Put on a baking sheet and bake, stem-side down, for 8 minutes. 4. Take out of the air fryer and divide the marinara sauce, Mozzarella cheese and pepperoni evenly among the caps. 5. Air fry for another 10 minutes until browned. 6. Serve hot.

Crispy Chickpeas

Prep time: 5 minutes | Cook time: 15 minutes | Serves 4

1 (15-ounces / 425-g) can chickpeas, drained but not

rinsed
2 tablespoons olive oil

1 teaspoon salt

2 tablespoons lemon juice

1. Preheat the air fryer to 400°F (204°C). 2. Add all the ingredients together in a bowl and mix. Transfer this mixture to the air fryer basket. 3. Air fry for 15 minutes, ensuring the chickpeas become nice and crispy. 4. Serve immediately.

Roasted Radishes with Sea Salt

Prep time: 5 minutes | Cook time: 18 minutes | Serves 4

1 pound (454 g) radishes, ends trimmed if needed

2 tablespoons olive oil
½ teaspoon sea salt

1. Preheat the air fryer to 360°F (182°C). 2. In a large bowl, combine the radishes with olive oil and sea salt. 3. Pour the radishes into the air fryer and roast for 10 minutes. Stir or turn the radishes over and roast for 8 minutes more, then serve.

Creamed Asparagus

Prep time: 10 minutes | Cook time: 18 minutes | Serves 4

½ cup heavy whipping cream
½ cup grated Parmesan cheese
2 ounces (57 g) cream cheese, softened
1 pound (454 g) asparagus,

ends trimmed, chopped into 1-inch pieces
¼ teaspoon salt
¼ teaspoon ground black pepper

1. In a medium bowl, whisk together heavy cream, Parmesan, and cream cheese until combined. 2. Place asparagus into an ungreased round nonstick baking dish. Pour cheese mixture over top and sprinkle with salt and pepper. 3. Place dish into air fryer basket. Adjust the temperature to 350°F (177°C) and set the timer for 18 minutes. Asparagus will be tender when done. Serve warm.

Spiced Butternut Squash

Prep time: 10 minutes | Cook time: 15 minutes | Serves 4

4 cups 1-inch-cubed butternut squash
2 tablespoons vegetable oil

1 to 2 tablespoons brown sugar
1 teaspoon Chinese five-spice powder

1. In a medium bowl, combine the squash, oil, sugar, and five-spice powder. Toss to coat. 2. Place the squash in the air fryer basket. Set the air fryer to 400°F (204°C) for 15 minutes or until tender.

Five-Spice Roasted Sweet Potatoes

Prep time: 10 minutes | Cook time: 12 minutes | Serves 4

½ teaspoon ground cinnamon
¼ teaspoon ground cumin
¼ teaspoon paprika
1 teaspoon chile powder
⅛ teaspoon turmeric
½ teaspoon salt (optional)

Freshly ground black pepper, to taste
2 large sweet potatoes, peeled and cut into ¾-inch cubes (about 3 cups)
1 tablespoon olive oil

1. In a large bowl, mix together cinnamon, cumin, paprika, chile powder, turmeric, salt, and pepper to taste. 2. Add potatoes and stir well. 3. Drizzle the seasoned potatoes with the olive oil and stir until evenly coated. 4. Place seasoned potatoes in a baking pan or an ovenproof dish that fits inside your air fryer basket. 5. Cook for 6 minutes at 390°F (199°C), stop, and stir well. 6. Cook for an additional 6 minutes.

Chapter 9   Vegetarian Mains

Quiche-Stuffed Peppers

Prep time: 5 minutes | Cook time: 15 minutes | Serves 2

2 medium green bell peppers	½ cup chopped broccoli
3 large eggs	½ cup shredded medium
¼ cup full-fat ricotta cheese	Cheddar cheese
¼ cup diced yellow onion	

1. Cut the tops off of the peppers and remove the seeds and white membranes with a small knife. 2. In a medium bowl, whisk eggs and ricotta. 3. Add onion and broccoli. Pour the egg and vegetable mixture evenly into each pepper. Top with Cheddar. Place peppers into a 4-cup round baking dish and place into the air fryer basket. 4. Adjust the temperature to 350°F (177°C) and bake for 15 minutes. 5. Eggs will be mostly firm and peppers tender when fully cooked. Serve immediately.

Broccoli Crust Pizza

Prep time: 15 minutes | Cook time: 12 minutes | Serves 4

3 cups riced broccoli, steamed and drained well	3 tablespoons low-carb Alfredo sauce
1 large egg	½ cup shredded Mozzarella
½ cup grated vegetarian Parmesan cheese	cheese

1. In a large bowl, mix broccoli, egg, and Parmesan. 2. Cut a piece of parchment to fit your air fryer basket. Press out the pizza mixture to fit on the parchment, working in two batches if necessary. Place into the air fryer basket. 3. Adjust the temperature to 370°F (188°C) and air fry for 5 minutes. 4. The crust should be firm enough to flip. If not, add 2 additional minutes. Flip crust. 5. Top with Alfredo sauce and Mozzarella. Return to the air fryer basket and cook an additional 7 minutes or until cheese is golden and bubbling. Serve warm.

Sweet Potatoes with Zucchini

Prep time: 20 minutes | Cook time: 20 minutes | Serves 4

2 large-sized sweet potatoes, peeled and quartered	1½ tablespoons maple syrup
1 medium zucchini, sliced	½ teaspoon porcini powder
1 Serrano pepper, deseeded and thinly sliced	¼ teaspoon mustard powder
	½ teaspoon fennel seeds
1 bell pepper, deseeded and thinly sliced	1 tablespoon garlic powder
	½ teaspoon fine sea salt
1 to 2 carrots, cut into matchsticks	¼ teaspoon ground black pepper
¼ cup olive oil	Tomato ketchup, for serving

1. Put the sweet potatoes, zucchini, peppers, and the carrot into the air fryer basket. Coat with a drizzling of olive oil. 2. Preheat the air fryer to 350°F (177°C). 3. Air fry the vegetables for 15 minutes. 4. In the meantime, prepare the sauce by vigorously combining the other ingredients, except for the tomato ketchup, with a whisk. 5. Lightly grease a baking dish. 6. Transfer the cooked vegetables to the baking dish, pour over the sauce and coat the vegetables well. 7. Increase the temperature to 390°F (199°C) and air fry the vegetables for an additional 5 minutes. 8. Serve warm with a side of ketchup.

Basmati Risotto

Prep time: 10 minutes | Cook time: 30 minutes | Serves 2

1 onion, diced	1 clove garlic, minced
1 small carrot, diced	¾ cup long-grain basmati rice
2 cups vegetable broth, boiling	1 tablespoon olive oil
½ cup grated Cheddar cheese	1 tablespoon unsalted butter

1. Preheat the air fryer to 390°F (199°C). 2. Grease a baking tin with oil and stir in the butter, garlic, carrot, and onion. 3. Put the tin in the air fryer and bake for 4 minutes. 4. Pour in the rice and bake for a further 4 minutes, stirring three times throughout the baking time. 5. Turn the temperature down to 320°F (160°C). 6. Add the vegetable broth and give the dish a gentle stir. Bake for 22 minutes, leaving the air fryer uncovered. 7. Pour in the cheese, stir once more and serve.

Roasted Spaghetti Squash

Prep time: 10 minutes | Cook time: 45 minutes | Serves 6

1 (4-pound / 1.8-kg) spaghetti squash, halved and seeded	melted
	1 teaspoon garlic powder
2 tablespoons coconut oil	2 teaspoons dried parsley
4 tablespoons salted butter,	

1. Brush shell of spaghetti squash with coconut oil. Brush inside with butter. Sprinkle inside with garlic powder and parsley. 2. Place squash skin side down into ungreased air fryer basket, working in batches if needed. Adjust the temperature to 350°F (177°C) and set the timer for 30 minutes. When the timer beeps, flip squash and cook an additional 15 minutes until fork-tender. 3. Use a fork to remove spaghetti strands from shell and serve warm.

Spinach-Artichoke Stuffed Mushrooms

Prep time: 10 minutes | Cook time: 10 to 14 minutes | Serves 4

2 tablespoons olive oil	crumbled
4 large portobello mushrooms, stems removed and gills scraped out	½ cup chopped marinated artichoke hearts
	1 cup frozen spinach, thawed and squeezed dry
½ teaspoon salt	½ cup grated Parmesan cheese
¼ teaspoon freshly ground pepper	2 tablespoons chopped fresh parsley
4 ounces (113 g) goat cheese,	

1. Preheat the air fryer to 400°F (204°C). 2. Rub the olive oil over the portobello mushrooms until thoroughly coated. Sprinkle both sides with the salt and black pepper. Place top-side down on a clean work surface. 3. In a small bowl, combine the goat cheese, artichoke hearts, and spinach. Mash with the back of a fork until thoroughly combined. Divide the cheese mixture among the mushrooms and sprinkle with the Parmesan cheese. 4. Air fry for 10 to 14 minutes until the mushrooms are tender and the cheese has begun to brown. Top with the fresh parsley just before serving.

Tangy Asparagus and Broccoli

Prep time: 25 minutes | Cook time: 22 minutes | Serves 4

½ pound (227 g) asparagus, cut into 1½-inch pieces	Salt and white pepper, to taste
½ pound (227 g) broccoli, cut into 1½-inch pieces	½ cup vegetable broth
2 tablespoons olive oil	2 tablespoons apple cider vinegar

1. Place the vegetables in a single layer in the lightly greased air fryer basket. Drizzle the olive oil over the vegetables. 2. Sprinkle with salt and white pepper. 3. Cook at 380ºF (193ºC) for 15 minutes, shaking the basket halfway through the cooking time. 4. Add ½ cup of vegetable broth to a saucepan; bring to a rapid boil and add the vinegar. Cook for 5 to 7 minutes or until the sauce has reduced by half. 5. Spoon the sauce over the warm vegetables and serve immediately. Bon appétit!

Eggplant Parmesan

Prep time: 15 minutes | Cook time: 17 minutes | Serves 4

1 medium eggplant, ends trimmed, sliced into ½-inch rounds	1 ounce (28 g) 100% cheese crisps, finely crushed
¼ teaspoon salt	½ cup low-carb marinara sauce
2 tablespoons coconut oil	½ cup shredded Mozzarella cheese
½ cup grated Parmesan cheese	

1. Sprinkle eggplant rounds with salt on both sides and wrap in a kitchen towel for 30 minutes. Press to remove excess water, then drizzle rounds with coconut oil on both sides. 2. In a medium bowl, mix Parmesan and cheese crisps. Press each eggplant slice into mixture to coat both sides. 3. Place rounds into ungreased air fryer basket. Adjust the temperature to 350ºF (177ºC) and air fry for 15 minutes, turning rounds halfway through cooking. They will be crispy around the edges when done. 4. Spoon marinara over rounds and sprinkle with Mozzarella. Continue cooking an additional 2 minutes at 350ºF (177ºC) until cheese is melted. Serve warm.

Crispy Tofu

Prep time: 30 minutes | Cook time: 15 to 20 minutes | Serves 4

1 (16-ounce / 454-g) block extra-firm tofu	1 tablespoon chili-garlic sauce
2 tablespoons coconut aminos	1½ teaspoons black sesame seeds
1 tablespoon toasted sesame oil	1 scallion, thinly sliced
1 tablespoon olive oil	

1. Press the tofu for at least 15 minutes by wrapping it in paper towels and setting a heavy pan on top so that the moisture drains. 2. Slice the tofu into bite-size cubes and transfer to a bowl. Drizzle with the coconut aminos, sesame oil, olive oil, and chili-garlic sauce. Cover and refrigerate for 1 hour or up to overnight. 3. Preheat the air fryer to 400ºF (204ºC). 4. Arrange the tofu in a single layer in the air fryer basket. Pausing to shake the pan halfway through the cooking time, air fry for 15 to 20 minutes until crisp. Serve with any juices that accumulate in the bottom of the air fryer, sprinkled with the sesame seeds and sliced scallion.

Black Bean and Tomato Chili

Prep time: 15 minutes | Cook time: 23 minutes | Serves 6

1 tablespoon olive oil	2 cans diced tomatoes
1 medium onion, diced	2 chipotle peppers, chopped
3 garlic cloves, minced	2 teaspoons cumin
1 cup vegetable broth	2 teaspoons chili powder
3 cans black beans, drained and rinsed	1 teaspoon dried oregano
	½ teaspoon salt

1. Over a medium heat, fry the garlic and onions in the olive oil for 3 minutes. 2. Add the remaining ingredients, stirring constantly and scraping the bottom to prevent sticking. 3. Preheat the air fryer to 400ºF (204ºC). 4. Take a dish and place the mixture inside. Put a sheet of aluminum foil on top. 5. Transfer to the air fryer and bake for 20 minutes. 6. When ready, plate up and serve immediately.

Whole Roasted Lemon Cauliflower

Prep time: 5 minutes | Cook time: 15 minutes | Serves 4

1 medium head cauliflower	1 medium lemon
2 tablespoons salted butter, melted	½ teaspoon garlic powder
	1 teaspoon dried parsley

1. Remove the leaves from the head of cauliflower and brush it with melted butter. Cut the lemon in half and zest one half onto the cauliflower. Squeeze the juice of the zested lemon half and pour it over the cauliflower. 2. Sprinkle with garlic powder and parsley. Place cauliflower head into the air fryer basket. 3. Adjust the temperature to 350ºF (177ºC) and air fry for 15 minutes. 4. Check cauliflower every 5 minutes to avoid overcooking. It should be fork tender. 5. To serve, squeeze juice from other lemon half over cauliflower. Serve immediately.

Spinach Cheese Casserole

Prep time: 15 minutes | Cook time: 15 minutes | Serves 4

1 tablespoon salted butter, melted	¼ cup chopped pickled jalapeños
¼ cup diced yellow onion	2 cups fresh spinach, chopped
8 ounces (227 g) full-fat cream cheese, softened	2 cups cauliflower florets, chopped
⅓ cup full-fat mayonnaise	1 cup artichoke hearts, chopped
⅓ cup full-fat sour cream	

1. In a large bowl, mix butter, onion, cream cheese, mayonnaise, and sour cream. Fold in jalapeños, spinach, cauliflower, and artichokes. 2. Pour the mixture into a round baking dish. Cover with foil and place into the air fryer basket. 3. Adjust the temperature to 370ºF (188ºC) and set the timer for 15 minutes. In the last 2 minutes of cooking, remove the foil to brown the top. Serve warm.

Pesto Spinach Flatbread

Prep time: 10 minutes | Cook time: 8 minutes | Serves 4

1 cup blanched finely ground almond flour	cheese
2 ounces (57 g) cream cheese	1 cup chopped fresh spinach leaves
2 cups shredded Mozzarella	2 tablespoons basil pesto

1. Place flour, cream cheese, and Mozzarella in a large microwave-safe bowl and microwave on high 45 seconds, then stir. 2. Fold in spinach and microwave an additional 15 seconds. Stir until a soft dough ball forms. 3. Cut two pieces of parchment paper to fit air fryer basket. Separate dough into two sections and press each out on ungreased parchment to create 6-inch rounds. 4. Spread 1 tablespoon pesto over each flatbread and place rounds on parchment into ungreased air fryer basket. Adjust the temperature to 350°F (177°C) and air fry for 8 minutes, turning crusts halfway through cooking. Flatbread will be golden when done. 5. Let cool 5 minutes before slicing and serving.

Cayenne Tahini Kale

Prep time: 5 minutes | Cook time: 15 minutes | Serves 2 to 4

Dressing:	Kale:
¼ cup tahini	4 cups packed torn kale leaves
¼ cup fresh lemon juice	(stems and ribs removed and
2 tablespoons olive oil	leaves torn into palm-size
1 teaspoon sesame seeds	pieces)
½ teaspoon garlic powder	Kosher salt and freshly ground
¼ teaspoon cayenne pepper	black pepper, to taste

1. Preheat the air fryer to 350°F (177°C). 2. Make the dressing: Whisk together the tahini, lemon juice, olive oil, sesame seeds, garlic powder, and cayenne pepper in a large bowl until well mixed. 3. Add the kale and massage the dressing thoroughly all over the leaves. Sprinkle the salt and pepper to season. 4. Place the kale in the air fryer basket in a single layer and air fry for about 15 minutes, or until the leaves are slightly wilted and crispy. 5. Remove from the basket and serve on a plate.

Garlicky Sesame Carrots

Prep time: 5 minutes | Cook time: 16 minutes | Serves 4 to 6

1 pound (454 g) baby carrots	Freshly ground black pepper,
1 tablespoon sesame oil	to taste
½ teaspoon dried dill	6 cloves garlic, peeled
Pinch salt	3 tablespoons sesame seeds

1. Preheat the air fryer to 380°F (193°C). 2. In a medium bowl, drizzle the baby carrots with the sesame oil. Sprinkle with the dill, salt, and pepper and toss to coat well. 3. Place the baby carrots in the air fryer basket and roast for 8 minutes. 4. Remove the basket and stir in the garlic. Return the basket to the air fryer and roast for another 8 minutes, or until the carrots are lightly browned. 5. Serve sprinkled with the sesame seeds.

Cheesy Cabbage Wedges

Prep time: 5 minutes | Cook time: 20 minutes | Serves 4

4 tablespoons melted butter	cheese
1 head cabbage, cut into wedges	Salt and black pepper, to taste
1 cup shredded Parmesan	½ cup shredded Mozzarella cheese

1. Preheat the air fryer to 380°F (193°C). 2. Brush the melted butter over the cut sides of cabbage wedges and sprinkle both sides with the Parmesan cheese. Season with salt and pepper to taste. 3. Place the cabbage wedges in the air fryer basket and air fry for 20 minutes, flipping the cabbage halfway through, or until the cabbage wedges are lightly browned. 4. Transfer the cabbage wedges to a plate and serve with the Mozzarella cheese sprinkled on top.

Zucchini and Spinach Croquettes

Prep time: 9 minutes | Cook time: 7 minutes | Serves 6

4 eggs, slightly beaten	½ cup Parmesan cheese, grated
½ cup almond flour	⅓ teaspoon red pepper flakes
½ cup goat cheese, crumbled	1 pound (454 g) zucchini,
1 teaspoon fine sea salt	peeled and grated
4 garlic cloves, minced	⅓ teaspoon dried dill weed
1 cup baby spinach	

1. Thoroughly combine all ingredients in a bowl. Now, roll the mixture to form small croquettes. Air fry at 340°F (171°C) for 7 minutes or until golden. Tate, adjust for seasonings and serve warm.

Buffalo Cauliflower Bites with Blue Cheese

Prep time: 10 minutes | Cook time: 8 to 10 minutes | Serves 4

1 large head cauliflower, chopped into florets	½ cup mayonnaise
1 tablespoon olive oil	¼ cup sour cream
Salt and freshly ground black pepper, to taste	2 tablespoons heavy cream
¼ cup unsalted butter, melted	1 tablespoon fresh lemon juice
¼ cup hot sauce	1 clove garlic, minced
Garlic Blue Cheese Dip:	¼ cup crumbled blue cheese
	Salt and freshly ground black pepper, to taste

1. Preheat the air fryer to 400°F (204°C). 2. In a large bowl, combine the cauliflower and olive oil. Season to taste with salt and black pepper. Toss until the vegetables are thoroughly coated. 3. Working in batches, place half of the cauliflower in the air fryer basket. Pausing halfway through the cooking time to shake the basket, air fry for 8 to 10 minutes until the cauliflower is evenly browned. Transfer to a large bowl and repeat with the remaining cauliflower. 4. In a small bowl, whisk together the melted butter and hot sauce. 5. To make the dip: In a small bowl, combine the mayonnaise, sour cream, heavy cream, lemon juice, garlic, and blue cheese. Season to taste with salt and freshly ground black pepper. 6. Just before serving, pour the butter mixture over the cauliflower and toss gently until thoroughly coated. Serve with the dip on the side.

Russet Potato Gratin

Prep time: 10 minutes | Cook time: 35 minutes | Serves 6

½ cup milk	½ cup heavy whipping cream
7 medium russet potatoes, peeled	½ cup grated semi-mature cheese
Salt, to taste	½ teaspoon nutmeg
1 teaspoon black pepper	

1. Preheat the air fryer to 390°F (199°C). 2. Cut the potatoes into wafer-thin slices. 3. In a bowl, combine the milk and cream and sprinkle with salt, pepper, and nutmeg. 4. Use the milk mixture to coat the slices of potatoes. Put in a baking dish. Top the potatoes with the rest of the milk mixture. 5. Put the baking dish into the air fryer basket and bake for 25 minutes. 6. Pour the cheese over the potatoes. 7. Bake for an additional 10 minutes, ensuring the top is nicely browned before serving.

Potato and Broccoli with Tofu Scramble

Prep time: 15 minutes | Cook time: 30 minutes | Serves 3

2½ cups chopped red potato	½ teaspoon onion powder
2 tablespoons olive oil, divided	½ teaspoon garlic powder
1 block tofu, chopped finely	½ cup chopped onion
2 tablespoons tamari	4 cups broccoli florets
1 teaspoon turmeric powder	

1. Preheat the air fryer to 400°F (204°C). 2. Toss together the potatoes and 1 tablespoon of the olive oil. 3. Air fry the potatoes in a baking dish for 15 minutes, shaking once during the cooking time to ensure they fry evenly. 4. Combine the tofu, the remaining 1 tablespoon of the olive oil, turmeric, onion powder, tamari, and garlic powder together, stirring in the onions, followed by the broccoli. 5. Top the potatoes with the tofu mixture and air fry for an additional 15 minutes. Serve warm.

Greek Stuffed Eggplant

Prep time: 15 minutes | Cook time: 20 minutes | Serves 2

1 large eggplant	1 cup fresh spinach
2 tablespoons unsalted butter	2 tablespoons diced red bell pepper
¼ medium yellow onion, diced	
¼ cup chopped artichoke hearts	½ cup crumbled feta

1. Slice eggplant in half lengthwise and scoop out flesh, leaving enough inside for shell to remain intact. Take eggplant that was scooped out, chop it, and set aside. 2. In a medium skillet over medium heat, add butter and onion. Sauté until onions begin to soften, about 3 to 5 minutes. Add chopped eggplant, artichokes, spinach, and bell pepper. Continue cooking 5 minutes until peppers soften and spinach wilts. Remove from the heat and gently fold in the feta. 3. Place filling into each eggplant shell and place into the air fryer basket. 4. Adjust the temperature to 320°F (160°C) and air fry for 20 minutes. 5. Eggplant will be tender when done. Serve warm.

Roasted Vegetable Mélange with Herbs

Prep time: 10 minutes | Cook time: 14 to 18 minutes | Serves 4

1 (8-ounce / 227-g) package sliced mushrooms	1 tablespoon olive oil
1 yellow summer squash, sliced	½ teaspoon dried basil
1 red bell pepper, sliced	½ teaspoon dried thyme
3 cloves garlic, sliced	½ teaspoon dried tarragon

1. Preheat the air fryer to 350°F (177°C). 2. Toss the mushrooms, squash, and bell pepper with the garlic and olive oil in a large bowl until well coated. Mix in the basil, thyme, and tarragon and toss again. 3. Spread the vegetables evenly in the air fryer basket and roast for 14 to 18 minutes, or until the vegetables are fork-tender. 4. Cool for 5 minutes before serving.

Rosemary Beets with Balsamic Glaze

Prep time: 5 minutes | Cook time: 10 minutes | Serves 2

Beet:	Salt and black pepper, to taste
2 beets, cubed	Balsamic Glaze:
2 tablespoons olive oil	⅓ cup balsamic vinegar
2 springs rosemary, chopped	1 tablespoon honey

1. Preheat the air fryer to 400°F (204°C). 2. Combine the beets, olive oil, rosemary, salt, and pepper in a mixing bowl and toss until the beets are completely coated. 3. Place the beets in the air fryer basket and air fry for 10 minutes until the beets are crisp and browned at the edges. Shake the basket halfway through the cooking time. 4. Meanwhile, make the balsamic glaze: Place the balsamic vinegar and honey in a small saucepan and bring to a boil over medium heat. When the sauce starts to boil, reduce the heat to medium-low heat and simmer until the liquid is reduced by half. 5. When ready, remove the beets from the basket to a platter. Pour the balsamic glaze over the top and serve immediately.

Rice and Eggplant Bowl

Prep time: 15 minutes | Cook time: 10 minutes | Serves 4

¼ cup sliced cucumber	paste
1 teaspoon salt	1 tablespoon mirin rice wine
1 tablespoon sugar	4 cups cooked sushi rice
7 tablespoons Japanese rice vinegar	4 spring onions
3 medium eggplants, sliced	1 tablespoon toasted sesame seeds
3 tablespoons sweet white miso	

1. Coat the cucumber slices with the rice wine vinegar, salt, and sugar. 2. Put a dish on top of the bowl to weight it down completely. 3. In a bowl, mix the eggplants, mirin rice wine, and miso paste. Allow to marinate for half an hour. 4. Preheat the air fryer to 400°F (204°C). 5. Put the eggplant slices in the air fryer and air fry for 10 minutes. 6. Fill the bottom of a serving bowl with rice and top with the eggplants and pickled cucumbers. 7. Add the spring onions and sesame seeds for garnish. Serve immediately.

Cheese Stuffed Peppers

Prep time: 20 minutes | Cook time: 15 minutes | Serves 2

1 red bell pepper, top and seeds removed	Salt and pepper, to taste
1 yellow bell pepper, top and seeds removed	1 cup Cottage cheese
	4 tablespoons mayonnaise
	2 pickles, chopped

1. Arrange the peppers in the lightly greased air fryer basket. Cook in the preheated air fryer at 400°F (204°C) for 15 minutes, turning them over halfway through the cooking time. 2. Season with salt and pepper. Then, in a mixing bowl, combine the cream cheese with the mayonnaise and chopped pickles. Stuff the pepper with the cream cheese mixture and serve. Enjoy!

Mushroom and Pepper Pizza Squares

Prep time: 10 minutes | Cook time: 10 minutes | Serves 10

1 pizza dough, cut into squares	¼ red bell pepper, chopped
1 cup chopped oyster mushrooms	2 tablespoons parsley
1 shallot, chopped	Salt and ground black pepper, to taste

1. Preheat the air fryer to 400°F (204°C). 2. In a bowl, combine the oyster mushrooms, shallot, bell pepper and parsley. Sprinkle some salt and pepper as desired. 3. Spread this mixture on top of the pizza squares. 4. Bake in the air fryer for 10 minutes. 5. Serve warm.

Roasted Vegetables with Rice

Prep time: 5 minutes | Cook time: 12 minutes | Serves 4

2 teaspoons melted butter	1 red onion, chopped
1 cup chopped mushrooms	1 garlic clove, minced
1 cup cooked rice	Salt and black pepper, to taste
1 cup peas	2 hard-boiled eggs, grated
1 carrot, chopped	1 tablespoon soy sauce

1. Preheat the air fryer to 380°F (193°C). Coat a baking dish with melted butter. 2. Stir together the mushrooms, cooked rice, peas, carrot, onion, garlic, salt, and pepper in a large bowl until well mixed. 3. Pour the mixture into the prepared baking dish and transfer to the air fryer basket. 4. Roast in the preheated air fryer for 12 minutes until the vegetables are tender. 5. Divide the mixture among four plates. Serve warm with a sprinkle of grated eggs and a drizzle of soy sauce.

Loaded Cauliflower Steak

Prep time: 5 minutes | Cook time: 7 minutes | Serves 4

1 medium head cauliflower	melted
¼ cup hot sauce	¼ cup blue cheese crumbles
2 tablespoons salted butter,	¼ cup full-fat ranch dressing

1. Remove cauliflower leaves. Slice the head in ½-inch-thick slices. 2. In a small bowl, mix hot sauce and butter. Brush the mixture over the cauliflower. 3. Place each cauliflower steak into the air fryer, working in batches if necessary. 4. Adjust the temperature to 400°F (204°C) and air fry for 7 minutes. 5. When cooked, edges will begin turning dark and caramelized. 6. To serve, sprinkle steaks with crumbled blue cheese. Drizzle with ranch dressing.

Sweet Pepper Nachos

Prep time: 10 minutes | Cook time: 5 minutes | Serves 2

6 mini sweet peppers, seeded and sliced in half	¼ cup sliced pickled jalapeños
¾ cup shredded Colby jack cheese	½ medium avocado, peeled, pitted, and diced
	2 tablespoons sour cream

1. Place peppers into an ungreased round nonstick baking dish. Sprinkle with Colby and top with jalapeños. 2. Place dish into air fryer basket. Adjust the temperature to 350°F (177°C) and bake for 5 minutes. Cheese will be melted and bubbly when done. 3. Remove dish from air fryer and top with avocado. Drizzle with sour cream. Serve warm.

Gold Ravioli

Prep time: 10 minutes | Cook time: 6 minutes | Serves 4

½ cup panko bread crumbs	Salt and ground black pepper, to taste
2 teaspoons nutritional yeast	¼ cup aquafaba
1 teaspoon dried basil	8 ounces (227 g) ravioli
1 teaspoon dried oregano	Cooking spray
1 teaspoon garlic powder	

1. Cover the air fryer basket with aluminum foil and coat with a light brushing of oil. 2. Preheat the air fryer to 400°F (204°C). Combine the panko bread crumbs, nutritional yeast, basil, oregano, and garlic powder. Sprinkle with salt and pepper to taste. 3. Put the aquafaba in a separate bowl. Dip the ravioli in the aquafaba before coating it in the panko mixture. Spritz with cooking spray and transfer to the air fryer. 4. Air fry for 6 minutes. Shake the air fryer basket halfway. 5. Serve hot.

Chapter 10   Desserts

Chocolate Bread Pudding

Prep time: 10 minutes | Cook time: 10 to 12 minutes | Serves 4

Nonstick flour-infused baking spray	2 tablespoons cocoa powder
1 egg	3 tablespoons light brown sugar
1 egg yolk	3 tablespoons peanut butter
¾ cup chocolate milk	1 teaspoon vanilla extract
	5 slices firm white bread, cubed

1. Spray a 6-by-2-inch round baking pan with the baking spray. Set aside. 2. In a medium bowl, whisk the egg, egg yolk, chocolate milk, cocoa powder, brown sugar, peanut butter, and vanilla until thoroughly combined. Stir in the bread cubes and let soak for 10 minutes. Spoon this mixture into the prepared pan. 3. Insert the crisper plate into the basket and the basket into the unit. Preheat the unit by selecting BAKE, setting the temperature to 325°F (163°C), and setting the time to 3 minutes. Select START/STOP to begin. 4. Once the unit is preheated, place the pan into the basket. Select BAKE, set the temperature to 325°F (163°C), and set the time to 12 minutes. Select START/STOP to begin. 5. Check the pudding after about 10 minutes. It is done when it is firm to the touch. If not, resume cooking. 6. When the cooking is complete, let the pudding cool for 5 minutes. Serve warm.

Cream Cheese Danish

Prep time: 20 minutes | Cook time: 15 minutes | Serves 6

¾ cup blanched finely ground almond flour	2 large egg yolks
1 cup shredded Mozzarella cheese	¾ cup powdered erythritol, divided
5 ounces (142 g) full-fat cream cheese, divided	2 teaspoons vanilla extract, divided

1. In a large microwave-safe bowl, add almond flour, Mozzarella, and 1 ounce (28 g) cream cheese. Mix and then microwave for 1 minute. 2. Stir and add egg yolks to the bowl. Continue stirring until soft dough forms. Add ½ cup erythritol to dough and 1 teaspoon vanilla. 3. Cut a piece of parchment to fit your air fryer basket. Wet your hands with warm water and press out the dough into a ¼-inch-thick rectangle. 4. In a medium bowl, mix remaining cream cheese, erythritol, and vanilla. Place this cream cheese mixture on the right half of the dough rectangle. Fold over the left side of the dough and press to seal. Place into the air fryer basket. 5. Adjust the temperature to 330°F (166°C) and bake for 15 minutes. 6. After 7 minutes, flip over the Danish. 7. When done, remove the Danish from parchment and allow to completely cool before cutting.

Baked Peaches with Yogurt and Blueberries

Prep time: 10 minutes | Cook time: 7 to 11 minutes | Serves 6

3 peaches, peeled, halved, and pitted	1 cup plain Greek yogurt
2 tablespoons packed brown sugar	¼ teaspoon ground cinnamon
	1 teaspoon pure vanilla extract
	1 cup fresh blueberries

1. Preheat the air fryer to 380°F (193°C). 2. Arrange the peaches in the air fryer basket, cut-side up. Top with a generous sprinkle of brown sugar. 3. Bake in the preheated air fryer for 7 to 11 minutes or until the peaches are lightly browned and caramelized. 4. Meanwhile, whisk together the yogurt, cinnamon, and vanilla in a small bowl until smooth. 5. Remove the peaches from the basket to a plate. Serve topped with the yogurt mixture and fresh blueberries.

Mixed Berry Hand Pies

Prep time: 5 minutes | Cook time: 30 minutes | Serves 4

¾ cup sugar	1 teaspoon water
½ teaspoon ground cinnamon	1 package refrigerated pie
1 tablespoon cornstarch	dough (or your own homemade
1 cup blueberries	pie dough)
1 cup blackberries	1 egg, beaten
1 cup raspberries, divided	

1. Combine the sugar, cinnamon, and cornstarch in a small saucepan. Add the blueberries, blackberries, and ½ cup of the raspberries. Toss the berries gently to coat them evenly. Add the teaspoon of water to the saucepan and turn the stovetop on to medium-high heat, stirring occasionally. Once the berries break down, release their juice and start to simmer (about 5 minutes), simmer for another couple of minutes and then transfer the mixture to a bowl, stir in the remaining ½ cup of raspberries and let it cool. 2. Preheat the air fryer to 370°F (188°C). 3. Cut the pie dough into four 5-inch circles and four 6-inch circles. 4. Spread the 6-inch circles on a flat surface. Divide the berry filling between all four circles. Brush the perimeter of the dough circles with a little water. Place the 5-inch circles on top of the filling and press the perimeter of the dough circles together to seal. Roll the edges of the bottom circle up over the top circle to make a crust around the filling. Press a fork around the crust to make decorative indentations and to seal the crust shut. Brush the pies with egg wash and sprinkle a little sugar on top. Poke a small hole in the center of each pie with a paring knife to vent the dough. 5. Air fry two pies at a time. Brush or spray the air fryer basket with oil and place the pies into the basket. Air fry for 9 minutes. Turn the pies over and air fry for another 6 minutes. Serve warm or at room temperature.

Grilled Peaches

Prep time: 5 minutes | Cook time: 10 minutes | Serves 4

Oil, for spraying	butter, cubed
¼ cup graham cracker crumbs	¼ teaspoon cinnamon
¼ cup packed light brown sugar	2 peaches, pitted and cut into quarters
8 tablespoons (1 stick) unsalted	4 scoops vanilla ice cream

1. Line the air fryer basket with parchment and spray lightly with oil. 2. In a small bowl, mix together the graham cracker crumbs, brown sugar, butter, and cinnamon with a fork until crumbly. 3. Place the peach wedges in the prepared basket, skin-side up. You may need to work in batches, depending on the size of your air fryer. 4. Air fry at 350°F (177°C) for 5 minutes, flip, and sprinkle with a spoonful of the graham cracker mixture. Cook for another 5 minutes, or until tender and caramelized. 5. Top with a scoop of vanilla ice cream and any remaining crumble mixture. Serve immediately.

Pecan Butter Cookies

Prep time: 5 minutes | Cook time: 24 minutes | Makes 12 cookies

1 cup chopped pecans	¾ cup erythritol, divided
½ cup salted butter, melted	1 teaspoon vanilla extract
½ cup coconut flour	

1. In a food processor, blend together pecans, butter, flour, ½ cup erythritol, and vanilla 1 minute until a dough forms. 2. Form dough into twelve individual cookie balls, about 1 tablespoon each. 3. Cut three pieces of parchment to fit air fryer basket. Place four cookies on each ungreased parchment and place one piece parchment with cookies into air fryer basket. Adjust air fryer temperature to 325°F (163°C) and set the timer for 8 minutes. Repeat cooking with remaining batches. 4. When the timer goes off, allow cookies to cool 5 minutes on a large serving plate until cool enough to handle. While still warm, dust cookies with remaining erythritol. Allow to cool completely, about 15 minutes, before serving.

Cinnamon-Sugar Almonds

Prep time: 5 minutes | Cook time: 8 minutes | Serves 4

1 cup whole almonds	1 tablespoon sugar
2 tablespoons salted butter, melted	½ teaspoon ground cinnamon

1. In a medium bowl, combine the almonds, butter, sugar, and cinnamon. Mix well to ensure all the almonds are coated with the spiced butter. 2. Transfer the almonds to the air fryer basket and shake so they are in a single layer. Set the air fryer to 300°F (149°C) for 8 minutes, stirring the almonds halfway through the cooking time. 3. Let cool completely before serving.

Strawberry Scone Shortcake

Prep time: 10 minutes | Cook time: 20 minutes | Serves 4 to 6

1⅓ cups all-purpose flour	Turbinado sugar, for sprinkling
3 tablespoons granulated sugar	2 tablespoons powdered sugar, plus more for dusting
1½ teaspoons baking powder	½ teaspoon vanilla extract
1 teaspoon kosher salt	1 cup quartered fresh strawberries
8 tablespoons (1 stick) unsalted butter, cubed and chilled	
1⅓ cups heavy cream, chilled	

1. In a large bowl, whisk together the flour, granulated sugar, baking powder, and salt. Add the butter and use your fingers to break apart the butter pieces while working them into the flour mixture, until pea-size pieces form. Pour ⅔ cup of the cream over the flour mixture and, using a rubber spatula, mix the ingredients together until just combined. 2. Transfer the dough to a work surface and form into a 7-inch-wide disk. Brush the top with water, then sprinkle with some turbinado sugar. Using a large metal spatula, transfer the dough to the air fryer and bake at 350°F (177°C) until golden brown and fluffy, about 20 minutes. Let cool in the air fryer basket for 5 minutes, then turn out onto a wire rack, right-side up, to cool completely. 3. Meanwhile, in a bowl, beat the remaining ⅔ cup cream, the powdered sugar, and vanilla until stiff peaks form. Split the scone like a hamburger bun and spread the strawberries over the bottom. Top with the whipped cream and cover with the top of the scone. Dust with powdered sugar and cut into wedges to serve.

Orange Gooey Butter Cake

Prep time: 5 minutes | Cook time: 1 hour 25 minutes | Serves 6 to 8

Crust Layer:	8 ounces (227 g) cream cheese, softened
½ cup flour	
¼ cup sugar	4 ounces (113 g) (1 stick) unsalted European style butter, melted
½ teaspoon baking powder	
⅛ teaspoon salt	
2 ounces (57 g) (½ stick) unsalted European style butter, melted	2 eggs
	2 teaspoons orange extract
	2 tablespoons orange zest
1 egg	4 cups powdered sugar
1 teaspoon orange extract	Garnish:
2 tablespoons orange zest	Powdered sugar
Gooey Butter Layer:	Orange slices

1. Preheat the air fryer to 350°F (177°C). 2. Grease a cake pan and line the bottom with parchment paper. Combine the flour, sugar, baking powder and salt in a bowl. Add the melted butter, egg, orange extract and orange zest. Mix well and press this mixture into the bottom of the greased cake pan. Lower the pan into the basket using an aluminum foil sling (fold a piece of aluminum foil into a strip about 2-inches wide by 24-inches long). Fold the ends of the aluminum foil over the top of the dish before returning the basket to the air fryer. Air fry uncovered for 8 minutes. 3. Make the gooey butter layer: Beat the cream cheese, melted butter, eggs, orange extract and orange zest in a large bowl using an electric hand mixer. Add the powdered sugar in stages, beat until smooth with each addition. Pour this mixture on top of the baked crust in the cake pan. Wrap the pan with a piece of greased aluminum foil, tenting the top of the foil to leave a little room for the cake to rise. 4. Air fry for 60 minutes at 350°F (177°C). Remove the aluminum foil and air fry for an additional 17 minutes. 5. Let the cake cool inside the pan for at least 10 minutes. Then, run a butter knife around the cake and let the cake cool completely in the pan. When cooled, run the butter knife around the edges of the cake again and invert it onto a plate and then back onto a serving platter. Sprinkle the powdered sugar over the top of the cake and garnish with orange slices.

Chocolate Croissants

Prep time: 5 minutes | Cook time: 24 minutes | Serves 8

1 sheet frozen puff pastry, thawed	spread
⅓ cup chocolate-hazelnut	1 large egg, beaten

1. On a lightly floured surface, roll puff pastry into a 14-inch square. Cut pastry into quarters to form 4 squares. Cut each square diagonally to form 8 triangles. 2. Spread 2 teaspoons chocolate-hazelnut spread on each triangle; from wider end, roll up pastry. Brush egg on top of each roll. 3. Preheat the air fryer to 375°F (191°C). Air fry rolls in batches, 3 or 4 at a time, 8 minutes per batch, or until pastry is golden brown. 4. Cool on a wire rack; serve while warm or at room temperature.

Vanilla Pound Cake

Prep time: 10 minutes | Cook time: 25 minutes | Serves 6

1 cup blanched finely ground almond flour	1 teaspoon baking powder
¼ cup salted butter, melted	½ cup full-fat sour cream
½ cup granular erythritol	1 ounce (28 g) full-fat cream cheese, softened
1 teaspoon vanilla extract	2 large eggs

1. In a large bowl, mix almond flour, butter, and erythritol. 2. Add in vanilla, baking powder, sour cream, and cream cheese and mix until well combined. Add eggs and mix. 3. Pour batter into a round baking pan. Place pan into the air fryer basket. 4. Adjust the temperature to 300ºF (149ºC) and bake for 25 minutes. 5. When the cake is done, a toothpick inserted in center will come out clean. The center should not feel wet. Allow it to cool completely, or the cake will crumble when moved.

Lush Chocolate Chip Cookies

Prep time: 7 minutes | Cook time: 9 minutes | Serves 4

3 tablespoons butter, at room temperature	chocolate
⅓ cup plus 1 tablespoon light brown sugar	¼ teaspoon baking soda
1 egg yolk	½ teaspoon vanilla extract
½ cup all-purpose flour	¾ cup semisweet chocolate chips
2 tablespoons ground white	Nonstick flour-infused baking spray

1. In medium bowl, beat together the butter and brown sugar until fluffy. Stir in the egg yolk. 2. Add the flour, white chocolate, baking soda, and vanilla and mix well. Stir in the chocolate chips. 3. Line a 6-by-2-inch round baking pan with parchment paper. Spray the parchment paper with flour-infused baking spray. 4. Insert the crisper plate into the basket and the basket into the unit. Preheat the unit by selecting BAKE, setting the temperature to 300ºF (149ºC), and setting the time to 3 minutes. Select START/STOP to begin. 5. Spread the batter into the prepared pan, leaving a ½-inch border on all sides. 6. Once the unit is preheated, place the pan into the basket. 7. Select BAKE, set the temperature to 300ºF (149ºC), and set the time to 9 minutes. Select START/STOP to begin. 8. When the cooking is complete, the cookie should be light brown and just barely set. Remove the pan from the basket and let cool for 10 minutes. Remove the cookie from the pan, remove the parchment paper, and let cool completely on a wire rack.

Almond Shortbread

Prep time: 10 minutes | Cook time: 12 minutes | Serves 8

½ cup (1 stick) unsalted butter	1 teaspoon pure almond extract
½ cup sugar	1 cup all-purpose flour

1. In bowl of a stand mixer fitted with the paddle attachment, beat the butter and sugar on medium speed until light and fluffy, 3 to 4 minutes. Add the almond extract and beat until combined, about 30 seconds. Turn the mixer to low. Add the flour a little at a time and beat for about 2 minutes more until well-incorporated. 2. Pat the dough into an even layer in a baking pan. Place the pan in the air fryer basket. Set the air fryer to 375ºF (191ºC) for 12 minutes. 3. Carefully remove the pan from air fryer basket. While the shortbread is still warm and soft, cut it into 8 wedges. 4. Let cool in the pan on a wire rack for 5 minutes. Remove the wedges from the pan and let cool completely on the rack before serving.

Tortilla Fried Pies

Prep time: 10 minutes | Cook time: 5 minutes per batch | Makes 12 pies

12 small flour tortillas (4-inch diameter)	2 tablespoons shredded, unsweetened coconut
½ cup fig preserves	Oil for misting or cooking spray
¼ cup sliced almonds	

1. Wrap refrigerated tortillas in damp paper towels and heat in microwave 30 seconds to warm. 2. Working with one tortilla at a time, place 2 teaspoons fig preserves, 1 teaspoon sliced almonds, and ½ teaspoon coconut in the center of each. 3. Moisten outer edges of tortilla all around. 4. Fold one side of tortilla over filling to make a half-moon shape and press down lightly on center. Using the tines of a fork, press down firmly on edges of tortilla to seal in filling. 5. Mist both sides with oil or cooking spray. 6. Place hand pies in air fryer basket close but not overlapping. It's fine to lean some against the sides and corners of the basket. You may need to cook in 2 batches. 7. Air fry at 390ºF (199ºC) for 5 minutes or until lightly browned. Serve hot. 8. Refrigerate any leftover pies in a closed container. To serve later, toss them back in the air fryer basket and cook for 2 or 3 minutes to reheat.

Chocolate Chip-Pecan Biscotti

Prep time: 15 minutes | Cook time: 20 to 22 minutes | Serves 10

1¼ cups finely ground blanched almond flour	1 teaspoon pure vanilla extract
¾ teaspoon baking powder	⅓ cup chopped pecans
½ teaspoon xanthan gum	¼ cup stevia-sweetened chocolate chips, such as Lily's Sweets brand
¼ teaspoon sea salt	
3 tablespoons unsalted butter, at room temperature	Melted stevia-sweetened chocolate chips and chopped pecans, for topping (optional)
⅓ cup Swerve	
1 large egg, beaten	

1. In a large bowl, combine the almond flour, baking powder, xanthan gum, and salt. 2. Line a cake pan that fits inside your air fryer with parchment paper. 3. In the bowl of a stand mixer, beat together the butter and Swerve. Add the beaten egg and vanilla, and beat for about 3 minutes. 4. Add the almond flour mixture to the butter-and-egg mixture; beat until just combined. 5. Stir in the pecans and chocolate chips. 6. Transfer the dough to the prepared pan, and press it into the bottom. 7. Set the air fryer to 325ºF (163ºC) and bake for 12 minutes. Remove from the air fryer and let cool for 15 minutes. Using a sharp knife, cut the cookie into thin strips, then return the strips to the cake pan with the bottom sides facing up. 8. Set the air fryer to 300ºF (149ºC). Bake for 8 to 10 minutes. 9. Remove from the air fryer and let cool completely on a wire rack. If desired, dip one side of each biscotti piece into melted chocolate chips, and top with chopped pecans.

Grilled Pineapple Dessert

Prep time: 5 minutes | Cook time: 12 minutes | Serves 4

Oil for misting or cooking spray	¼ teaspoon brandy
4½-inch-thick slices fresh pineapple, core removed	2 tablespoons slivered almonds, toasted
1 tablespoon honey	Vanilla frozen yogurt or coconut sorbet

1. Spray both sides of pineapple slices with oil or cooking spray. Place into air fryer basket. 2. Air fry at 390°F (199°C) for 6 minutes. Turn slices over and cook for an additional 6 minutes. 3. Mix together the honey and brandy. 4. Remove cooked pineapple slices from air fryer, sprinkle with toasted almonds, and drizzle with honey mixture. 5. Serve with a scoop of frozen yogurt or sorbet on the side.

Caramelized Fruit Skewers

Prep time: 10 minutes | Cook time: 3 to 5 minutes | Serves 4

2 peaches, peeled, pitted, and thickly sliced	½ teaspoon ground cinnamon
3 plums, halved and pitted	¼ teaspoon ground allspice
3 nectarines, halved and pitted	Pinch cayenne pepper
1 tablespoon honey	Special Equipment:
	8 metal skewers

1. Preheat the air fryer to 400°F (204°C). 2. Thread, alternating peaches, plums, and nectarines, onto the metal skewers that fit into the air fryer. 3. Thoroughly combine the honey, cinnamon, allspice, and cayenne in a small bowl. Brush generously the glaze over the fruit skewers. 4. Transfer the fruit skewers to the air fryer basket. You may need to cook in batches to avoid overcrowding. 5. Air fry for 3 to 5 minutes, or until the fruit is caramelized. 6. Remove from the basket and repeat with the remaining fruit skewers. 7. Let the fruit skewers rest for 5 minutes before serving.

Protein Powder Doughnut Holes

Prep time: 25 minutes | Cook time: 6 minutes | Makes 12 holes

½ cup blanched finely ground almond flour	½ teaspoon baking powder
½ cup low-carb vanilla protein powder	1 large egg
½ cup granular erythritol	5 tablespoons unsalted butter, melted
	½ teaspoon vanilla extract

1. Mix all ingredients in a large bowl. Place into the freezer for 20 minutes. 2. Wet your hands with water and roll the dough into twelve balls. 3. Cut a piece of parchment to fit your air fryer basket. Working in batches as necessary, place doughnut holes into the air fryer basket on top of parchment. 4. Adjust the temperature to 380°F (193°C) and air fry for 6 minutes. 5. Flip doughnut holes halfway through the cooking time. 6. Let cool completely before serving.

Peach Cobbler

Prep time: 15 minutes | Cook time: 12 to 14 minutes | Serves 4

16 ounces (454 g) frozen peaches, thawed, with juice (do not drain)	Crust:
	½ cup flour
6 tablespoons sugar	¼ teaspoon salt
1 tablespoon cornstarch	3 tablespoons butter
1 tablespoon water	1½ tablespoons cold water
	¼ teaspoon sugar

1. Place peaches, including juice, and sugar in a baking pan. Stir to mix well. 2. In a small cup, dissolve cornstarch in the water. Stir into peaches. 3. In a medium bowl, combine the flour and salt. Cut in butter using knives or a pastry blender. Stir in the cold water to make a stiff dough. 4. On a floured board or wax paper, pat dough into a square or circle slightly smaller than your baking pan. Cut diagonally into 4 pieces. 5. Place dough pieces on top of peaches, leaving a tiny bit of space between the edges. Sprinkle very lightly with sugar, no more than about ¼ teaspoon. 6. Bake at 360°F (182°C) for 12 to 14 minutes, until fruit bubbles and crust browns.

Chocolate Soufflés

Prep time: 5 minutes | Cook time: 14 minutes | Serves 2

Butter and sugar for greasing the ramekins	3 tablespoons sugar
	½ teaspoon pure vanilla extract
3 ounces (85 g) semi-sweet chocolate, chopped	2 tablespoons all-purpose flour
¼ cup unsalted butter	Powdered sugar, for dusting the finished soufflés
2 eggs, yolks and white separated	Heavy cream, for serving

1. Butter and sugar two 6-ounce (170-g) ramekins. (Butter the ramekins and then coat the butter with sugar by shaking it around in the ramekin and dumping out any excess.) 2. Melt the chocolate and butter together, either in the microwave or in a double boiler. In a separate bowl, beat the egg yolks vigorously. Add the sugar and the vanilla extract and beat well again. Drizzle in the chocolate and butter, mixing well. Stir in the flour, combining until there are no lumps. 3. Preheat the air fryer to 330°F (166°C). 4. In a separate bowl, whisk the egg whites to soft peak stage (the point at which the whites can almost stand up on the end of your whisk). Fold the whipped egg whites into the chocolate mixture gently and in stages. 5. Transfer the batter carefully to the buttered ramekins, leaving about ½-inch at the top. (You may have a little extra batter, depending on how airy the batter is, so you might be able to squeeze out a third soufflé if you want to.) Place the ramekins into the air fryer basket and air fry for 14 minutes. The soufflés should have risen nicely and be brown on top. (Don't worry if the top gets a little dark, you'll be covering it with powdered sugar in the next step.) 6. Dust with powdered sugar and serve immediately with heavy cream to pour over the top at the table.

Luscious Coconut Pie

Prep time: 5 minutes | Cook time: 45 minutes | Serves 6

1 cup plus ¼ cup unsweetened shredded coconut, divided	1½ teaspoons vanilla extract
2 eggs	¼ teaspoon salt
1½ cups almond milk	2 tablespoons powdered Swerve (optional)
½ cup granulated Swerve	½ cup sugar-free whipped topping (optional)
½ cup coconut flour	
¼ cup unsalted butter, melted	

1. Spread ¼ cup of the coconut in the bottom of a pie plate and place in the air fryer basket. Set the air fryer to 350°F (177°C) and air fry the coconut while the air fryer preheats, about 5 minutes, until golden brown. Transfer the coconut to a small bowl and set aside for garnish. Brush the pie plate with oil and set aside. 2. In a large bowl, combine the remaining 1 cup shredded coconut, eggs, milk, granulated Swerve, coconut flour, butter, vanilla, and salt. Whisk until smooth. Pour the batter into the prepared pie plate and air fry for 40 to 45 minutes, or until a toothpick inserted into the center of the pie comes out clean. (Check halfway through the baking time and rotate the pan, if necessary, for even baking.) 3. Remove the pie from the air fryer and place on a baking rack to cool completely. Garnish with the reserved toasted coconut and the powdered Swerve or sugar-free whipped topping, if desired. Cover and refrigerate leftover pie for up to 3 days.

Cream-Filled Sponge Cakes

Prep time: 10 minutes | Cook time: 10 minutes | Makes 4 cakes

Oil, for spraying	4 cream-filled sponge cakes
1 (8-ounce / 227-g) can refrigerated crescent rolls	1 tablespoon confectioners' sugar

1. Line the air fryer basket with parchment and spray lightly with oil. 2. Unroll the dough into a single flat layer and cut it into 4 equal pieces. 3. Place 1 sponge cake in the center of each piece of dough. Wrap the dough around the cake, pinching the ends to seal. 4. Place the wrapped cakes in the prepared basket and spray lightly with oil. 5. Bake at 200°F (93°C) for 5 minutes, flip, spray with oil, and cook for another 5 minutes, or until golden brown. 6. Dust with the confectioners' sugar and serve.

Cinnamon and Pecan Pie

Prep time: 10 minutes | Cook time: 25 minutes | Serves 4

1 pie dough	⅛ teaspoon nutmeg
½ teaspoons cinnamon	3 tablespoons melted butter, divided
¾ teaspoon vanilla extract	
2 eggs	2 tablespoons sugar
¾ cup maple syrup	½ cup chopped pecans

1. Preheat the air fryer to 370°F (188°C). 2. In a small bowl, coat the pecans in 1 tablespoon of melted butter. 3. Transfer the pecans to the air fryer and air fry for about 10 minutes. 4. Put the pie dough in a greased pie pan and add the pecans on top. 5. In a bowl, mix the rest of the ingredients. Pour this over the pecans. 6. Put the pan in the air fryer and bake for 25 minutes. 7. Serve immediately.

Fried Oreos

Prep time: 7 minutes | Cook time: 6 minutes per batch | Makes 12 cookies

Oil for misting or nonstick spray	½ cup water, plus 2 tablespoons
1 cup complete pancake and waffle mix	12 Oreos or other chocolate sandwich cookies
1 teaspoon vanilla extract	1 tablespoon confectioners' sugar

1. Spray baking pan with oil or nonstick spray and place in basket. 2. Preheat the air fryer to 390°F (199°C). 3. In a medium bowl, mix together the pancake mix, vanilla, and water. 4. Dip 4 cookies in batter and place in baking pan. 5. Cook for 6 minutes, until browned. 6. Repeat steps 4 and 5 for the remaining cookies. 7. Sift sugar over warm cookies.

Peach Fried Pies

Prep time: 15 minutes | Cook time: 20 minutes | Makes 8 pies

1 (14.75-ounce / 418-g) can sliced peaches in heavy syrup	1 large egg
1 teaspoon ground cinnamon	All-purpose flour, for dusting
1 tablespoon cornstarch	2 refrigerated piecrusts

1. Reserving 2 tablespoons of syrup, drain the peaches well. Chop the peaches into bite-size pieces, transfer to a medium bowl, and stir in the cinnamon. 2. In a small bowl, stir together the reserved peach juice and cornstarch until dissolved. Stir this slurry into the peaches. 3. In another small bowl, beat the egg. 4. Dust a cutting board or work surface with flour and spread the piecrusts on the prepared surface. Using a knife, cut each crust into 4 squares (8 squares total). 5. Place 2 tablespoons of peaches onto each dough square. Fold the dough in half and seal the edges. Using a pastry brush, spread the beaten egg on both sides of each hand pie. Using a knife, make 2 thin slits in the top of each pie. 6. Preheat the air fryer to 350°F (177°C). 7. Line the air fryer basket with parchment paper. Place 4 pies on the parchment. 8. Cook for 10 minutes. Flip the pies, brush with beaten egg, and cook for 5 minutes more. Repeat with the remaining pies.

Chocolate Lava Cakes

Prep time: 5 minutes | Cook time: 15 minutes | Serves 2

2 large eggs, whisked	½ teaspoon vanilla extract
¼ cup blanched finely ground almond flour	2 ounces (57 g) low-carb chocolate chips, melted

1. In a medium bowl, mix eggs with flour and vanilla. Fold in chocolate until fully combined. 2. Pour batter into two ramekins greased with cooking spray. Place ramekins into air fryer basket. Adjust the temperature to 320°F (160°C) and bake for 15 minutes. Cakes will be set at the edges and firm in the center when done. Let cool 5 minutes before serving.

Nutty Pear Crumble

Prep time: 10 minutes | Cook time: 30 minutes | Serves 2 to 4

2 ripe d'Anjou pears (1 pound / 454 g), peeled, cored, and roughly chopped	at room temperature
	⅓ cup all-purpose flour
¼ cup packed light brown sugar	2½ tablespoons Dutch-process cocoa powder
2 tablespoons cornstarch	¼ cup chopped blanched hazelnuts
1 teaspoon kosher salt	Vanilla ice cream or whipped
¼ cup granulated sugar	cream, for serving (optional)
3 tablespoons unsalted butter,	

1. In a cake pan, combine the pears, brown sugar, cornstarch, and ½ teaspoon salt and toss until the pears are evenly coated in the sugar. 2. In a bowl, combine the remaining ½ teaspoon salt with the granulated sugar, butter, flour, and cocoa powder and pinch and press the butter into the other ingredients with your fingers until a sandy, shaggy crumble dough forms. Stir in the hazelnuts. Sprinkle the crumble topping evenly over the pears. 3. Place the pan in the air fryer and bake at 320°F (160°C) until the crumble is crisp and the pears are bubbling in the center, about 30 minutes. 4. Carefully remove the pan from the air fryer and serve the hot crumble in bowls, topped with ice cream or whipped cream, if you like.

Lime Bars

Prep time: 10 minutes | Cook time: 33 minutes | Makes 12 bars

1½ cups blanched finely ground almond flour, divided	4 tablespoons salted butter, melted
¾ cup confectioners' erythritol, divided	½ cup fresh lime juice
	2 large eggs, whisked

1. In a medium bowl, mix together 1 cup flour, ¼ cup erythritol, and butter. Press mixture into bottom of an ungreased round nonstick cake pan. 2. Place pan into air fryer basket. Adjust the temperature to 300°F (149°C) and bake for 13 minutes. Crust will be brown and set in the middle when done. 3. Allow to cool in pan 10 minutes. 4. In a medium bowl, combine remaining flour, remaining erythritol, lime juice, and eggs. Pour mixture over cooled crust and return to air fryer for 20 minutes at 300°F (149°C). Top will be browned and firm when done. 5. Let cool completely in pan, about 30 minutes, then chill covered in the refrigerator 1 hour. Serve chilled.

Brown Sugar Banana Bread

Prep time: 20 minutes | Cook time: 22 to 24 minutes | Serves 4

1 cup packed light brown sugar	1 teaspoon ground cinnamon
1 large egg, beaten	½ teaspoon salt
2 tablespoons butter, melted	1 banana, mashed
½ cup milk, whole or 2%	1 to 2 tablespoons oil
2 cups all-purpose flour	¼ cup confectioners' sugar
1½ teaspoons baking powder	(optional)

1. In a large bowl, stir together the brown sugar, egg, melted butter, and milk. 2. In a medium bowl, whisk the flour, baking powder, cinnamon, and salt until blended. Add the flour mixture to the sugar mixture and stir just to blend. 3. Add the mashed banana and stir to combine. 4. Preheat the air fryer to 350°F (177°C). Spritz 2 mini loaf pans with oil. 5. Evenly divide the batter between the prepared pans and place them in the air fryer basket. 6. Cook for 22 to 24 minutes, or until a knife inserted into the middle of the loaves comes out clean. 7. Dust the warm loaves with confectioners' sugar (if using).

Air Fryer Apple Fritters

Prep time: 30 minutes | Cook time: 7 to 8 minutes | Serves 6

1 cup chopped, peeled Granny Smith apple	2 tablespoons milk
	2 tablespoons butter, melted
½ cup granulated sugar	1 large egg, beaten
1 teaspoon ground cinnamon	Cooking spray
1 cup all-purpose flour	¼ cup confectioners' sugar
1 teaspoon baking powder	(optional)
1 teaspoon salt	

1. Mix together the apple, granulated sugar, and cinnamon in a small bowl. Allow to sit for 30 minutes. 2. Combine the flour, baking powder, and salt in a medium bowl. Add the milk, butter, and egg and stir to incorporate. 3. Pour the apple mixture into the bowl of flour mixture and stir with a spatula until a dough forms. 4. Make the fritters: On a clean work surface, divide the dough into 12 equal portions and shape into 1-inch balls. Flatten them into patties with your hands. 5. Preheat the air fryer to 350°F (177°C). Line the air fryer basket with parchment paper and spray it with cooking spray. 6. Transfer the apple fritters onto the parchment paper, evenly spaced but not too close together. Spray the fritters with cooking spray. 7. Bake for 7 to 8 minutes until lightly browned. Flip the fritters halfway through the cooking time. 8. Remove from the basket to a plate and serve with the confectioners' sugar sprinkled on top, if desired.

New York Cheesecake

Prep time: 1 hour | Cook time: 37 minutes | Serves 8

1½ cups almond flour	½ cup heavy cream
3 ounces (85 g) Swerve	1¼ cups granulated Swerve
½ stick butter, melted	3 eggs, at room temperature
20 ounces (567 g) full-fat cream cheese	1 tablespoon vanilla essence
	1 teaspoon grated lemon zest

1. Coat the sides and bottom of a baking pan with a little flour. 2. In a mixing bowl, combine the almond flour and Swerve. Add the melted butter and mix until your mixture looks like bread crumbs. 3. Press the mixture into the bottom of the prepared pan to form an even layer. Bake at 330°F (166°C) for 7 minutes until golden brown. Allow it to cool completely on a wire rack. 4. Meanwhile, in a mixer fitted with the paddle attachment, prepare the filling by mixing the soft cheese, heavy cream, and granulated Swerve; beat until creamy and fluffy. 5. Crack the eggs into the mixing bowl, one at a time; add the vanilla and lemon zest and continue to mix until fully combined. 6. Pour the prepared topping over the cooled crust and spread evenly. 7. Bake in the preheated air fryer at 330°F (166°C) for 25 to 30 minutes; leave it in the air fryer to keep warm for another 30 minutes. 8. Cover your cheesecake with plastic wrap. Place in your refrigerator and allow it to cool at least 6 hours or overnight. Serve well chilled.

Mixed Berries with Pecan Streusel Topping

Prep time: 5 minutes | Cook time: 17 minutes | Serves 3

½ cup mixed berries	2 tablespoons chopped walnuts
Cooking spray	3 tablespoons granulated
Topping:	Swerve
1 egg, beaten	2 tablespoons cold salted
3 tablespoons almonds, slivered	butter, cut into pieces
3 tablespoons chopped pecans	½ teaspoon ground cinnamon

1. Preheat the air fryer to 340°F (171°C). Lightly spray a baking dish with cooking spray. 2. Make the topping: In a medium bowl, stir together the beaten egg, nuts, Swerve, butter, and cinnamon until well blended. 3. Put the mixed berries in the bottom of the baking dish and spread the topping over the top. 4. Bake in the preheated air fryer for 17 minutes, or until the fruit is bubbly and topping is golden brown. 5. Allow to cool for 5 to 10 minutes before serving.

Vanilla Cookies with Hazelnuts

Prep time: 20 minutes | Cook time: 10 minutes | Serves 6

1 cup almond flour	1 cup Swerve
½ cup coconut flour	2 teaspoons vanilla
1 teaspoon baking soda	2 eggs, at room temperature
1 teaspoon fine sea salt	1 cup hazelnuts, coarsely
1 stick butter	chopped

1. Preheat the air fryer to 350°F (177°C). 2. Mix the flour with the baking soda, and sea salt. 3. In the bowl of an electric mixer, beat the butter, Swerve, and vanilla until creamy. Fold in the eggs, one at a time, and mix until well combined. 4. Slowly and gradually, stir in the flour mixture. Finally, fold in the coarsely chopped hazelnuts. 5. Divide the dough into small balls using a large cookie scoop; drop onto the prepared cookie sheets. Bake for 10 minutes or until golden brown, rotating the pan once or twice through the cooking time. 6. Work in batches and cool for a couple of minutes before removing to wire racks. Enjoy!

5-Ingredient Brownies

Prep time: 10 minutes | Cook time: 25 minutes | Serves 6

Vegetable oil	3 large eggs
½ cup (1 stick) unsalted butter	½ cup sugar
½ cup chocolate chips	1 teaspoon pure vanilla extract

1. Generously grease a baking pan with vegetable oil. 2. In a microwave-safe bowl, combine the butter and chocolate chips. Microwave on high for 1 minute. Stir very well. (You want the heat from the butter and chocolate to melt the remaining clumps. If you microwave until everything melts, the chocolate will be overcooked. If necessary, microwave for an additional 10 seconds, but stir well before you try that.) 3. In a medium bowl, combine the eggs, sugar, and vanilla. Whisk until light and frothy. While whisking continuously, slowly pour in the melted chocolate in a thin stream and whisk until everything is incorporated. 4. Pour the batter into the prepared pan. Set the pan in the air fryer basket. Set the air fryer to 350°F (177°C) for 25 minutes, or until a toothpick inserted into the

center comes out clean. 5. Let cool in the pan on a wire rack for 30 minutes before cutting into squares.

Berry Crumble

Prep time: 10 minutes | Cook time: 15 minutes | Serves 4

For the Filling:	¼ cup rolled oats
2 cups mixed berries	1 tablespoon sugar
2 tablespoons sugar	2 tablespoons cold unsalted
1 tablespoon cornstarch	butter, cut into small cubes
1 tablespoon fresh lemon juice	Whipped cream or ice cream
For the Topping:	(optional)
¼ cup all-purpose flour	

1. Preheat the air fryer to 400°F (204°C). 2. For the filling: In a round baking pan, gently mix the berries, sugar, cornstarch, and lemon juice until thoroughly combined. 3. For the topping: In a small bowl, combine the flour, oats, and sugar. Stir the butter into the flour mixture until the mixture has the consistency of bread crumbs. 4. Sprinkle the topping over the berries. 5. Put the pan in the air fryer basket and air fry for 15 minutes. Let cool for 5 minutes on a wire rack. 6. Serve topped with whipped cream or ice cream, if desired.

Gingerbread

Prep time: 5 minutes | Cook time: 20 minutes | Makes 1 loaf

Cooking spray	⅛ teaspoon salt
1 cup flour	1 egg
2 tablespoons sugar	¼ cup molasses
¾ teaspoon ground ginger	½ cup buttermilk
¼ teaspoon cinnamon	2 tablespoons oil
1 teaspoon baking powder	1 teaspoon pure vanilla extract
½ teaspoon baking soda	

1. Preheat the air fryer to 330°F (166°C). 2. Spray a baking dish lightly with cooking spray. 3. In a medium bowl, mix together all the dry ingredients. 4. In a separate bowl, beat the egg. Add molasses, buttermilk, oil, and vanilla and stir until well mixed. 5. Pour liquid mixture into dry ingredients and stir until well blended. 6. Pour batter into baking dish and bake at 330°F (166°C) for 20 minutes or until toothpick inserted in center of loaf comes out clean.

Dark Chocolate Lava Cake

Prep time: 5 minutes | Cook time: 10 minutes | Serves 4

Olive oil cooking spray	½ teaspoon baking powder
¼ cup whole wheat flour	¼ cup raw honey
1 tablespoon unsweetened dark	1 egg
chocolate cocoa powder	2 tablespoons olive oil
⅛ teaspoon salt	

1. Preheat the air fryer to 380°F(193°C). Lightly coat the insides of four ramekins with olive oil cooking spray. 2. In a medium bowl, combine the flour, cocoa powder, salt, baking powder, honey, egg, and olive oil. 3. Divide the batter evenly among the ramekins. 4. Place the filled ramekins inside the air fryer and bake for 10 minutes. 5. Remove the lava cakes from the air fryer and slide a knife around

the outside edge of each cake. Turn each ramekin upside down on a saucer and serve.

Lemon Raspberry Muffins

Prep time: 5 minutes | Cook time: 15 minutes | Serves 6

2 cups almond flour	¼ teaspoon salt
¾ cup Swerve	2 eggs
1¼ teaspoons baking powder	1 cup sour cream
⅓ teaspoon ground allspice	½ cup coconut oil
⅓ teaspoon ground anise star	½ cup raspberries
½ teaspoon grated lemon zest	

1. Preheat the air fryer to 345ºF (174ºC). Line a muffin pan with 6 paper liners. 2. In a mixing bowl, mix the almond flour, Swerve, baking powder, allspice, anise, lemon zest, and salt. 3. In another mixing bowl, beat the eggs, sour cream, and coconut oil until well mixed. Add the egg mixture to the flour mixture and stir to combine. Mix in the raspberries. 4. Scrape the batter into the prepared muffin cups, filling each about three-quarters full. 5. Bake for 15 minutes, or until the tops are golden and a toothpick inserted in the middle comes out clean. 6. Allow the muffins to cool for 10 minutes in the muffin pan before removing and serving.

Ricotta Lemon Poppy Seed Cake

Prep time: 10 minutes | Cook time: 55 minutes | Serves 4

Unsalted butter, at room temperature	¼ cup coconut oil, melted
1 cup almond flour	2 tablespoons poppy seeds
½ cup sugar	1 teaspoon baking powder
3 large eggs	1 teaspoon pure lemon extract
¼ cup heavy cream	Grated zest and juice of 1
¼ cup full-fat ricotta cheese	lemon, plus more zest for garnish

1. Generously butter a baking pan. Line the bottom of the pan with parchment paper cut to fit. 2. In a large bowl, combine the almond flour, sugar, eggs, cream, ricotta, coconut oil, poppy seeds, baking powder, lemon extract, lemon zest, and lemon juice. Beat with a hand mixer on medium speed until well blended and fluffy. 3. Pour the batter into the prepared pan. Cover the pan tightly with aluminum foil. Set the pan in the air fryer basket. Set the air fryer to 325ºF (163ºC) for 45 minutes. Remove the foil and cook for 10 to 15 minutes more, until a knife (do not use a toothpick) inserted into the center of the cake comes out clean. 4. Let the cake cool in the pan on a wire rack for 10 minutes. Remove the cake from pan and let it cool on the rack for 15 minutes before slicing. 5. Top with additional lemon zest, slice and serve.

Indian Toast and Milk

Prep time: 10 minutes | Cook time: 20 minutes | Serves 4

1 cup sweetened condensed milk	4 slices white bread
1 cup evaporated milk	2 to 3 tablespoons ghee or butter, softened
1 cup half-and-half	2 tablespoons crushed pistachios, for garnish (optional)
1 teaspoon ground cardamom, plus additional for garnish	
1 pinch saffron threads	

1. In a baking pan, combine the condensed milk, evaporated milk, half-and-half, cardamom, and saffron. Stir until well combined. 2. Place the pan in the air fryer basket. Set the air fryer to 350ºF (177ºC) for 15 minutes, stirring halfway through the cooking time. Remove the sweetened milk from the air fryer and set aside. 3. Cut each slice of bread into two triangles. Brush each side with ghee. Place the bread in the air fryer basket. Set the air fryer to 350ºF (177ºC) for 5 minutes or until golden brown and toasty. 4. Remove the bread from the air fryer. Arrange two triangles in each of four wide, shallow bowls. Pour the hot milk mixture on top of the bread and let soak for 30 minutes. 5. Garnish with pistachios if using, and sprinkle with additional cardamom.

Appendix 1: Measurement Conversion Chart

MEASUREMENT CONVERSION CHART

VOLUME EQUIVALENTS(DRY)

US STANDARD	METRIC (APPROXIMATE)
1/8 teaspoon	0.5 mL
1/4 teaspoon	1 mL
1/2 teaspoon	2 mL
3/4 teaspoon	4 mL
1 teaspoon	5 mL
1 tablespoon	15 mL
1/4 cup	59 mL
1/2 cup	118 mL
3/4 cup	177 mL
1 cup	235 mL
2 cups	475 mL
3 cups	700 mL
4 cups	1 L

VOLUME EQUIVALENTS(LIQUID)

US STANDARD	US STANDARD (OUNCES)	METRIC (APPROXIMATE)
2 tablespoons	1 fl.oz.	30 mL
1/4 cup	2 fl.oz.	60 mL
1/2 cup	4 fl.oz.	120 mL
1 cup	8 fl.oz.	240 mL
1 1/2 cup	12 fl.oz.	355 mL
2 cups or 1 pint	16 fl.oz.	475 mL
4 cups or 1 quart	32 fl.oz.	1 L
1 gallon	128 fl.oz.	4 L

TEMPERATURES EQUIVALENTS

FAHRENHEIT(F)	CELSIUS(C) (APPROXIMATE)
225 °F	107 °C
250 °F	120 °C
275 °F	135 °C
300 °F	150 °C
325 °F	160 °C
350 °F	180 °C
375 °F	190 °C
400 °F	205 °C
425 °F	220 °C
450 °F	235 °C
475 °F	245 °C
500 °F	260 °C

WEIGHT EQUIVALENTS

US STANDARD	METRIC (APPROXIMATE)
1 ounce	28 g
2 ounces	57 g
5 ounces	142 g
10 ounces	284 g
15 ounces	425 g
16 ounces (1 pound)	455 g
1.5 pounds	680 g
2 pounds	907 g

Appendix 2: Air Fryer Cooking Chart

Air Fryer Cooking Chart

Beef

Item	Temp (°F)	Time (mins)	Item	Temp (°F)	Time (mins)
Beef Eye Round Roast (4 lbs.)	400 °F	45 to 55	Meatballs (1-inch)	370 °F	7
Burger Patty (4 oz.)	370 °F	16 to 20	Meatballs (3-inch)	380 °F	10
Filet Mignon (8 oz.)	400 °F	18	Ribeye, bone-in (1-inch, 8 oz)	400 °F	10 to 15
Flank Steak (1.5 lbs.)	400 °F	12	Sirloin steaks (1-inch, 12 oz)	400 °F	9 to 14
Flank Steak (2 lbs.)	400 °F	20 to 28			

Chicken

Item	Temp (°F)	Time (mins)	Item	Temp (°F)	Time (mins)
Breasts, bone in (1 ¼ lb.)	370 °F	25	Legs, bone-in (1 ¾ lb.)	380 °F	30
Breasts, boneless (4 oz)	380 °F	12	Thighs, boneless (1 ½ lb.)	380 °F	18 to 20
Drumsticks (2 ½ lb.)	370 °F	20	Wings (2 lb.)	400 °F	12
Game Hen (halved 2 lb.)	390 °F	20	Whole Chicken	360 °F	75
Thighs, bone-in (2 lb.)	380 °F	22	Tenders	360 °F	8 to 10

Pork & Lamb

Item	Temp (°F)	Time (mins)	Item	Temp (°F)	Time (mins)
Bacon (regular)	400 °F	5 to 7	Pork Tenderloin	370 °F	15
Bacon (thick cut)	400 °F	6 to 10	Sausages	380 °F	15
Pork Loin (2 lb.)	360 °F	55	Lamb Loin Chops (1-inch thick)	400 °F	8 to 12
Pork Chops, bone in (1-inch, 6.5 oz)	400 °F	12	Rack of Lamb (1.5 – 2 lb.)	380 °F	22

Fish & Seafood

Item	Temp (°F)	Time (mins)	Item	Temp (°F)	Time (mins)
Calamari (8 oz)	400 °F	4	Tuna Steak	400 °F	7 to 10
Fish Fillet (1-inch, 8 oz)	400 °F	10	Scallops	400 °F	5 to 7
Salmon, fillet (6 oz)	380 °F	12	Shrimp	400 °F	5
Swordfish steak	400 °F	10			

Air Fryer Cooking Chart

Vegetables					
INGREDIENT	AMOUNT	PREPARATION	OIL	TEMP	COOK TIME
Asparagus	2 bunches	Cut in half, trim stems	2 Tbsp	420°F	12-15 mins
Beets	1½ lbs	Peel, cut in ½-inch cubes	1 Tbsp	390°F	28-30 mins
Bell peppers (for roasting)	4 peppers	Cut in quarters, remove seeds	1 Tbsp	400°F	15-20 mins
Broccoli	1 large head	Cut in 1-2-inch florets	1 Tbsp	400°F	15-20 mins
Brussels sprouts	1 lb	Cut in half, remove stems	1 Tbsp	425°F	15-20 mins
Carrots	1 lb	Peel, cut in ¼-inch rounds	1 Tbsp	425°F	10-15 mins
Cauliflower	1 head	Cut in 1-2-inch florets	2 Tbsp	400°F	20-22 mins
Corn on the cob	7 ears	Whole ears, remove husks	1 Tbps	400°F	14-17 mins
Green beans	1 bag (12 oz)	Trim	1 Tbps	420°F	18-20 mins
Kale (for chips)	4 oz	Tear into pieces, remove stems	None	325°F	5-8 mins
Mushrooms	16 oz	Rinse, slice thinly	1 Tbps	390°F	25-30 mins
Potatoes, russet	1½ lbs	Cut in 1-inch wedges	1 Tbps	390°F	25-30 mins
Potatoes, russet	1 lb	Hand-cut fries, soak 30 mins in cold water, then pat dry	½-3 Tbps	400°F	25-28 mins
Potatoes, sweet	1 lb	Hand-cut fries, soak 30 mins in cold water, then pat dry	1 Tbps	400°F	25-28 mins
Zucchini	1 lb	Cut in eighths lengthwise, then cut in half	1 Tbps	400°F	15-20 mins

Appendix 3: Recipe Index

Printed in Great Britain
by Amazon